ENDURING TIES

Enduring Ties

POEMS *of* FAMILY RELATIONSHIPS

Edited by Grant Hardy

STEERFORTH PRESS • SOUTH ROYALTON, VERMONT

For information about permission to reproduce selections from this book, write to:
Steerforth Press L.C., P.O. Box 70,
South Royalton, Vermont 05068

Library of Congress Cataloging-in-Publication Data
Enduring ties : poems of family relationships / edited by Grant Hardy.—
1st ed.
    p. cm.
  Includes bibliographical references and index.
  ISBN 1-58642-064-x (alk. paper)
  1. Family—Poetry. 2. Family life—Poetry. I. Hardy, Grant.
PN6110.F32 E53 2003
808.81'0355—dc21

                          2002154281

FIRST EDITION

For Herb and Karleen
Liza and Elliot
And especially, Heather

願生生世世為夫婦

Todd,

Congratulations to you and your wife on your recent marriage and on your new child. I thought this book doubly appropriate. Though I'm not particularly prone to poetry, this is an excellent book on family that is edited by my brother-in-law.

You know how I feel about family and this book covers all aspects across time and many cultures - I hope you enjoy it. Although I have several favorites, from what you've told me, the poem "Men Marry What They Need" seems particularly appropriate. I hope the thoughts found herein help your family's journey and you will have "Enduring Tie."

Mike & Tina   Aug 2011

CONTENTS

I only perceive
the strange idea of family
travelling through the flesh.

from "Family Portrait"
CARLOS DRUMMOND DE ANDRADE
(translated by Elizabeth Bishop)

INTRODUCTION

This anthology began as a folder in a file cabinet. I am not a poet or an English teacher, but I enjoy reading poetry, and when I find something I like I photocopy it and put it in my "Favorite Poems" file. Of the many ways to make poetry a part of your life, this is probably the most basic (it's certainly easier than memorizing). A few years ago, I noticed that many of these poems shared a common theme — they were about family life in some way or another — and I looked for a collection of poems about living within families. To my surprise, there didn't seem to be one. There were books of mother–daughter poems, marriage poems, grandparent poems, and so forth, but no single volume that captured the full range of family connections that make up most people's lives. So I started reading more widely and collecting more systematically. The result is an anthology that tells the human story through poetic glimpses of our most intimate and committed relationships, arranged as they might be encountered over the stages of a typical lifetime.

Given the proportion of my own life that has been devoted to enjoying or tending to these connections of biology and love, it now seems obvious why I was attracted to poems that took up family themes. Poetry allows us to see more clearly and feel more deeply, with a level of reflection that the demands of daily living seem to work against. The poems collected here share not only a topic, but also a particular perspective. This is a celebration of family life, an affirmation of the worth of those relationships in which we have invested so much of ourselves. Yet it conveys these sentiments without sentimentality. These poems are the work of fine poets who, as Matthew Arnold once said of Sophocles, "saw life steadily, and saw it whole." They know both the strength and fragility of family ties; that joy and pleasure have to be set against the real possibility of disappointment and loss; and that an awareness of our vulnerability in these most intimate of bonds makes them all the more valuable.

The theme of family relationships over time is reflected in the historical scope of this anthology, which brings together poems from twenty-five hundred years of world literature. Poets ancient and modern; Christian, Jewish, Buddhist, Hindu, and agnostic; American, Asian, European, Hispanic,

Black, and White, all join in a conversation about one significant aspect of what makes us human. When I read of Sappho's delight in her daughter, or T'ao Yüan-ming's complaints about his children's laziness, I am surprised at how similar they seem to my own feelings, despite vast differences of time and culture. Obviously, there have been many variations in the organization of families — some of which are mentioned in the biographical notes — but there nevertheless seems to be a core of human experience at work here. It is astonishing that partings that took place a thousand years ago can still move us, or that John Milton and Su Tung-p'o (who certainly never heard of each other) had similar dreams of deceased wives. When Jacqueline Osherow and Anne Bradstreet write of an imminent childbirth, the contrast is striking — Osherow is taken by newness, life, and potential, while Bradstreet, writing in the seventeenth century, thinks immediately of the possibility of her own death — but both joyful anticipation and anxiety seem like genuine, even typical, responses to a rapidly advancing pregnancy.

The arrangement of this anthology offers yet another perspective on family relations over time, for it roughly follows the course of an individual life span: from growing up, to marriage and children, to full maturity. The poems here reflect the experience not only of humanity as a whole, but also of individuals. As you thumb through this volume, you can track your own life — seeing at a glance where you've been and where you're headed. Of course, not everyone has siblings or a spouse or children (including a number of the poets in this collection), but we are all deeply enmeshed in this basic story of existence, either through extended family ties or through the lives of friends. Indeed, our close involvement in the daily rounds of caregiving and compromise that sustained relationships require can make it difficult to appreciate what happens over the course of months and years. To take time to look back thoughtfully (as Linda Pastan does in "The Happiest Day") or to anticipate future transitions (as in C. K. Williams's "Grace") may help us find meaning in the flurry of activities and emotions and concerns that constitute our lives. Poetry offers one route to a spirituality of dailiness.

On closer inspection, however, my arrangement by life stages breaks down, because we play different roles in the lives of different family members. When I read James Merrill's "The World and the Child," with its recurring refrain of "the child awake and wearied of," I realize that I have been both that boy and that tired parent. I was once the grateful groom of Michael Blumenthal's "A Marriage," and someday, when I am called upon for a father's blessing at my own son's wedding, I hope that my words will have at least a fraction of the eloquence of Richard Wilbur's "A Wedding Toast." And so it goes — poets in the section on "parting" contemplate the loss of loved ones and also their own inevitable passing; in "inheriting" we both give and acquire. The life of a single person, through family ties, flows into the larger story of the regular succession of generations. And this makes it easier, perhaps, to think of one's own life as something received and shared and handed on, rather than as a solitary journey that abruptly comes to an end.

Given the universality of family life, what might poetry add to the wisdom of lived experience? Part of the answer is the way that poets give tangible form to chaotic, complicated emotions. Some feelings may ultimately be inexpressible, but words help; they concentrate our attention and seal things for memory. And poets find words that are lovely, memorable, and often surprisingly apt. Indeed, individual poems can shape the way that we think of our lives. Sometime in the course of its making, this book became a family project, and around my house when someone leaves we speak of the "bad monkeys [at] the windows" (anonymous). "If ever two were one, then surely we" (Anne Bradstreet) is inscribed in my wedding band. Announcements of family reunions are met with "reconciliation was our long work, not all of it joyful" (William Meredith). We sent our reluctant son to kindergarten with the words "great kindness came of it in the end" (Howard Nemerov). And the dedication for this volume was chosen with T. S. Eliot's earlier dedication in mind — "private words addressed to you in public."

Poetry helps us to perceive and articulate emotion, but it can also create it anew, so that in reading a poem about, say, holding a newborn child or trying to communicate with a sullen teenager, we not only remember doing this, but actually reexperience those feelings. Yet the result is not simply nostalgic; as we mature and gain perspective, the full meaning of such incidents becomes clearer. There is a crucial transaction at work here — poets inspire emotion within us, and we in turn bring our life experiences to the text. In an important sense, each reader completes a poem, as something significant is expressed and then grasped. This is also why good poems can be read and reread many times over — as we change, so does our understanding of a given poem; each reading becomes a unique encounter that brings together the intimately personal voice of the poet and our own particular life situation (especially if we read aloud and make the words our own). Astonishingly, the intensity of poetic communication can even let us feel something of how we might respond to events only now imagined — perhaps the death of a spouse, or the departure of a grown child, or the arrival of a grandchild. Although in the end it may remain a mystery as to how squiggles on a page can make us weep or fill us with joy, poets tend to draw on a range of long-established techniques — including form, rhythm, repetitions, doubled meanings, and arresting imagery.

There is so much I would like say about what makes particular poems engaging — how Elizabeth Bishop's "Sestina" is the most successful poem I know in re-çreating a child's-eye view of a world laden with meaning, but only vaguely perceived; how Edward Hirsch's memories of his grandmother involve all five senses; how Seamus Heaney's "Honeymoon Flight" evokes the strange and wonderful emotions of a new marriage almost entirely through the description of a landscape as seen through an airplane window. I would point out how astonishing it is that the joke underlying Su Tung-p'o's "On the Birth of His Son" is still funny after nine hundred years, or how Fleur Adcock's "For a Five-Year-Old" suggests that parents sometimes discover their true values only as they try to pass them on. I would want you to notice how Stephen Dunn's exuberant "I Come Home Wanting to Touch Everyone" contrasts with the grim understatement of Raymond Carver's "My Daughter and Apple Pie." I am taken by George Meredith's portrait of a marriage in trouble (actually his own), in which the husband, though no longer in love, still admires his wife's style and grace; I am entranced by John Donne's rapid succession of varied metaphors — a death scene, an earthquake, planetary motion, the malleability of gold, and a geometer's compass — as well as the convoluted syntax of the single sentence in C. K. Williams's "Instinct"; and I would remark at length on the chilling psychological insight in these lines from Mei Yao-ch'en's "Mourning for My Son":

> I felt only astonishment looking down at him;
> Strange, but the greatest sorrows bring no tears.
> Not until my feelings settled did awareness come,
> And searing fires seemed to mass inside.

(It is perhaps a measure of the universal nature of such relationships that this lament is still heartbreaking today, despite the fact that even if this child had lived to a ripe old age, he still would have died nearly a thousand years ago.)

But you would be better served by going to the poems themselves. They are concise and accessible enough to be enjoyed the first time through, but rich enough to repay numerous rereadings. If it so happens that you, like me, enjoy poems more if you puzzle over them a bit, there is an appendix of poetic forms, and there are the biographical notes printed at the end of each poem. Poets do not always write from firsthand experience — Emily Dickinson, for example, was never married, and the speaker of "John Anderson, My Jo," is clearly not Robert Burns, who was never that old, that well married, or female — but they often do, especially when they are exploring family relationships. Strong poems can certainly stand on their own, yet imagining their origin in someone's life lets us focus on the act of creation, on the way that poets bring order and beauty out of what are often messy or tragic circumstances (though perhaps no more messy or tragic than those of their readers). In this volume, several poets are represented by multiple poems, so that readers can get a sense of how poetry can track the course of a single life.

I should probably also say something about the number of medieval Chinese poems in this collection. This partly reflects my own interests — I teach Asian history — but there is a startling convergence at work here. Traditional Chinese verse is filled with meditations on the everyday tasks of raising and caring for family members. This is a result of the extraordinary intersection of an ideology that found spiritual and ethical meaning in family life (Confucianism) with a highly literate culture in which everyone who was educated was expected to compose poems on any and all occasions. Not every Chinese poet transformed family into poetry, but those who did — Po Chü-i and Mei Yao-ch'en are notable examples — wrote verses that are surprisingly resonant with modern sensibilities. (Remarkably my own mother, not a regular reader of poetry, read through an early draft of this book and told me that she felt like she understood the Chinese poems the best.)

To my mind, each of the poems in this volume is an expression of deep and abiding love, the kind that calls forth what is best in us, that motivates us to keep trying. As we negotiate our way through the various stages of life, we are not always as generous or as wise as we might wish. But it matters that there are people who love us anyway. And the trust they exhibit can sometimes provoke us to unexpected strength and courage. As Celia Gilbert writes in a poem about her mother: "everything in us that answers to good / crowds round her lap / hearing itself spoken for." These lovely lines, of course, were written in retrospect. The other side of motherhood

— the tedium and isolation — appears in Katha Pollitt's "Playground": "Mama! Was it like this? / Did I do this to you?" Both observations are enriched by their juxtaposition. There is a radical notion at the heart of this volume — that meaning in life is found not through individual accomplishment, but in our connections with others. Love is perhaps most genuinely manifest in committed relationships over time, and family connections are usually the most constant, most enduring relationships in our lives.

Yet they cannot last forever. Sometimes the significance of a particular relationship is fully realized only in its absence — hence this collection includes poems not only on the deaths of loved ones, but also about not marrying, infertility, separation, and the ways in which relationships change over time. Indeed, the passing of time is constantly in the background here, and an anthology organized by life stages will inevitably end with the unpleasant prospect of one's own demise. Poetry may be a poor consolation at a time of personal tragedy, but it can remind us that there are other perspectives from which human comings and goings are part of a larger scheme, a narrative that we are blessed to have a part in. As Sharon Olds wryly notes: "It's an old / story — the oldest on the planet — / the story of replacement." Within the context of family relationships across generations, this somehow seems okay. There is something spiritually comforting in reading poems of loss that are hundreds of years old; as painful as parting is, a world where no one ever dies is absurd. I only hope that such lofty, mature reflections don't desert me at my own moments of crisis. And this again is where poetry comes in. I believe that poetry can help us work our way through life with increased grace, compassion, and understanding. Insightful, skilled poets can both prepare us for the worst, and also show us how to appreciate our present circumstances, whatever they may be.

The last poem in the book, James Merrill's "A Timepiece," brings together many of the themes in this anthology. Merrill takes an ordinary moment — his older sister, pregnant and heavy with her third child, gently rocks in a hammock in the yard, trying to get some rest while her two daughters play nearby — and creates a meditation on the passage of time, the succession of generations, and the importance of family. This modest summer afternoon holds out both the promise of new life and the assurance of inevitable partings. In their mother, the girls vaguely perceive their own futures, while she in turn is made aware by the double heartbeat within her that this moment and these relationships are slowly but surely ticking away. In the meantime, however, *this* is life. And the poet on the sidelines (as a loving relative, not a neutral observer), takes it all in — the "partial fullnesses," the merging of lives, the need for constant nourishment — and weaves a delicate pattern of *abba* stanzas, enriched by internal rhymes and off-rhymes. "Let us each have some milk," his sister says. And the milk — that will someday become bone — suggests the sustenance and strength that come from these long-term ties of kinship and love.

I

GROWING UP

from There Was a Child Went Forth

His own parents, he that had father'd him and she that had
      conceiv'd him in her womb and birth'd him,
They gave this child more of themselves than that,
They gave him afterward every day, they became part of him.

The mother at home quietly placing the dishes on the supper-table,
The mother with mild words, clean her cap and gown, a wholesome
      odor falling off her person and clothes as she walks by,
The father, strong, self-sufficient, manly, mean, anger'd, unjust,
The blow, the quick loud word, the tight bargain, the crafty lure,
The family usages, the language, the company, the furniture, the
      yearning and swelling heart,
Affection that will not be gainsay'd, the sense of what is real, the
      thought if after all it should prove unreal,
The doubts of day-time and the doubts of night-time, the curious
      whether and how,
Whether that which appears so is so, or is it all flashes and specks?

WALT WHITMAN
(1819–1892)

Walt Whitman was born on Long Island, and then moved with his family to Brooklyn when he was four. At twelve, he learned the printer's trade, and he later worked as a journalist, a carpenter, an editor, and a schoolteacher. During the Civil War, he served as a wound dresser. Whitman's first book was *Leaves of Grass* in 1855, which he continued to revise throughout his life (the poem above was Whitman's later revision of lines from the first edition of *Leaves of Grass*). In 1873, he suffered a paralytic stroke and moved to Camden, New Jersey, where — though a semi-invalid — he continued to write until his death.

The World and the Child

Letting his wisdom be the whole of love,
The father tiptoes out, backwards. A gleam
Falls on the child awake and wearied of,

Then, as the door clicks shut, is snuffed. The glove —
Gray afterglow appalls him. It would seem
That letting wisdom be the whole of love

Were pastime even for the bitter grove
Outside, whose owl's white hoot of disesteem
Falls on the child awake and wearied of.

He lies awake in pain, he does not move,
He will not call. The women, hearing him,
Would let their wisdom be the whole of love.

People have filled the room he lies above.
Their talk, mild variation, chilling theme,
Falls on the child. Awake and wearied of

Mere pain, mere wisdom also, he would have
All the world waking from its winter dream,
Letting its wisdom be. The whole of love
Falls on the child awake and wearied of.

JAMES MERRILL
(1926–1995)

James Merrill was born in New York City to the very wealthy Charles E. Merrill (cofounder of the brokerage firm Merrill Lynch) and his second wife, Hellen Ingram. His parents divorced when he was twelve — he later wrote a sequence of seven sonnets, "The Broken Home," about this experience. He was educated at Amherst College, with a two-year interruption to serve in the U.S. Army during World War II. In 1955, he bought a house with his longtime companion, David Jackson, in Stonington, Connecticut, which he kept for the rest of his life, though he also had residences at different times in Manhattan, Key West, and Athens, Greece. He never married. Merrill was the winner of two National Book Awards (1967, 1979), a Bollingen Prize (1973), and a Pulitzer (1977). For other poems by Merrill, see pages 57 and 178.

Nikki-Rosa

childhood remembrances are always a drag
if you're Black
you always remember things like living in Woodlawn
with no inside toilet
and if you become famous or something
they never talk about how happy you were to have
your mother
all to yourself and
how good the water felt when you got your bath
from one of those
big tubs that folk in chicago barbecue in
and somehow when you talk about home
it never gets across how much you
understood their feelings
as the whole family attended meetings about Hollydale
and even though you remember
your biographers never understand
your father's pain as he sells his stock
and another dream goes
And though you're poor it isn't poverty that
concerns you
and though they fought a lot
it isn't your father's drinking that makes any difference
but only that everybody is together and you
and your sister have happy birthdays and very good

Christmases
and I really hope no white person ever has cause
to write about me
because they never understand
Black love is Black wealth and they'll
probably talk about my hard childhood
and never understand that
all the while I was quite happy

NIKKI GIOVANNI
(1943–)

Nikki Giovanni was born in Knoxville, Tennessee, and raised in Ohio. She began college at sixteen at Fisk University, was expelled after her first semester, and then returned to finish her degree. Later she studied at the University of Pennsylvania and Columbia. Giovanni has been active in the civil rights and Black arts movements throughout her life. She gave birth to a son, Thomas, in 1969.

Five Years Old

Stars fell all night.
The iceman had been very generous that day
with his chips and slivers.

And I buried my pouch of jewels
inside a stone casket under the porch,
their beauty saved for another world.

And then my sister came home
and I threw a dart through her cheek
and cried all night,

so much did I worship her.

JAMES TATE
(1943–)

A native of Kansas City, Missouri, James Tate was educated at the University of Missouri, Kansas State, and the University of Iowa. The title poem of his first book, *The Lost Pilot*, refers to his father, who was lost in World War II. He won a Pulitzer Prize in 1992 and a National Book Award in 1994.

My Grandmother's Bed

How she pulled it out of the wall
To my amazement. How it rattled and
Creaked, how it sagged in the middle
And smelled like a used-clothing store.
I was ecstatic to be sleeping on wheels!

It rolled when I moved; it trembled
When she climbed under the covers
In her flannel nightgown, kissing me
Softly on the head, turning her back.
Soon I could hear her snoring next to me —

Her clogged breath roaring in my ears,
Filling her tiny apartment like the ocean
Until I, too, finally swayed and slept
While a radiator hissed in the corner
And traffic droned on Lawrence Avenue. . . .

I woke up to the color of light pouring
Through the windows, the odor of soup
Simmering in the kitchen, my grandmother's
Face. It felt good to be ashore again
After sleeping on rocky, unfamiliar waves.

I loved to help her straighten the sheets
And lift the Murphy back into the wall.
It was like putting the night away
When we closed the wooden doors again
And her bed disappeared without a trace.

EDWARD HIRSCH
(1950–)

Murphy — brand name of a bed that folded up into a wall for storage

Edward Hirsch was born in Chicago and educated at Grinnell College and the University of Pennsylvania. He married Janet Landay in 1977; they have one son. A recipient of a MacArthur Fellowship in 1998, he is the author of an introduction to poetry titled *How to Read a Poem and Fall in Love with Poetry*. For another poem by Hirsch, see page 64.

Sestina

September rain falls on the house.
In the failing light, the old grandmother
sits in the kitchen with the child
beside the Little Marvel Stove,
reading the jokes from the almanac,
laughing and talking to hide her tears.

She thinks that her equinoctial tears
and the rain that beats on the roof of the house
were both foretold by the almanac,
but only known to a grandmother.
The iron kettle sings on the stove.
She cuts some bread and says to the child,

It's time for tea now; but the child
is watching the teakettle's small hard tears
dance like mad on the hot black stove,
the way the rain must dance on the house.
Tidying up, the old grandmother
hangs up the clever almanac

on its string. Birdlike, the almanac
hovers half open above the child,
hovers above the old grandmother
and her teacup full of dark brown tears.
She shivers and says she thinks the house
feels chilly, and puts more wood in the stove.

It was to be, says the Marvel Stove.
I know what I know, says the almanac.
With crayons the child draws a rigid house
and a winding pathway. Then the child
puts in a man with buttons like tears
and shows it proudly to the grandmother.

But secretly, while the grandmother
busies herself about the stove,
the little moons fall down like tears
from between the pages of the almanac
into the flower bed the child
has carefully placed in the front of the house.

Time to plant tears, says the almanac.
The grandmother sings to the marvellous stove
and the child draws another inscrutable house.

ELIZABETH BISHOP
(1911–1979)

equinoctial — pertaining to the equinox, when day and night are equal in length; the
    autumnal equinox, in late September, is often a time of fierce rainstorms
Little Marvel Stove — brand name of a wood-burning stove

Elizabeth Bishop was born in Worcester, Massachusetts, as the only child of an American
father and a Canadian mother. Her father died when she was eight months old, and her
mother, after a series of mental breakdowns, was locked away in a mental hospital when
Elizabeth was five. She never saw her mother again. She went to Nova Scotia to live with
her grandparents and six years later returned to Worcester to live with an aunt. After
graduating from Vassar, she spent nine years in Key West, Florida, and then sixteen years
in Brazil, where she lived with the architect Lota de Macedo Soares (who later commit-
ted suicide). Bishop never married, though she once wrote, "Happiness does not consist
in worldly goods but in a peaceful home, in family affection, — things that fortune can-
not bring and often takes away." Despite the fact that she did not publish many poems
(her *Complete Poems 1927–1979* includes only about one hundred titles), she has been
enormously influential, winning both a Pulitzer Prize (1956) and a National Book Award
(1970). She was consultant in poetry to the Library of Congress, 1949–1950.

Grandfather's Heaven

My grandfather told me I had a choice.
Up or down, he said. Up or down.
He never mentioned east or west.

Grandpa stacked newspapers on his bed
and read them years after the news was relevant.
He even checked the weather reports.

Grandma was afraid of Grandpa
for some reason I never understood.
She tiptoed while he snored, rarely disagreed.

I liked Grandma because she gave me cookies
and let me listen to the ocean in her shell.
Grandma liked me even though my daddy was a Moslem.

I think Grandpa liked me too
though he wasn't sure what to do with it.
Just before he died, he wrote me a letter.

"I hear you're studying religion," he said.
"That's how people get confused.
Keep it simple. Down or up."

NAOMI SHIHAB NYE
(1952–)

Naomi Shihab Nye was born and raised in St. Louis, Missouri, as the daughter of a Palestinian father and an American mother of German descent. Her family moved to Jerusalem for a year while she was in high school and then relocated to San Antonio, Texas. She was educated at Trinity University in San Antonio, where she still lives with her photographer husband Michael Nye (whom she married in 1978) and their son. In addition to her poetry, she has written books for children and edited several anthologies of poetry for young readers.

The Journey

I am looking for a past
I can rely on
in order to look to death
with equanimity.
What was given me:
my mother's largeness
to protect me,
my father's regularity
in coming home from work
at night, his opening the door
silently and smiling,
pleased to be back
and the lights on
in all the rooms
through which I could run
freely or sit at ease
at table and do my homework
undisturbed: love arranged
as order directed at the next day.
Going to bed was a journey.

DAVID IGNATOW
(1914–1997)

The son of Jewish Russian immigrants, David Ignatow was born in Brooklyn. His father's education consisted of reading Russian literature while he was apprenticed to a bookbinder in Kiev; his mother grew up illiterate, though her husband taught her to read the Yiddish newspaper, the *Jewish Forward*. Ignatow entered his father's bookbinding business at eighteen when the onset of the Great Depression forced him to drop out of college his freshman year. He worked at a series of low-paying jobs and eventually managed his father's business for a time. He never graduated from college, though he later taught at a number of universities. In 1937, he married Rose Graubart, a writer and painter whom he had met in a poetry class in Manhattan. He adopted her son, and then together they had a daughter, some nineteen years younger than their son. During difficult times, Rose supported her husband's writing by working in factories as a seamstress. Ignatow won the Bollingen Prize in 1977. For other poems by Ignatow, see pages 108, 119, and 120.

Drawing from the Past

Only Mama and I were at home.
We ate tomato sandwiches
with sweeps of mayonnaise
on indifferent white bread.

Surely it was September
my older brother at school.
The tomatoes were fragrant
and richly red, perhaps the last
before frost.

I was alert to the joy of eating
sandwiches alone with Mama, bare
feet braced on the underpinnings
of the abraded kitchen table.

Once I'd made a mark in the wood
by pressing too hard as I traced
the outline of a horse.

I was no good at drawing — from life,
or from imagination. My brother
was good at it, and I was alert
to that, too.

JANE KENYON
(1947–1995)

Jane Kenyon was born and educated in Ann Arbor, Michigan. Her father was a jazz pianist, her mother a nightclub singer and a seamstress. She had one older brother. In 1972, she married the poet Donald Hall (whose poems appear on pages 76 and 139). They lived in New Hampshire from 1975 until her death from leukemia twenty years later. She struggled with depression her whole life, but found solace in her art and her faith. Her two poems in this anthology were among the last that she wrote. For another poem by Kenyon, see page 143.

Childhood

My father mounted his horse and rode away into the country.
My mother stayed behind, sewing in her chair.
My little brother lay asleep.
I, a lonely child under the mango trees,
read the story of Robinson Crusoe,
a long story that never came to an end.

In the white sunlight of noontime a voice that had learned
to sing us to sleep long ago in the slave quarters — and had
        never been forgotten —
called us to coffee.
Coffee black as the old negress herself
savoury coffee,
good coffee.

My mother sat sewing,
looking at me:
— Hush . . . Don't wake the baby! —
at the cradle on which a mosquito had lit,
and sighed from the depths of her being.

Somewhere far off my father was exploring
the endless woods of the plantation.

And I never knew that my own story
was more beautiful than Robinson Crusoe's.

CARLOS DRUMMOND DE ANDRADE
(1902–1987)
Translated from the Portuguese by Dudley Poore

Often considered Brazil's foremost poet, Carlos Drummond was born in the state of Minas
Gerais, about three hundred miles from Rio de Janeiro. He was educated as a pharmacist,
but earned a living as a journalist and a civil servant in the ministries of education and
culture. He married Dolores Dutra de Morais in 1925; they had a son who died in infancy
and one daughter.

Only Child

Sister to no one,
I watched
the children next door
quarrel and make up
in a code
I never learned
to break.

Go play!
my mother told me.
Play! said the aunts,
their heads all nodding
on their stems,
a family of rampant
flowers

and I a single shoot.
At night I dreamed
I was a twin
the way my two hands,
my eyes,
my feet were twinned.
I married young.

In the fractured light
of memory — that place

of blinding sun or shade,
I stand waiting
on the concrete stoop
for my own children
to find me.

LINDA PASTAN
(1932–)

Raised in New York City, Linda Pastan was educated at Radcliffe College, Simmons College, and Brandeis University. She married Ira Pastan in 1953, and they have two sons, one daughter, and seven grandchildren. She has lived most of her life in Potomoc, Maryland, a suburb of Washington, D.C. For other poems by Pastan, see pages 71 and 125.

Sonnet to My Mother

Most near, most dear, most loved and most far,
Under the window where I often found her
Sitting as huge as Asia, seismic with laughter,
Gin and chicken helpless in her Irish hand,
Irresistible as Rabelais but most tender for
The lame dogs and hurt birds that surround her, —
She is a procession no one can follow after
But be like a little dog following a brass band.

She will not glance up at the bomber, or condescend
To drop her gin and scuttle to a cellar,
But lean on the mahogany table like a mountain
Whom only faith can move, and so I send
O all my faith and all my love to tell her
That she will move from mourning into morning.

GEORGE BARKER
(1913–1991)

Rabelais — French writer (1494?–1553) known for his love of life and irreverent humor
mountain . . . faith can move — Matthew 17:20

Written in 1940, just after Barker left a teaching position in Japan for one in the United States. His mother was back home in London; in July of that year, Germany began bombing Britain.

Born in Essex, George Barker was raised in London, where his father was a constable. Though he dropped out of high school and never had any further formal education after the age of fourteen, he eventually taught at universities in both Japan and the United States, then made a living primarily from his writing, which included essays and novels as well as poetry. He married Elspeth Langlands in 1964 (his third marriage), and they had five children.

Portrait of My Mother on Her Wedding Day

A young woman,
lilies gathered to her breast —
the moment of the wave
before it crests —
bride,
incandescent,
even in this sepia image
dazzling me, like a wedding guest.

Fifty years later, I uncover
in the movement of her swept-back veil
the life that was to come,
seeing revealed
the cunning of those hands
that clasp the flowers;
the will to shape a world
of her devising.

And once again I feel
how evil seems to fall away
before the power of her candid gaze
while everything in us that answers to good
crowds round her lap
hearing itself spoken for.

CELIA GILBERT
(1932–)

Celia Gilbert was born in Philadelphia, Pennsylvania, and educated at Smith College
and Boston University. She has worked as a journalist and a teacher. She married Walter
Gilbert in 1953, and they have a son and a daughter. Another daughter died as a child.
For other poems by Gilbert, see pages 103 and 153.

Clearances

in memoriam M. K. H., 1911–1984

#3

When all the others were away at Mass
I was all hers as we peeled potatoes.
They broke the silence, let fall one by one
Like solder weeping off the soldering iron:
Cold comforts set between us, things to share
Gleaming in a bucket of clean water.
And again let fall. Little pleasant splashes
From each other's work would bring us to our senses.

So while the parish priest at her bedside
Went hammer and tongs at the prayers for the dying
And some were responding and some crying
I remembered her head bent towards my head,
Her breath in mine, our fluent dipping knives —
Never closer the whole rest of our lives.

SEAMUS HEANEY
(1939–)

From an eight-sonnet sequence commemorating Heaney's mother, Margaret Kathleen Heaney.

Born in 1939 to a Roman Catholic family in Protestant Northern Ireland, Seamus Heaney was the eldest of nine children. He studied at St. Columb's College in Londonderry and Queen's University, Belfast. In 1965, he married Marie Devlin, and they have two sons and a daughter. He won the Nobel Prize for Literature in 1995. For other poems by Heaney, see pages 41 and 147.

Piano

Softly, in the dusk, a woman is singing to me;
Taking me back down the vista of years, till I see
A child sitting under the piano, in the boom of the tingling strings
And pressing the small, poised feet of a mother who smiles as she sings.

In spite of myself, the insidious mastery of song
Betrays me back, till the heart of me weeps to belong
To the old Sunday evenings at home, with winter outside
And hymns in the cozy parlor, the tinkling piano our guide.

So now it is vain for the singer to burst into clamor
With the great black piano appassionato. The glamour

Of childish days is upon me, my manhood is cast
Down in the flood of remembrance, I weep like a child for the past.

D. H. LAWRENCE
(1885–1930)

D. H. Lawrence was the fourth son of a coal-mining father in Nottinghamshire. His schoolteacher mother (who had come from a middle-class background) desperately wanted her son to become something more. His close attachment to his mother and the tension between his parents became important in his later fiction. He gained an education at University College, Nottingham, and worked briefly as a clerk and schoolteacher. In 1912, he eloped to Germany with Frieda von Richthofen Weekley, the wife of his former French professor (she was six years older than he and had three young children), and while abroad he finished his first novel, *Sons and Lovers*. They returned to England for the war, and then lived briefly in Italy, Ceylon, Australia, New Mexico, and Mexico. Lawrence died in France at forty-four of tuberculosis.

I Ask My Mother to Sing

She begins, and my grandmother joins her.
Mother and daughter sing like young girls.
If my father were alive, he would play
his accordion and sway like a boat.

I've never been in Peking, or the Summer Palace,
nor stood on the great Stone Boat to watch
the rain begin on Kuen Ming Lake, the picnickers
running away in the grass.

But I love to hear it sung;
how the waterlilies fill with rain until
they overturn, spilling water into water,
then rock back, and fill with more.

Both women have begun to cry.
But neither stops her song.

LI-YOUNG LEE
(1957–)

Li-Young Lee was born in Jakarta, Indonesia, of Chinese parents. His great-grandfather
was the first president of the Republic of China in 1912, his mother was a member of the
Chinese royal family, and his father was once the personal physician to Chairman Mao.
A few years before his birth, his family fled the political turmoil of China to Indonesia,
where his father spent a year incarcerated as a political prisoner. In 1959, the family
escaped Indonesia, and after several years of wandering through Hong Kong, Macao, and
Japan, they came to America in 1964, where Lee's father became a minister. Lee studied
at the University of Pittsburgh, the University of Arizona, and SUNY Brockport. He and
his wife, Donna, have two children. For another poem by Lee, see page 173.

My Papa's Waltz

The whiskey on your breath
Could make a small boy dizzy;
But I hung on like death:
Such waltzing was not easy.

We romped until the pans
Slid from the kitchen shelf;
My mother's countenance
Could not unfrown itself.

The hand that held my wrist
Was battered on one knuckle;
At every step you missed
My right ear scraped a buckle.

You beat time on my head
With a palm caked hard by dirt,
Then waltzed me off to bed
Still clinging to your shirt.

THEODORE ROETHKE
(1908–1963)

Born in Saginaw, Michigan, Theodore Roethke was the son of a wholesale florist who owned a large greenhouse. He was educated at the University of Michigan and Harvard. In 1953, he married Beatrice Heath O'Connell, who had been his student at Bennington College some ten years earlier. He was briefly institutionalized several times for mental illness, but continued to write innovative and widely respected poetry. He died of a heart attack while swimming at the age of fifty-five. He won a Pulitzer in 1954, two National Book Awards (1959, 1965), and a Bollingen Prize in 1959. For another poem by Roethke, see page 42.

Those Winter Sundays

Sundays too my father got up early
and put his clothes on in the blueblack cold,
then with cracked hands that ached
from labor in the weekday weather made
banked fires blaze. No one ever thanked him.

I'd wake and hear the cold splintering, breaking.
When the rooms were warm, he'd call,
and slowly I would rise and dress,
fearing the chronic angers of that house,

Speaking indifferently to him,
who had driven out the cold
and polished my good shoes as well.
What did I know, what did I know
of love's austere and lonely offices?

ROBERT HAYDEN
(1913–1980)

Originally named Asa Bundy Sheffey, Robert Hayden was born in a Detroit ghetto to parents who divorced shortly before his birth, and his mother gave him to her neighbors William and Sue Ellen Hayden to raise. Hayden's general bookishness, combined with poor eyesight that kept him out of sports, made relations with his stern father difficult. He attended college at Wayne State University and Michigan University. In 1940, he married Emma Inez Morris, and they had one daughter. In 1976, Hayden was the first African American to be appointed consultant in poetry to the Library of Congress.

Letter of Recommendation

On summer nights I sleep naked
in Jerusalem on my bed,
which stands on the brink
of a deep valley
without rolling down into it.

During the day I walk about,
the Ten commandments on my lips
like an old song someone is humming to himself.

Oh, touch me, touch me, you good woman!
This is not a scar you feel under my shirt.
It's a letter of recommendation, folded,
from my father:
"He is still a good boy and full of love."

I remember my father waking me up
for early prayers. He did it caressing
my forehead, not tearing the blanket away.

Since then I love him even more.
And because of this
let him be woken up
gently and with love
on the Day of Resurrection.

YEHUDA AMICHAI
(1924–2000)
Translated from the Hebrew by the author and Ted Hughes

Perhaps the most widely translated Hebrew poet since King David, Yehuda Amichai was
born in Wurzburg, Germany, and then emigrated with his family to Palestine in 1935. He
fought in the British Army in World War II, and then against the British in the Israeli
War of Independence. He married twice and had three children, living most of his life in
Jerusalem and teaching Hebrew literature.

Lesson

It was 1963 or 4, summer,
and my father was driving our family
from Ft. Hood to North Carolina in our 56 Buick.
We'd been hearing about Klan attacks, and we knew

Mississippi to be more dangerous than usual.
Dark lay hanging from trees the way moss did,
and when it moaned light against the windows
that night, my father pulled off the road to sleep.

Noises
that usually woke me from rest afraid of monsters
kept my father awake that night, too,
and I lay in the quiet noticing him listen, learning
that he might not be able always to protect us

from everything and the creatures besides;
perhaps not even from the fury suddenly loud
through my body about this trip from Texas
to settle us home before he would go away

to a place no place in the world
he named Viet Nam. A boy needs a father
with him, I kept thinking, fixed against noise
from the dark.

FORREST HAMER
(1956–)

Forrest Hamer grew up in Goldsboro, North Carolina, an African American in the years
of freedom marches and school desegregation. He was educated at Yale and Berkeley, and
he is now a psychologist in Oakland, California.

✦ II ✦
Marrying

Poor Girls

A poor girl can't hope for scented silks,
Thoughts of a matchmaker just make her miserable.
Who really cares for refined taste or lofty ideals —
Even strangers take pity when virtue is packaged so plainly.
In the needlework of her fingers she might claim some skill,
But she can't compete with delicately fashioned eyebrows.
So grieving year after year, she stitches with golden thread —
Making bridal gowns for others to wear.

CH'IN T'AO-YÜ
(LATE NINTH CENTURY)
Translated from the Chinese by Grant Hardy

A native of the Chinese capital Ch'ang-an (now Xi'an) in Shensi Province, Ch'in T'ao-yü gained his *chin-shih* degree — similar to earning a doctorate in the West — in the year 882, after passing the highest level of the Chinese civil service exams. He served in various official posts and from a young age had a considerable reputation as a poet.

Old Bachelor Brother

Here from his prominent but thankfully
uncentral position at the head of the church —
a flanking member of the groom's large party —
he stands and waits to watch the women march

up the wide aisle, just the way they did
at last night's long and leaden-joked rehearsal.
Only this time, it's all changed. There's now a crowd,
of course, and walls of lit stained glass, and Purcell

ringing from the rented organist,
and yet the major difference, the one
that hits his throat as a sort of smoky thirst,
is how, so far away, the church's main

doors are flung back, uncovering a square
of sun that streams into the narthex, so that
the women who materialize there
do so in blinding silhouette,

and these are not the women he has helloed
and kissed, and who have bored, ignored, or teased him,
but girls — whose high, garlanded hair goes haloed
by the noon-light . . . The years have dropped from them.

One by one they're bodied forth, edged with flame,
as new as flame, destined to part the sea
of faces on each side, and approaching him
in all their passionate anonymity.

BRAD LEITHAUSER
(1953–)

Purcell — Henry Purcell (ca. 1659–1695), an English composer
narthex — a porch or vestibule at the main entrance of a church

Born in Detroit, Brad Leithauser was educated at Harvard and Harvard Law School. He
is married to the poet Mary Jo Salter, with whom he has two daughters, and he spent
three years as a research fellow at the Kyoto Comparative Law Center in Japan
(1980–1983). He has also written several novels. Leithauser was a MacArthur Fellow in
1983. For another poem by Leithauser, see page 66.

A Wedding Toast
M. C. H.
C. H. W.
14 July 1971

St. John tells how, at Cana's wedding-feast,
The water-pots poured wine in such amount
That by his sober count
There were a hundred gallons at the least.

It made no earthly sense, unless to show
How whatsoever love elects to bless
Brims to a sweet excess
That can without depletion overflow.

Which is to say that what love sees is true;
That the world's fullness is not made but found.
Life hungers to abound
And pour its plenty out for such as you.

Now if your loves will lend an ear to mine,
I toast you both, good son and dear new daughter.
May you not lack for water,
And may that water smack of Cana's wine.

RICHARD WILBUR
(1921–)

St. John tells how — John 2:1–11

Written for the marriage of Wilbur's second child, Christopher.

Richard Wilbur was born in New York City, raised in New Jersey, and educated at Amherst College and Harvard. He began writing poetry while serving in the U.S. Army during World War II, and he later explained, "One does not use poetry for its major purposes, as a means to organize oneself and the world, until one's world somehow gets out of hand." In 1942, he married Charlotte Ward, and he has been writing love poetry to this same woman for more than fifty years. They have one daughter and three sons. Wilbur was the second poet laureate of the United States (1987–1988), and he is also prominent as a translator. He won Pulitzer Prizes in 1957 and 1989, a National Book Award in 1957, and a Bollingen in 1971.

Honeymoon Flight

Below, the patchwork earth, dark hems of hedge,
The long grey tapes of road that bind and loose
Villages and fields in casual marriage:
We bank above the small lough and farmhouse

And the sure green world goes topsy-turvy
As we climb out of our familiar landscape.
The engine noises change. You look at me.
The coastline slips away beneath the wing-tip.

And launched right off the earth by force of fire
We hang, miraculous, above the water,
Dependent on the invisible air
To keep us airborne and to bring us further.

Ahead of us the sky's a geyser now.
A calm voice talks of cloud yet we feel lost.
Air-pockets jolt our fears and down we go.
Travellers, at this point, can only trust.

SEAMUS HEANEY
(1939–)

lough — a bay or inlet of the sea

For a biography, see page 27. For other poems by Heaney, see pages 27 and 147.

Wish for a Young Wife

My lizard, my lively writher,
May your limbs never wither,
May the eyes in your face
Survive the green ice
Of envy's mean gaze;
May you live out your life
Without hate, without grief,
And your hair ever blaze,
In the sun, in the sun,
When I am undone,
When I am no one.

THEODORE ROETHKE
(1908–1963)

From a sequence of love poems Roethke wrote for his wife, Beatrice O'Connell, who had once been his student. It was one of the last poems that he wrote and was published posthumously.

For a biography, see page 30.

Written to the Tune: "Song of Picking Mulberry"

Evening comes with an onslaught of wind and rain,
washing clean the heat and glare.
I put away my reed pipes,
face the flower-formed mirror, applying light makeup.

Red silk gauze so sheer my white skin shines through,
snowy-smooth, cream-fragrant:
I smile and say to my husband,
Tonight inside the light curtains, pillow and mat will be cool!

LI CH'ING-CHAO
(1084–CA. 1151)
Translated from the Chinese by Burton Watson

Li Ch'ing-chao was the foremost female poet in Chinese history. She was born into a literary, scholar-official family in Shantung. Her father was a noted prose writer and a close friend of Su Tung-p'o (whose poems appear on pages 75 and 158), and her mother was a poet in her own right. At the age of eighteen, Li married Chao Ming-ch'eng, a student in the imperial academy, whose father was a powerful statesman opposed to the conservative faction to which her own father belonged. The couple was nonetheless very happily married, enjoying books, poetry, and art, and they worked together on a catalog of ancient stone and bronze inscriptions. Li's husband became an official, but when the Jurchens invaded North China in 1127, the couple fled south, losing nearly all of their art collection in the scramble for safety. Her husband died two years later, and their relationship figures in most of Li's extant poems. She married again, but with much less success. Li sued her new husband for embezzling funds, and when he was found guilty and exiled she divorced him. They had been married for less than one hundred days. Li never had any children. Very little is known of her later life, and out of the hundreds of poems she wrote, we now have only eighteen *shih* poems and seventy-eight *tz'u*.

A Marriage

For Margie Smigel and Jon Dopkeen

You are holding up a ceiling
with both arms. It is very heavy,
but you must hold it up, or else
it will fall down on you. Your arms
are tired, terribly tired,
and, as the day goes on, it feels
as if either your arms or the ceiling
will soon collapse.

But then,
unexpectedly,
something wonderful happens:
Someone,
a man or a woman,
walks into the room
and holds their arms up
to the ceiling beside you.

So you finally get
to take down your arms.
You feel the relief of respite,
the blood flowing back
to your fingers and arms.
And when your partner's arms tire,
you hold up your own
to relieve him again.

And it can go on like this
for many years
without the house falling.

MICHAEL BLUMENTHAL
(1949–)

Raised in a German-speaking household in New York City, Michael Blumenthal took degrees from SUNY Binghamton and Cornell Law School. He has worked as an antitrust lawyer, a high school German teacher, a television producer, an editor, and an administrator for the National Endowment for the Arts. He has a son from his second marriage.

A Dedication to My Wife

To whom I owe the leaping delight
That quickens my senses in our wakingtime
And the rhythm that governs the repose of our sleepingtime,
    The breathing in unison

Of lovers whose bodies smell of each other
Who think the same thoughts without need of speech
And babble the same speech without need of meaning.

No peevish winter wind shall chill
No sullen tropic sun shall wither
The roses in the rose-garden which is ours and ours only

But this dedication is for others to read:
These are private words addressed to you in public.

    T. S. ELIOT
    (1888–1965)

Addressed to his second wife, Valerie Fletcher, and included as the dedication in his *Collected Poems: 1909–1962*; this was Eliot's last poem.

T. S. Eliot was born in St. Louis, Missouri, as one of seven children. He studied at Harvard and then emigrated to England in 1914 and became a British citizen in 1927. He worked as a banker, an editor, a publisher, and a critic. His first marriage, to Vivien Haigh-Wood in 1915, was not happy, and they separated in the 1930s. Vivien was eventually committed to a mental hospital until her death in 1947. They had no children. Ten years later he married Valerie Fletcher, his secretary at the publishing firm of Faber and Faber. In 1948, Eliot received both the Nobel Prize for Literature and the British Order of Merit.

To My Dear and Loving Husband

If ever two were one, then surely we.
If ever man were loved by wife, then thee;
If ever wife was happy in a man,
Compare with me, ye women, if you can.
I prize thy love more than whole mines of gold
Or all the riches that the East doth hold.
My love is such that rivers cannot quench,
Nor ought but love from thee, give recompense.
Thy love is such I can no way repay,
The heavens reward thee manifold, I pray.
Then while we live, in love let's so persevere
That when we live no more, we may live ever.

ANNE BRADSTREET
(1612–1672)

This poem was never intended for publication, but was found among Bradstreet's papers
after her death and inserted in the second, posthumous edition of her poetry.

Born in Northhampton, England, Anne Bradstreet was the daughter of Thomas Dudley,
who would later become the first governor of Massachusetts. She married Simon
Bradstreet (another future governor) in 1628, at sixteen, and immigrated to New England
two years later. There she gave birth to eight children and was so happily married that
she worried, in good Puritan fashion, whether her love for her husband would compro-
mise her devotion to God. She became the first poet in America when her brother-in-
law, without her knowledge, published a book of her poetry in England in 1650.
Remarkably, all but one of her children were alive when she died. For other poems by
Bradstreet, see pages 70 and 164.

Men Marry What They Need

Men marry what they need. I marry you,
morning by morning, day by day, night by night,
and every marriage makes this marriage new.

In the broken name of heaven, in the light
that shatters granite, by the spitting shore,
in air that leaps and wobbles like a kite,

I marry you from time and a great door
is shut and stays shut against wind, sea, stone,
sunburst, and heavenfall. And home once more

inside our walls of skin and struts of bone,
man-woman, woman-man, and each the other,
I marry you by all dark and all dawn

and have my laugh at death. Why should I bother
the flies about me? Let them buzz and do.
Men marry their queen, their daughter, or their mother

by hidden names, but that thin buzz whines through:
where reasons are no reason, cause is true.
Men marry what they need. I marry you.

JOHN CIARDI
(1916–1986)

From a series of poems dedicated to the poet's wife, Judith Hostetter.

John Ciardi was born in Boston, where his parents were Italian immigrants. When he was three, his father died in a car accident. He was educated at Bates, Tufts, and the University of Michigan, and he served in the U.S. Air Force from 1942 to 1945. In 1946, he married Judith Hostetter, and they had two sons and a daughter.

She Rose to His Requirement — Dropt

She rose to His Requirement — dropt
The Playthings of Her Life
To take the honorable Work
Of Woman, and of Wife —

If ought She missed in Her new Day
Of Amplitude, or Awe —
Or first Prospective — Or the Gold
In using, wear away,

It lay unmentioned — as the Sea
Develope Pearl, and Weed,
But only to Himself — be known
The Fathoms they abide —

EMILY DICKINSON
(1830–1886)

Born into a prominent Amherst, Massachussets, family, Emily Dickinson was educated at Amherst Academy, and for a year at Mount Holyoke Female Seminary. In contrast to her astonishingly rich mental life, Dickenson's outer life was almost entirely uneventful. She never married, and she died in the same house in which she was born. Indeed, from the age of twenty-six until her death she almost never left that house, breaking off contact (aside from letters) with all but a few close friends. Nearly eighteen hundred of her poems have survived, written in small, handmade booklets and on scraps of paper tucked into boxes and drawers. For the most part she kept her poems secret, though about ten were published during her lifetime by friends, without her permission.

My Husband before Leaving

My husband
before leaving on a journey
is still in the house speaking
to the gods and already
separation is climbing like
bad monkeys to the windows.

ANONYMOUS
(TWELFTH CENTURY)
Translated from the Sanskrit by
J. Moussaieff Masson and W. S. Merwin

From a medieval Indian grammar that used verses to illustrate grammatical points.

A Valediction: Forbidding Mourning

As virtuous men pass mildly away,
　　And whisper to their souls to go,
Whilst some of their sad friends do say
　　The breath goes now, and some say, No;

So let us melt, and make no noise,
　　No tear-floods, nor sigh-tempests move,
'Twere profanation of our joys
　　To tell the laity our love.

Moving of th' earth brings harms and fears,
　　Men reckon what it did and meant;
But trepidation of the spheres,
　　Though greater far, is innocent.

Dull sublunary lovers' love
　　(Whose soul is sense) cannot admit
Absence, because it doth remove
　　Those things which elemented it.

But we by a love so much refined
　　That our selves know not what it is,
Inter-assuréd of the mind,
　　Care less, eyes, lips, and hands to miss.

Our two souls therefore, which are one,
　　Though I must go, endure not yet
A breach, but an expansion,
　　Like gold to airy thinness beat.

If they be two, they are two so
　　As stiff twin compasses are two;
Thy soul, the fixed foot, makes no show
　　To move, but doth, if th' other do.

And though it in the center sit,
   Yet when the other far doth roam,
It leans and hearkens after it,
   And grows erect, as that comes home.

Such wilt thou be to me, who must
   Like th' other foot, obliquely run;
Thy firmness makes my circle just,
   And makes me end where I begun.

JOHN DONNE
(1572–1631)

---

valediction — a farewell speech
profanation — desecration
laity — uninitiated
moving of th' earth — earthquakes
trepidation of the spheres — irregularities in planetary orbits thought to produce the
   precession of the equinoxes
innocent — harmless
sublunary — under the moon, earthly (and hence changeable)
elemented — composed
just — perfect or complete

Probably written as Donne's farewell to his wife, Ann More, before a long trip to France in 1611. While he was away, she gave birth to a stillborn child.

The son of prosperous London Catholic parents, John Donne studied at both Oxford and Cambridge. In 1593, his brother Henry died in prison after being arrested for harboring a priest, and about this time John converted to the Church of England. He eventually became secretary to the powerful Sir Thomas Egerton, but his prospects for a successful career were dashed when his secret marriage in 1601 to Egerton's seventeen-year-old niece, Ann More, was discovered. John was dismissed and Ann disinherited. Although they struggled financially, their marriage was happy enough that after thirteen years Donne could write "we had not one another at so cheap a rate, as that we should ever be weary of one another." Ann bore twelve children in fifteen years (not counting miscarriages), seven of whom survived. In 1615, John entered the ministry, in time becoming famous as a preacher. After Ann died in childbirth in 1617 (at the age of thirty-three), he turned entirely to God. His poems, mostly written in his youth, include both erotic love poetry and sacred verse.

When Will I Be Home?

When will I be home? I don't know.
In the mountains, in the rainy night,
The Autumn lake is flooded.
Someday we will be back together again.
We will sit in the candlelight by the West window,
And I will tell you how I remembered you
Tonight on the stormy mountain.

LI SHANG-YIN
(813?–858)
Translated from the Chinese by Kenneth Rexroth

Written while Li was in Szechwan, and then sent to his wife in Honan, several hundred miles to the northeast.

———

Often thought to be the greatest of late T'ang dynasty poets, Li Shang-yin was born in Honan, the son of a junior official. His father died when he was eight. He gained his *chin-shih* degree in 837, and the next year married the daughter of the military governor for whom he was working. They had a son and a daughter before her death in 851. Li had a lackluster official career, serving in posts all over China. He never gained high rank and died out of office in Cheng-chou at the age of forty-five.

Song of a Woman Whose Husband
Had Gone to the Coast to Earn Money

Whenever I go out of the village
and see a stone
or a tree in the distance,
I think:
It is my husband.

ANONYMOUS
(TWENTIETH CENTURY?)
*Adapted from a German translation of
the original Baule by Willard R. Trask*

This song, from the Baule tribe of Ivory Coast, first appeared in 1951 in a German ethnographic study of West Africa. It was later translated and included in an anthology of traditional oral poetry from around the world called *The Unwritten Song*.

An Ancient Gesture

I thought, as I wiped my eyes on the corner of my apron:
Penelope did this too.
And more than once: you can't keep weaving all day
And undoing it all through the night;
Your arms get tired, and the back of your neck gets tight;
And along toward morning, when you think it will never be light,
And your husband has been gone, and you don't know where, for years,
Suddenly you burst into tears;
There is simply nothing else to do.

And I thought, as I wiped my eyes on the corner of my apron:
This is an ancient gesture, authentic, antique,
In the very best tradition, classic, Greek;
Ulysses did this too.
But only as a gesture, — a gesture which implied
To the assembled throng that he was much too moved to speak.
He learned it from Penelope . . .
Penelope, who really cried.

EDNA ST. VINCENT MILLAY
(1892–1950)

Penelope — the wife of Ulysses in Homer's *Odyssey;*
    her husband was away for twenty years
weaving all day . . . undoing it — *Odyssey* II, 91–110
Ulysses did this too — *Odyssey* VIII, 83–95, 521–541

Edna St. Vincent Millay was born in Rockland, Maine. Her parents separated and then divorced when she was eight. She and her two sisters were raised by their mother, who took on work as a practical nurse to support them. After studying at Barnard College and graduating from Vassar, Millay worked in New York as an actress and playwright, writing poetry and living a bohemian life in Greenwich Village. In 1923, she married Eugen Boissevain, a Dutch businessman. They traveled extensively in the Orient and lived for a time in New York before buying and moving to a farm in Austerlitz, New York, which became home base for them between further travels and reading tours. In 1923, Millay was awarded the Pulitzer Prize for poetry — the first for a woman. Eugen died in 1949; grief-stricken and alone, Millay survived her husband by only a year.

Modern Love

#17

At dinner, she is hostess, I am host.
Went the feast ever cheerfuller? She keeps
The Topic over intellectual deeps
In buoyancy afloat. They see no ghost.
With sparkling surface-eyes we ply the ball:
It is in truth a most contagious game:
HIDING THE SKELETON, shall be its name.
Such play as this the devils might appall!
But here's the greater wonder; in that we,
Enamored of an acting naught can tire,
Each other, like true hypocrites, admire;
Warm-lighted looks, Love's ephemerioe,
Shoot gaily o'er the dishes and the wine.
We waken envy of our happy lot.
Fast, sweet, and golden, shows the marriage-knot.
Dear guests, you now have seen Love's corpse-light shine.

GEORGE MEREDITH
(1828–1909)

---

ephemerioe — insects that live for only one day
corpse-light — a natural phosphorescent light seen in marshes or over graves; believed to
be an omen of death

Part of a sequence of fifty sixteen-line sonnets on the breakup of Meredith's first marriage.

George Meredith was born in Portsmouth, England, as the son of a naval outfitter who went bankrupt. His mother died when he was five, and he was educated for a time in Germany. He began to study law but was more interested in literature. At twenty-one, without a job, he married the widowed Mary Nicolls (daughter of the satirical novelist Thomas Love Peacock), who was six years his senior and had a five-year-old daughter. Their marriage lasted for nine years, during which finances were always uncertain and quarrels were frequent. Several children were born to them, but only one, a son, survived infancy. In 1857, Mary eloped to Europe with the painter Henry Wallis. She returned the next year deserted and ill, but the couple were never reconciled. Three years later she died of kidney disease, and George refused her dying request to come see her. Nevertheless, within a few months he had written a fifty-sonnet sequence narrating and analyzing their marriage, in which he acknowledged both her talents and his own faults. He married again, this time happily, to Marie Vulliamy; they lived in Surrey from 1864 to the end of his life. He is known for his novels as well as his poetry, and was awarded the British Order of Merit in 1905.

Upon a Second Marriage

For H. I. P.

Orchards, we linger here because
Women we love stand propped in your green prisons,
Obedient to such justly bending laws
    Each one longs to take root,
  Lives to confess whatever season's
Pride of blossom or endeavor's fruit
    May to her rustling boughs have risen.

Then autumn reddens the whole mind.
No more, she vows, the dazzle of a year
Shall woo her from your bare cage of loud wind,
    Promise the ring and run
  To burn the altar, reappear
With apple blossoms for the credulous one.
    Orchards, we wonder that we linger here!

Orchards we planted, trees we shook
To learn what you were bearing, say we stayed
Because one winter dusk we half-mistook
    Frost on a bleakened bough
  For blossoms, and were half-afraid
To miss the old persuasion, should we go.
    And spring did come, and discourse made

Enough of weddings to us all
That, loving her for whom the whole world grows
Fragrant and white, we linger to recall
    As down aisles of cut trees
    How a tall trunk's cross-section shows
Concentric rings, those many marriages
    That life on each live thing bestows.

JAMES MERRILL
(1926–1995)

Written for the second marriage of Merrill's mother, Hellen Ingram Plummer.

For a biography, see page 12. For other poems by Merrill, see pages 12 and 178.

John Anderson My Jo

John Anderson my jo, John,
    When we were first acquent;
Your locks were like the raven,
    Your bonny brow was brent;
But now your brow is beld, John,
    Your locks are like the snaw
But blessings on your frosty pow,
    John Anderson my jo.

John Anderson my jo, John,
    We clamb the hill thegither;
And mony a canty day, John,
    We've had wi' ane anither:
Now we maun totter down, John,
    And hand in hand we'll go;
And sleep together at the foot,
    John Anderson my jo.

ROBERT BURNS
(1759–1796)

---

jo — sweetheart • *acquent* — acquainted • *brent* — unwrinkled • *beld* — bald
pow — head • *clamb* — climbed • *canty* — happy • *maun* — must

---

These were new words written to an old Scottish tune, which the Burns scholar Thomas Crawford called "one of the most beautiful in the whole of Scottish folk-music." For the melody, see page 195.

Robert Burns is often regarded as the national poet of Scotland. He was born in south-west Scotland as the first of seven children. His father was an unsuccessful farmer, and Burns was largely self-taught. He worked as a farm laborer and flax dresser until his first book made him famous and allowed him to buy a farm of his own. Then he married Jean Armour, with whom he had already fathered two sets of twins (three of these children had died), and they had five more children together. (Burns fathered several illegitimate children as well.) They lost the farm in 1792, and Burns worked as a tax inspector. He died four years later of heart disease, at the age of thirty-seven. His last child was born on the day of his funeral, and his remarkably forgiving wife was left a widow at thirty-one. For another poem by Burns, see page 161.

✦ III ✦
CHILDBEARING

Sonnet

#3

Look in thy glass and tell the face thou viewest,
Now is the time that face should form another,
Whose fresh repair if now thou not renewest,
Thou dost beguile the world, unbless some mother.
For where is she so fair whose uneared womb
Disdains the tillage of thy husbandry?
Or who is he so fond will be the tomb
Of his self-love to stop posterity?
Thou art thy mother's glass, and she in thee
Calls back the lovely April of her prime;
So thou through windows of thine age shalt see,
Despite of wrinkles, this thy golden time.
    But if thou live rememb'red not to be,
    Die single, and thine image dies with thee.

WILLIAM SHAKESPEARE
(1564–1616)

glass — mirror
repair — condition
beguile — cheat
uneared — unplowed
fond — foolish

From a sequence of 150 sonnets, most of which are addressed to an unidentified male friend. This sequence defined the sonnet form in English.

We know surprisingly little about William Shakespeare's life. His father was a prominent tradesman in Stratford-upon-Avon. He attended grammar school in Stratford (and never studied at a university). At eighteen, he married Anne Hathaway, who was eight years his senior, and in six months they became the parents of a daughter, Susanna. Twins Judith and Hamnet were born two years later. In the 1590s, he left his home village for London, where he acted and wrote the three dozen plays that make him the most famous dramatist in the world. Hamnet died in 1596. Shakespeare retired to Stratford in 1610, at the age of forty-six; he died six years later, shortly after his daughter Judith's marriage. Most of his works were published without his supervision or even his permission. For more verse by Shakespeare, see page 167.

Infertility

We don't know how to name

                    the long string of zeros
Stretching across winter,

                the barren places,
The missing birthdates of the unborn.

We'd like to believe in their souls

                   drifting through space
Between the Crab and the Northern Cross,
Smoky and incandescent,

                longing for incarnation.

We'd like to believe in their spirits descending,
But month after month, year after year,
We have laid ourselves down

                and raised ourselves up
And not one has ever entered our bodies.

We'd like to believe that we have planted
And tended seeds

            in their honor,
But the spirits never appear

             in darkness or light.

We don't know whether to believe in their non-existence
Or their secrecy and evasiveness,

                               their invisible spite.

Maybe it's past us, maybe it's the shape of nothing
Being born,

                  the cold slopes of the absolute.

EDWARD HIRSCH
(1950–)

the Crab and the Northern Cross — two constellations, also known as Cancer and
    Cygnus

Both of the Hirsch poems in this anthology come from his book *The Night Parade*, whose
contents he described (borrowing a line from the poet John Clare) as "memorandums of
my affections."

For a biography, see page 16.

A Honeymoon Conception (1952)

All night, though not a flake fell, the snow deepened . . .
From Grand Central their train joggled forth (stray
   snow scraps wadded in gulleys, like
a leafletting not fully swept away)
at dusk; in Connecticut, the darkness opened

(but here and there, a street lamp's sliding glow
showed how the scraps had formed a quilt) as they
   toasted themselves in the dining car,
their glances, given the press of what still lay
before them, sometimes shying toward the window.

In Vermont (though in the sleeping car they kept
the shade drawn and so never saw the play
   of bridal white on white on white,
dark pine fastnesses suddenly giving way
to snow-packed moon-limned stands of birch), they slept,

part of the time. But neither one had ever
been wider awake than on the following day,
   in Quebec, Canada (a city
of foreign signs — *gare, rue, petit déjeuner* —
and everything wrapped in white except the river,

whose fierce black urgings made of the whole place
a kind of high-piled dockyard, every slipway
   loaded with crates of lace and crystal).
On a noon walk, happily mapless, they
chanced a side street and soon came face to face

with a colossal, larger-than-life snowman
in red scarf and blue cape, who, in his warm,
    generous, featureless way, smiled
blessings upon them. (Or snow*woman*? — it was a form
smooth and rich-bellied, as if big with child.)

BRAD LEITHAUSER
(1953–)

In an author's note, Leithauser dedicated this poem to his mother, Gladys Garner
Leithauser.

For a biography, see page 39.

After Midnight, the Fifth Month

I am becoming a cathedral! My
Belly rises from the bed like a tiny
Model of the Florence *Cupolone*.
Probably a belly just like this
Inspired Brunelleschi's great design:
The original, the perfect, home.
There is a tapping from the inside,
Gentle, almost imperceptible,
Like piano hammers touching piano strings.
And I am fluent in these first attempts
At language; I am turned to someone else.
There *is* life beyond our own. Gabriel
Whispers, softly fluttering his wings,
With every touch a hushed annunciation.

JACQUELINE OSHEROW
(1956–)

Brunelleschi — Italian architect (1377–1446) who designed the massive dome (*cupola*)
   atop the Florence Cathedral
Gabriel — Luke 1:26–28

Written in 1987 when Osherow was pregnant with her first child, Magda.

Jacqueline Osherow was born in Philadelphia, and educated at Harvard-Radcliffe and
Princeton. Her more recent work explores her Jewish heritage. She lives in Salt Lake City
with her three daughters. See the next poem as well, from the same pregnancy.

Five A.M., the Ninth Month

Your kick awakens me to wild geese
Honking overhead, the stirring trees
Just visible beneath the new, pale blue.
Everything is coming: day, spring, you;
The geese above all seem to shout, "Make way!"
But I would almost keep you where you are,
Your pulse at breakneck speed turning the air
I breathe into a future, wind on clay,
Your heart galloping beneath my heart
And every living thing I hear, its echo,
Geese and wind in trees and my own heart,
The whole unwakened world resounds with you,
Shaking until life itself will part
And you — imagine — you'll come screaming through.

JACQUELINE OSHEROW
(1956–)

Before the Birth of One of Her Children

All things within this fading world hath end,
Adversity doth still our joys attend;
No ties so strong, no friends so dear and sweet,
But with death's parting blow is sure to meet.
The sentence past is most irrevocable,
A common thing, yet oh, inevitable.
How soon, my Dear, death may my steps attend,
How soon't may be thy lot to lose thy friend,
We both are ignorant, yet love bids me
These farewell lines to recommend to thee,
That when that knot's untied that made us one,
I may seem thine, who in effect am none.
And if I see not half my days that's due,
What nature would, God grant to yours and you;
The many faults that well you know I have
Let be interred in my oblivious grave;
If any worth or virtue were in me,
Let that live freshly in thy memory
And when thou feel'st no grief, as I no harms,
Yet love thy dead, who long lay in thine arms.
And when thy loss shall be repaid with gains
Look to my little babes, my dear remains.
And if thou love thyself, or loved'st me,
Then O protect from step-dame's injury.
And if chance to thine eyes shall bring this verse,
With some sad sighs honour my absent hearse;
And kiss this paper for thy love's dear sake,
Who with salt tears this last farewell did take.

ANNE BRADSTREET
(1612–1672)

step-dame — stepmother

Probably written during the pregnancy of Bradstreet's sixth child, Mercy, born in 1646. Like "To My Dear and Loving Husband," this poem was not originally intended for publication.

For a biography, see page 47. For other poems by Bradstreet, see pages 47 and 164.

Notes from the Delivery Room

Strapped down,
victim in an old comic book,
I have been here before,
this place where pain winces
off the walls
like too bright light.
Bear down a doctor says,
foreman to sweating laborer,
but this work, this forcing
of one life from another
is something that I signed for
at a moment when I would have signed anything.
Babies should grow in fields;
common as beets or turnips
they should be picked and held
root end up, soil spilling
from between their toes —
and how much easier it would be later,
returning them to earth.
Bear up . . . bear down . . . the audience
grows restive, and I'm a new magician
who can't produce the rabbit
from my swollen hat.
She's crowning, someone says,
but there is no one royal here,
just me, quite barefoot,
greeting my barefoot child.

LINDA PASTAN
(1932–)

For a biography, see page 24. For other poems by Pastan, see pages 23 and 125.

Morning Song

Love set you going like a fat gold watch.
The midwife slapped your footsoles, and your bald cry
Took its place among the elements.

Our voices echo, magnifying your arrival. New statue.
In a drafty museum, your nakedness
Shadows our safety. We stand round blankly as walls.

I'm no more your mother
Than the cloud that distills a mirror to reflect its own slow
Effacement at the wind's hand.

All night your moth-breath
Flickers among the flat pink roses. I wake to listen:
A far sea moves in my ear.

One cry, and I stumble from bed, cow-heavy and floral
In my Victorian nightgown.
Your mouth opens clean as a cat's. The window square

Whitens and swallows its dull stars. And now you try
Your handful of notes;
The clear vowels rise like balloons.

SYLVIA PLATH
(1932–1963)

Written a few months after the birth of Plath's first child, Frieda, in 1960.

Sylvia Plath was a native of Boston. Her father, a German immigrant from Poland, taught biology at Boston University and died when she was eight. After her graduation from Smith College, she attended Cambridge on a Fulbright scholarship, where she met and married British poet Ted Hughes (later poet laureate of England). They had two children. The strains of ill health, depression, motherhood, a marital separation, and writing overwhelmed her; she committed suicide at age thirty-one. She was awarded a Pulitzer Prize posthumously in 1982.

The Tempest
To my daughter Miranda

If you name your daughter *vision*,
or *wondrous to behold*, you should not be surprised
if she comes to you in anger or in shame,
wishing to be known as *Mary* or *Ann*.
That will be the moment to carry her out
to the things of the world she is not,
speaking other sounds that were almost hers:
aspen, lily-white, cumulo-nimbus glow.

Soon enough she'll realize the world,
too often, gets named in hope of profit,
or deceit, or the scientist's exactitude.
But on the greening island of the family
testing its voice in the months of waiting,
the sought-after words are music and the past:
Grandparent. Aunt. Child deceased.

Spirits of fashion and monsters of commerce
lurk, bedfellows eager to keep us
from our own best inventions and songs.
Some days it seems we grow from wailing silence
into speech, only that we might curse
the coming return to silence.
But if you've named your daughter *wondrous to behold,*

she'll someday learn she heard those words
before all others, and then again, and again.
When you are gone beyond all roaring
she'll know, should you ever brave return,
which words are the first you'll speak.

STEPHEN COREY
(1948–)

Written at the birth of Corey's second daughter, Miranda — a name chosen for its sound, its meaning (as noted in the first two lines of the poem), and the character in Shakespeare's *Tempest*. Corey explains: "I loved . . . the attitude of wonder and hopefulness that attend Prospero's famous child."

Stephen Corey was born in Buffalo, New York, and educated at SUNY Binghamton and the University of Florida. In 1970, he married Mary Gibson; they have four daughters and two grandchildren. He has lived in the South since 1975 and has been a longtime editor of *The Georgia Review*.

On the Birth of His Son

Families, when a child is born
Want it to be intelligent.
I, through intelligence,
Having wrecked my whole life,
Only hope the baby will prove
Ignorant and stupid.
Then he will crown a tranquil life
By becoming a Cabinet Minister.

SU TUNG-P'O
(1037–1101)
Translated from the Chinese by Arthur Waley

Also known as Su Shih, Su Tung-p'o was the dominant literary figure of China's Northern Sung period. He was born into a gentry family of limited means in Szechwan and was educated primarily by his father Su Hsün, a self-educated man who later gained fame as an essayist. Both he and his younger brother attained their *chin-shih* degrees in 1057. He became an important official, but his career fluctuated with court politics, and he endured a series of demotions, transfers, exiles, and pardons. He married the fifteen-year-old Wang Fu in 1054, and shortly after her death in 1065 he married Wang Jun-chih, her first cousin. About ten years later he took Chaoyun as a concubine, and she lived with them for twenty years, until her death in 1095, two years after the death of his second wife. These three women bore four sons, three of whom survived into adulthood. Unfortunately, Tun-erh, Chaoyun's only child and the son whose birth was marked by this poem, died at ten months. Su wrote about twenty-eight hundred *shih* poems and 350 *tz'u*, and he was also famous for his essays, calligraphy, and paintings. For another poem by Su, see page 158.

My Son, My Executioner

My son, my executioner,
  I take you in my arms,
Quiet and small and just astir,
  And whom my body warms.

Sweet death, small son, our instrument
  Of immortality,
Your cries and hungers document
  Our bodily decay.

We twenty-five and twenty-two
  Who seemed to live forever,
Observe enduring life in you
  And start to die together.

DONALD HALL
(1928–)

Written a few weeks after the birth of Hall's first child, Andrew.
_____

Born in New Haven, Connecticut, Donald Hall was educated at Harvard and Oxford. He has two children and five grandchildren. In 1975, he retired from teaching to live with his second wife, Jane Kenyon, in the ancestral farmhouse where both his grandmother and his mother were born, in Danbury, New Hampshire. For another poem by Hall, see page 139; for poems by Kenyon, see pages 21 and 143.

Infant Joy

"I have no name:
I am but two days old."
What shall I call thee?
"I happy am,
Joy is my name."
Sweet joy befall thee!

Pretty joy!
Sweet joy but two days old,
Sweet joy I call thee:
Thou dost smile,
I sing the while,
Sweet joy befall thee!

Infant Sorrow

My mother groaned, my father wept!
Into the dangerous world I leapt,
Helpless, naked, piping loud,
Like a fiend hid in a cloud.

Struggling in my father's hands,
Striving against my swaddling bands,
Bound and weary, I thought best
To sulk upon my mother's breast.

WILLIAM BLAKE
(1757–1827)

The son of a London haberdasher, William Blake was educated at home, chiefly by his mother. He studied art for a few months and then at fourteen was apprenticed to an engraver. At twenty-four he married Catherine Boucher, who was illiterate at the time. Blake taught her to read and she later assisted him in his work. The couple remained childless. He became a painter and engraver as well as a poet, but his unconventional style, in both art and religion, meant that he never achieved popular acclaim. Plagued by poverty his entire life, he was buried in an unmarked grave in a public cemetery.

Upon Her Soothing Breast

Upon her soothing breast
She lulled her little child;
A winter sunset in the west
A dreary glory smiled.

EMILY BRONTË
(1818–1848)

Best known for her novel *Wuthering Heights*, Emily Brontë was the second of three liter-
ary sisters. The girls, along with a brother, Branwell, grew up in a remote village in
Yorkshire where their father was a parson (two other sisters died in childhood). Their
mother died when Emily was two, and the children entertained themselves by creating
long narratives, dialogues, and poems about an imaginary island they called Gondal.
Many of her poems, including this one, were originally written about events in Gondal.
She lived in her father's parsonage for her entire life, with the exception of six months as
a governess and a year as a student. She died at age thirty of tuberculosis, without ever
having married.

Rocking

The sea its thousand of waves
rocks, divinely.
Listening to the loving seas,
I rock my child.

The erratic wind in the night
rocks the wheat.
Listening to the loving winds
I rock my child.

God, the Father, his thousands of worlds
rocks silently.
Sensing his hand in the shadow
I rock my child.

GABRIELA MISTRAL
(1889–1957)
Translated from the Spanish by John Eric Gant

Gabriela Mistral was the pseudonym of Lucila Godoy Alcayaga, who was born in rural Chile of mixed Basque, Spanish, Indian, and Jewish descent. Her father left when she was three, and she was raised and educated by her elder sister Emeline. At fifteen she began to teach school, and she made a living as a teacher, a school administrator, and educational consultant to the governments of Chile and Mexico. Later she worked as a Chilean diplomat and a university professor in the United States. Her early poetry was inspired by the suicide of Romilie Ureta in 1909, whom she had hoped to wed. Despite other loves, she never did marry, though in 1926 she adopted her half brother's nine-month-old son shortly after the death of his mother. She was heartbroken when the boy died at age seventeen. Two years later, Mistral won the Nobel Prize in Literature (1945), the first Latin American writer to receive that honor.

A Cradle Song

*"Coth yani me von gilli beg,
'N heur ve thu more a creena."*

The angels are bending
   Above your white bed,
They weary of tending
   The souls of the dead.

God smiles in high heaven
   To see you so good,
The old planets seven
   Grow gay with his mood.

I kiss you and kiss you,
   With arms round my own,
Ah, how shall I miss you,
   When, dear, you have grown.

W. B. YEATS
(1865–1939)

---

old planets seven — in ancient astronomy, the celestial bodies that had motions independent of the fixed stars — Mercury, Venus, Mars, Jupiter, Saturn, the sun, and the moon

---

The last two lines are adapted from the Gaelic song quoted in the inscription.

W. B. Yeats was born in Dublin to an Anglo-Irish Protestant family who shortly thereafter moved to London. When he was sixteen, they moved back to Dublin, where he studied art, hoping to become a painter like his father. After publishing his first book of poems, he fell desperately in love with the actress and Irish activist Maude Gonne, who persistently refused to marry him (she married someone else, unhappily, in 1903). He remained single until his fifties, and then he married Georgie Hyde-Lees in 1917, with whom he had a son and a daughter. He served as a senator of the Irish Free State from 1922 to 1928, and he was awarded the Nobel Prize for Literature in 1923.

Golden Bells' First Birthday

When my fortieth birthday was almost upon me
Along came a daughter, Golden Bells.
Now she's survived her first full year
And is learning to sit but can't yet talk.

I'm somewhat shamed of my unsaintly sentiments,
But I can't help having normal feelings.
From now on I'm trapped by outside attachments,
And must simply find solace in my daily delights.

If only she is spared from premature death,
Soon I'm entangled in marriage arrangements!
This means that my plans to retire to the hills
Will just have to wait for some fifteen years more!

Po Chü-i
(772–846)
Translated from the Chinese by Charles Hucker

Written in 810. Sadly, Po's hopes were in vain. Golden Bells, his first child, died a year later after a ten-day illness.

———

Po Chü-i was born in Honan to an impoverished, scholarly family. He gained his *chin-shih* degree in 800, and then had a long and checkered career in government. At times he held important posts at the capital, though he was repeatedly demoted and sent to the provinces (apparently his passion for social reform did not endear him to everyone); he retired from government in 832. He wrote more than twenty-eight hundred poems, which he took care to edit and organize himself. We know little about his wife, Miss Yang, other than that she was the younger sister of a close friend. They were married for some thirty-eight years. When he was seventy and she about fifty-two, he wrote, "A companion till old age is hard to get / But to one who has her, what do white hairs matter?" His only son, A-ts'ui, was born in 829, when Po was fifty-seven, but the boy died at age two. For other poems by Po, see pages 94, 134, and 136.

After Making Love We Hear Footsteps

For I can snore like a bullhorn
or play loud music
or sit up talking with any reasonably sober Irishman
and Fergus will only sink deeper
into his dreamless sleep, which goes by all in one flash,
but let there be that heavy breathing
or a stifled come-cry anywhere in the house
and he will wrench himself awake
and make for it on the run — as now, we lie together,
after making love, quiet, touching along the length of our bodies,
familiar touch of the long-married,
and he appears — in his baseball pajamas, it happens,
the neck opening so small
he has to screw them on, which one day may make him wonder
about the mental capacity of baseball players —
and says, "Are you loving and snuggling? May I join?"
He flops down between us and hugs us and snuggles himself to sleep,
his face gleaming with satisfaction at being this very child.

In the half darkness we look at each other
and smile
and touch arms across his little, startlingly muscled body —
this one whom habit of memory propels to the ground of his making,
sleeper only the mortal sounds can sing awake,
this blessing love gives again into our arms.

GALWAY KINNELL
(1927–)

Galway Kinnell was born in Providence, Rhode Island, as the youngest of four children of immigrant parents (from Ireland and Scotland). He was educated at Princeton and the University of Rochester, and he served in the U.S. Navy during World War II. He has held visiting positions at universities in Europe, the Middle East, and the United States. He was awarded a Pulitzer Prize in 1983, the same year he won a National Book Award, and was named a MacArthur Fellow in 1984. He has two children.

35/10

Brushing out my daughter's dark
silken hair before the mirror
I see the gray gleaming on my head,
the silver-haired servant behind her. Why is it
just as we begin to go
they begin to arrive, the fold in my neck
clarifying as the fine bones of her
hips sharpen? As my skin shows
its dry pitting, she opens like a small
pale flower on the tip of a cactus;
as my last chances to bear a child
are falling through my body, the duds among them,
her full purse of eggs, round and
firm as hard-boiled yolks, is about
to snap its clasp. I brush her tangled
fragrant hair at bedtime. It's an old
story — the oldest we have on our planet —
the story of replacement.

SHARON OLDS
(1942–)

Born in San Francisco, Sharon Olds was educated at Stanford and Columbia. She has lived most of her adult life in New York City, teaching at NYU for more than twenty years.

·IV·
$\mathscr{P}$ARENTING

To My Daughter

Bright clasp of her whole hand around my finger,
My daughter, as we walk together now.
All my life I'll feel a ring invisibly
Circle this bone with shining: when she is grown
Far from today as her eyes are far already.

STEPHEN SPENDER
(1909–1995)

Written when his daughter, Elizabeth, was two or three, and Spender was in his early forties.

———

Stephen Spender was born in London and educated at Oxford. His parents died while he was in his teens. He became one of the major British poets of the 1930s along with his friends W. H. Auden and Louis MacNeice (whose poem appears on page 127). Always politically active, he moved from espousing left-wing causes to fervent anti-Communism. He married Inez Pearn in 1936 and then divorced three years later. In 1941, he married Natasha Litvin, with whom he had one son and one daughter. During the war he served as a fireman in London with the National Fire Service. He taught in the United States during the 1950s and 1960s, serving as consultant in poetry at the Library of Congress from 1965 to 1966. He returned to England in the 1970s and was knighted in 1983.

Instinct

Although he's apparently the youngest (his little Rasta-beard is barely
    down and feathers),
most casually connected (he hardly glances at the girl he's with, though
    she might be his wife),
half-sloshed (or more than half) on picnic-whiskey teen-aged father,
    when his little son,
two or so, tumbles from the slide, hard enough to scare himself, hard
    enough to make him cry,
really cry, not partly cry, not pretend the fright for what must be some
    scarce attention,
but really let it out, let loudly be revealed the fear of having been so
    close to real fear,
he, the father, knows just how quickly he should pick the child up, then
    how firmly hold it,
fit its head into the muscled socket of his shoulder, rub its back, croon
    and whisper to it,
and finally pull away a little, about a head's length, looking, still concerned,
    into its eyes,
then smiling, broadly, brightly, as though something had been shared,
    something of importance,
not dreadful, or not very, not at least now that it's past, but rather
    something . . . funny,
funny, yes, it was funny, wasn't it, to fall and cry like that, though one
    certainly can understand,

we've all had glimpses of a premonition of the anguish out there, you're
    better now, though,
aren't you, why don't you go back and try again, I'll watch you, maybe
    have another drink,
yes, my son, my love, I'll go back and be myself now: you go be the
    person you are, too.

C. K. WILLIAMS
(1936–)

Born in Newark, New Jersey, C. K. Williams graduated from the University of Pennsylvania. He has worked as an editor, a group therapist for adolescents, a teacher, and a translator. He splits his time between Paris and Princeton University, where he teaches. In 1975, he married Catherine Mauger, with whom he has a son; he has a daughter by a previous marriage, and two grandsons. He was awarded the Pulitzer Prize in 2000 for his book *Repair*, and he published a prose memoir in the same year titled *Misgivings: My Mother, My Father, Myself*. For other poems by Williams, see pages 132 and 140.

Night Terrors

Whose voice is it in mine when the child cries,
terrified in sleep, and half asleep myself I'm there
beside him saying, shh, now easy, shh,

whose voice — too intimate with all the ways
of solace to be merely mine; so prodigal
in desiring to give, yet so exact in giving

that even before I reach the little bed,
before I touch him, as I do anyway,
already he is breathing quietly again.

Is it my mother's voice in mine, the memory
no memory at all but just the vocal trace,
sheer bodily sensation on the lips and tongue,

of what I may have heard once in the pre-
remembering of infancy — heard once and then
forgot entirely till it was wakened by the cry,

brought back, as if from exile, by the child's cry, —
here to the father's voice, where the son again
can ask the mother, and the mother, too, the son —

Why has it taken you so long to come?

ALAN SHAPIRO
(1952–)

Alan Shapiro was born in Boston, Massachusetts, and educated at Brandeis University.
He teaches at the University of North Carolina, Chapel Hill, and lives with his son and
daughter in Hillsborough, North Carolina.

I Have a Beautiful Daughter

I have a beautiful daughter, golden
like a flower, my beloved Cleis,
for her, in her place, I would not accept
the whole of Lydia, nor lovely . . .

SAPPHO
(LATE SEVENTH CENTURY B.C.)
Translated from the Greek by Josephine Balmer

Lydia, a large kingdom in present-day Turkey, was the dominant political and economic power in the region during Sappho's time. Lydia's military capabilities constantly threatened the island of Lesbos, whose inhabitants were very familiar with its vast resources.

Sappho was an early Greek lyric poet and a native of the island of Lesbos. Her father was Scamandronymus and her mother, Cleis. As a child, her family went into exile in Sicily, but later she returned to Lesbos. There she married Cercylas, a rich man from the island of Andros, and had a daughter Cleis, named for her grandmother. She is known for her passionate love poetry and her close friendships with other women. Although she was enormously influential in the ancient world and wrote some nine books of poetry, everything was lost by the eighth or ninth century, and all that survived were quotations of her poems by other authors. These included only one complete poem (of twenty-eight lines), the first seventeen lines of another, and about one hundred fragments — none longer than four lines and many just single words or phrases. The four lines above (Fragment # 132) survived because they were quoted in a second-century A.D. grammatical handbook. Many more fragments of Sappho's poems were discovered in the twentieth century on ancient bits of papyrus.

An Excuse for Not Returning the Visit of a Friend

Do not be offended because
I am slow to go out. You know
Me too well for that. On my lap
I hold my little girl. At my
Knees stands my handsome little son.
One has just begun to talk.
The other chatters without
Stopping. They hang on my clothes
And follow my every step.
I can't get any farther
Than the door. I am afraid
I will never make it to your house.

MEI YAO-CH'EN
(1002–1060)
Translated from the Chinese by Kenneth Rexroth

Mei Yao-ch'en was born into a scholar-official family in Anhwei Province, educated by an uncle, and after many attempts finally passed the *chin-shih* examination in 1051. Through his uncle's connections, he had secured a number of minor government posts starting in 1030, three years after he had married the daughter of the statesman Hsieh T'ao. His wife's death in 1044 at the age of thirty-six inspired a number of heartbreaking poems. She had borne him two sons (including a baby who died within a month of her own death) and a daughter. Mei's second wife, from the Tiao family, gave birth to three more sons and two daughters (including one who lived only half a year). In the preface to Mei's collected works, his good friend Ou-yang Hsiu wrote, "a man must undergo hardship before he can become an accomplished poet." For another poem by Mei, see page 144.

For a Five-Year-Old

A snail is climbing up the window-sill
into your room, after a night of rain.
You call me in to see, and I explain
that it would be unkind to leave it there:
It might crawl to the floor; we must take care
that no one squashes it. You understand,
and carry it outside, with careful hand,
to eat a daffodil.

I see, then, that a kind of faith prevails:
your gentleness is moulded still by words
from me, who have trapped mice and shot wild birds,
from me, who drowned your kittens, who betrayed
four closest relatives, and who purveyed
the harshest kind of truth to many another.
But that is how things are: I am your mother,
and we are kind to snails.

FLEUR ADCOCK
(1934–)

By the time the eldest of Adcock's boys turned five, she had divorced their father.

Fleur Adcock was born in Papakura, New Zealand. She spent the war years in England
and then returned to New Zealand, where she was educated at Victoria University in
Wellington. At the age of eighteen she married Alistair Campbell, and they had two sons
before their divorce in 1958. Adcock has worked as a librarian in both New Zealand and
Britain, where she has lived since 1963. She now has five grandchildren.

Children

My nephew, who is six years old, is called "Tortoise";
My daughter of three, — little "Summer Dress."
One is beginning to learn to joke and talk;
The other can already recite poems and songs.
At morning they play clinging about my feet;
At night they sleep pillowed against my dress.
Why, children, did you reach the world so late,
Coming to me just when my years are spent?
Young things draw our feelings to them;
Old people easily give their hearts.
The sweetest vintage at last turns sour;
The full moon in the end begins to wane.
And so with men the bonds of love and affection
Soon may change to a load of sorrow and care.
But all the world is bound by love's ties;
Why did I think that I alone should escape?

Po Chü-i
(772–846)
Translated from the Chinese by Arthur Waley

Written in 818, when the poet was forty-six. Of his four children, Summer Dress was the only one to survive to adulthood; Tortoise was the son of his younger brother and was also raised by Po Chü-i.

For a biography, see page 81. For other poems by Po, see pages 81, 134, and 136.

Daystar

She wanted a little room for thinking:
but she saw diapers steaming on the line,
a doll slumped behind the door.

So she lugged a chair behind the garage
to sit out the children's naps.

Sometimes there were things to watch —
the pinched armor of a vanished cricket,
a floating maple leaf. Other days
she stared until she was assured
when she closed her eyes
she'd see only her own vivid blood.

She had an hour, at best, before Liza appeared
pouting from the top of the stairs.
And just *what* was mother doing
out back with the field mice? Why,

building a palace. Later
that night when Thomas rolled over and
lurched into her, she would open her eyes
and think of the place that was hers
for an hour — where
she was nothing,
pure nothing, in the middle of the day.

RITA DOVE
(1952–)

From *Thomas and Beulah*, a book of poems that narrates the lives of Dove's maternal grandparents.

Rita Dove was born in Akron, Ohio, in 1952, the daughter of the first Black research chemist in the American tire and rubber industry. She was educated at Miami University in Ohio, the University of Tübingen in Germany, and the University of Iowa, and married the German writer Fred Viebahn in 1979; they have a daughter, Aviva Dove-Viebahn. Dove won the 1987 Pulitzer Prize in poetry for *Thomas and Beulah* and became the first Black poet laureate of the United States in 1993. Her literary career was sparked when she was in the twelfth grade and went to a book signing by John Ciardi (whose poem appears on page 48).

Playground

In the hygienic sand
of the new municipal sandbox,
toddlers with names from the soaps,
Brandon and Samantha,
fill and empty, fill and empty
their bright plastic buckets
alongside children with names
from obscure books of the Bible.
We are all mothers here,
friendly and polite.
We are teaching our children to share.

A man could slice his way
through us like a pirate!
And why not? Didn't we open
our bodies recklessly
to any star, say, Little one,
whoever you are, come in?
But the men are busy elsewhere.
Broad-hipped in fashionable sweatpants,
we discuss the day — a tabloid
murder, does cold cream work,
those students in China —
and as we talk

not one of us isn't thinking,
Mama! Was it like this?
Did I do this to you?
But Mama is too busy,
she is dead, or in Florida,
or taking up new interests,
and the children want apple juice
and Cheerios, diapers and naps.
We have no one to ask but each other.
But we do not ask each other.

KATHA POLLITT
(1949–)

Katha Pollitt was born in New York City and educated at Harvard-Radcliffe and Columbia University. She lives in Manhattan with her daughter, Sophie, and writes a bimonthly column on politics, feminism, and culture for *The Nation*. Her most recent books are *Reasonable Creatures* and *Subject to Debate*, both collections of prose.

September, the First Day of School

#1

My child and I hold hands on the way to school,
And when I leave him at the first-grade door
He cries a little but is brave; he does
Let go. My selfish tears remind me how
I cried before that door a life ago.
I may have had a hard time letting go.

Each fall the children must endure together
What every child also endures alone:
Learning the alphabet, the integers,
Three dozen bits and pieces of a stuff
So arbitrary, so peremptory,
That worlds invisible and visible

Bow down before it, as in Joseph's dream
The sheaves bowed down and then the stars bowed down
Before the dreaming of a little boy.
That dream got him such hatred of his brothers
As cost the greater part of life to mend
And yet great kindness came of it in the end.

HOWARD NEMEROV
(1920–1991)

as in Joseph's dream — Genesis 37:5–11
great kindness — Genesis 45

Howard Nemerov was born in New York City and educated at Harvard. He served as a pilot in the Second World War with both the Royal Air Force and the U.S. Eighth Army Air Corps. In 1944, he married Margaret Russell, an Englishwoman, with whom he had three sons. He won a Pulitzer and a National Book Award in 1978, won a Bollingen in 1981, and served as the poet laureate of the United States from 1988 to 1990.

Blaming Sons

White hair shrouds both my temples,
my skin and flesh have lost their fullness.
Though I have five male children,
not a one of them loves brush and paper,
A-shu's already twice times eight —
in laziness he's never been rivaled.
A-hsüan's going on fifteen
but cares nothing for letters or learning.
Yung and Tuan are thirteen
and can't tell a 6 from a 7!
T'ung-tzu's approaching age nine —
all he does is hunt for chestnuts and pears.
If this is the luck Heaven sends me,
then pour me the "thing in the cup"!

T'AO YÜAN-MING
(365–427)
Translated from the Chinese by Burton Watson

can't tell a 6 from a 7 — the characters for "6" and "7" are not at all similar in Chinese
"thing in the cup" — wine

T'ao Yüan-ming, also known as T'ao Ch'ien, is generally considered one of the two or three greatest pre-T'ang poets. He was born in a time of political instability in China as a member of the Hsi minority. Though his family had once had powerful connections, his own father (whose name we do not know) was an impoverished official. T'ao served in a number of minor government positions though he was often unhappy with the hypocrisy and compromises required by official life. Finally, through an uncle's connections, he secured the post of magistrate of P'eng-tse. He lasted only eighty days, however, before resigning and giving up politics for good. For the next twenty-two years he lived as a farmer, with all the hardships and difficulties that life entails. We know from this poem that he had five sons.

Twelfth Birthday

As if because you lay
(deeply embarrassing) inside
my body, I could *(inconceivable)*
follow your swift thoughts into their blue
immersion even now,
stilettoes flickering, or schools of fish
maneuvering, first clear and then occluded,
though now and then a piercing gleam cuts through;

as if the snow reflections that glaze
the winter afternoon to porcelain
could penetrate the secrets of a skull
that happens to have lodged *(improbable)*
inside me once. Your liberation
twelve years ago today is the occasion
you and your friends are celebrating now
behind a door that's firmly shut.

The fantasy you've lately been devouring
features an evil mage with hourglass eyes.
Last week, when you were furious at me
(I must have thrown some precious thing away),
you swiftly slipped into your parents' room
and turned the bedside clock an hour ahead.
Discovered as the culprit, wickedly
you smiled. You knew time was my enemy.

RACHEL HADAS
(1948–)

mage — magician, sorcerer

Born in New York City, Rachel Hadas was educated at Radcliffe, Johns Hopkins, and Princeton. She teaches English at the Newark campus of Rutgers University and is the author of more than a dozen books of poetry, essays, and translations. Having grown up in an academic family, she often writes about families and books. She is married to George Edwards, a composer; they have one son, Jonathan. For another poem by Hadas, see page 174.

Mother and Daughter

#6

Sometimes, as young things will, she vexes me,
  Wayward, or too unheeding, or too blind.
  Like aimless birds that, flying on a wind,
Strike slant against their own familiar tree;
Like venturous children pacing with the sea,
  That turn but when the breaker spurts behind
  Outreaching them with spray: she in such kind
Is borne against some fault, or does not flee.

And so, may be, I blame her for her wrong,
  And she will frown and lightly plead her part,
And then I bid her go. But 'tis not long:
  Then comes she lip to ear and heart to heart.
And thus forgiven her love seems newly strong,
  And, oh my penitent, how dear thou art!

AUGUSTA WEBSTER
(1837–1894)

One of twenty-seven sonnets from an unfinished sonnet sequence on the poet's relationship with her daughter, Davies. These poems were mostly written when Davies was in her twenties, over a period of about fifteen years. In 1890, this daughter appeared on the London stage as the heroine in one of her mother's plays.

Augusta Davies Webster was born in Dorset, England, as the daughter of a vice admiral. She lived much of her early childhood aboard naval ships at various harbors and islands (which may explain the seaside imagery in the poem above). She eventually attended the Cambridge School of Art and studied ancient Greek to help a younger brother; later she published her translations of two Greek tragedies. At thirty, she married Thomas Webster; the couple moved to London, where he practiced law and she became active in local politics (including serving two terms on the London School Board). They had one child, a daughter. Webster published several books of poetry, but her "Mother and Daughter" sonnets appeared only in 1895, the year after her death.

Maps

In his cluttered room, socks and comics
on the floor, a Metro map spreads its tangles
of blue and red and green above the bed.
On Saturdays he travels to unexplored stations,
returns and circles them in triumph.
"Do you walk in the neighborhoods?" I ask.

No, he just wants to follow the mind
that worked the system out, to play
the boards where flashing lights
spell the routes to destinations.

Together we chant the names
of my favorite stations: *Gaité, Abbesses,
Bonne-Nouvelle.* He's gone where I have never been . . .
Michel-Ange-Molitor . . . Eglise de Pantin . . .
exotic urban ports of call.

But Agnès scolds, "Madame doesn't understand.
Paris is dangerous. There are men who harm
boys. He shouldn't be alone."

Give him one more element to fear? Never.
Looking in his eyes, I wonder how he sees
the city I worshipped at twenty, idolized
like a first lover.

"Don't worry," he says unexpectedly one day,
"I have a map and I don't talk to anyone."

CELIA GILBERT
(1932–)

Written of a time when Gilbert and her family were living in Paris for a year.

For a biography, see page 26. For other poems by Gilbert, see pages 26 and 153.

To a Daughter at Fourteen, Forsaking the Violin

All year, Mozart went under
the sea of rock punk reggae
that crashed into your room every
night and wouldn't recede however
I sandbagged our shore
and swore to keep the house dry.
Your first violin, that halfsize
rented model, slipped out of tune
as you played Bach by ear
Suzuki method with forty other virtuosos
who couldn't tie their shoes.
Then such progress: your own
fiddle, the trellised notes you read,
recitals where I sat on hard chairs.
Your playing made me the kid.
If I had those fingers! . . .
Five of yours grasped my pinky,
the world before you grew teeth.
Okay. They're your fingers,
To paint the nails of, put rings on,
hold cigarettes in, make obscene
gestures or farewells with.

CAROLE SIMMONS OLES
(1939–)

Carole Simmons Oles was born in New York City and educated at Queens College and
the University of California at Berkeley. She is currently professor of English at California
State University, Chico, where she directs the creative writing program. She has two
children, Thomas and Julia, and a grandson, Logan.

Daughter

My next poem will be happy,
I promise myself. Then you come
with your deep eyes, your tall jeans,
your narrow hands, your wit,
your uncanny knowledge, and
your loneliness. All the flowers
your father planted, all
the green beans that have made it,
all the world's recorded pianos
and this exhilarating day
cannot change that.

LISEL MUELLER
(1924–)

Mueller writes that this poem "comes from a period when one of my two daughters, then a teenager, went through a period of sadness and loneliness, a condition many gifted adolescents go through, and I, her mother, could not help her because she had to work through it herself."

Born in Hamburg, Germany, Mueller immigrated to the United States in 1939 at the age of fifteen. She was educated at the University of Evansville and Indiana University. In 1943, she married Pat Mueller; they have two daughters. In her poem "Curriculum Vitae," she explained the familial origins of her poetic voice: "The death of the mother hurt the daughter into poetry. The daughter became a mother of daughters." Mueller won a National Book Award in 1981 and a Pulitzer in 1997.

Elena

My Spanish isn't enough.
I remember how I'd smile
listening to my little ones,
understanding every word they'd say,
their jokes, their songs, their plots.
   Vamos a pedirle dulces a mamá. Vamos.
But that was in Mexico.
Now my children go to American high schools.
They speak English. At night they sit around
the kitchen table, laugh with one another.
I stand by the stove and feel dumb, alone.
I bought a book to learn English.
My husband frowned, drank more beer.
My oldest said, "*Mamá,* he doesn't want you
to be smarter than he is." I'm forty,
embarrassed at mispronouncing words,
embarrassed at the laughter of my children,
the grocer, the mailman. Sometimes I take
my English book and lock myself in the bathroom,
say the thick words softly,
for if I stop trying, I will be deaf
when my children need my help.

PAT MORA
(1942–)

Vamos . . . — "Let's go ask Mama for sweets. Let's go."

Pat Mora, born in El Paso, Texas, was raised by her grandmother and aunt along with her parents (both sets of her grandparents migrated from Mexico to El Paso during the Mexican Revolution of 1910). She was educated at Texas Western College and the University of Texas at El Paso. Mora has taught at all levels and been a university administrator, museum director, and foundation consultant. Her family memoir, *House of Houses*, was published in 1997. Married, with three grown children, she divides her time between Santa Fe, New Mexico, and the Cincinnati/northern Kentucky area.

Mother to Son

Well, son, I'll tell you:
Life for me ain't been no crystal stair.
It's had tacks in it,
And splinters,
And boards torn up,
And places with no carpet on the floor —
Bare;
But all the time
I'se been a-climbin' on,
And reachin' landin's,
And turnin' corners,
And sometimes goin' in the dark
Where there ain't been no light.
So boy, don't you turn back;
Don't you sit down on the steps,
'Cause you finds it's kinder hard;
Don't you fall now —
For I'se still goin', honey,
I'se still climbin',
And life for me ain't been no crystal stair.

LANGSTON HUGHES
(1902–1967)

First published in 1922 in *The Crisis*, the official magazine of the NAACP and one of the oldest Black periodicals in the United States.

Langston Hughes was born in Joplin, Missouri. His parents separated when he was young, with his father moving to Mexico and Langston living by turns with his mother and grandmother in Kansas, Illinois, and Ohio. He started at Columbia University in 1921, but after a year dropped out to work as a delivery boy, a merchant seaman, and a cook in a Paris nightclub, among many other jobs. In 1925, he was a busboy at the Wardman Park Hotel in Washington, D.C. When the poet Vachal Lindsay came for a performance, Hughes left some of his poems on Lindsay's table. Lindsay was impressed and brought him to the attention of a wider public. Eventually he was able to attend Lincoln University in Pennsylvania. He wrote plays, essays, and short stories about the Black experience in America and became one of the leaders of the Harlem Renaissance. He never married.

In Limbo

I have a child in limbo
I must bring back.
My experience grows
but there is no wisdom
without a child in the house.

DAVID IGNATOW
(1914–1983)

For a biography, see page 20. For other poems by Ignatow, see pages 20, 119, and 120.

Sent to Her Elder Daughter from the Capital

I cherished you, my darling,
As the Sea God the pearls
He treasures in his comb-box.
But you, led by your lord husband —
Such is the way of the world —
And torn from me like a vine,
Left for distant Koshi;
Since then, your lovely eyebrows
Curving like the far-off waves,
Ever linger in my eyes,
My heart unsteady as a rocking boat;
Under such a longing
I, now weak with age,
Come near to breaking.

Envoy

If I had foreknown such longing,
I would have lived with you,
Gazing on you every hour of the day
As in a shining mirror.

LADY ŌTOMO OF SAKANOÉ
(CA. 700–750)
Translated from the Japanese by the Nippon Gakujutsu Shinkōkai

Lady Ōtomo of Sakanoé was the author of eighty-four poems in the Japanese *Manyōshū*; of these, about two-thirds are love poems. She was born into a family of literary courtiers and high-ranking officials. She first married Fujiwara no Maro, but after he died in the smallpox epidemic of 737 she married Ōtomo Sukanamaro and gave birth to two daughters, the eldest of whom became a prominent poet herself. After the wife of her older brother died in Kyushu, Lady Ōtomo traveled there to look after his children, and later in life she seems to have played an important role in clan affairs.

❖ V ❖
GROWING OLDER

I Come Home Wanting to Touch Everyone

The dogs greet me, I descend
into their world of fur and tongues
and then my wife and I embrace
as if we'd just closed the door
in a motel, our two girls slip in
between us and we're all saying
each other's names and the dogs
Buster and Sundown are on their hind legs,
people-style, seeking more love.
I've come home wanting to touch
everyone, everything; usually I turn
the key and they're all lost
in food or homework, even the dogs
are preoccupied with themselves,
I desire only to ease
back in, the mail, a drink,
but tonight the body-hungers have sent out
their long-range signals
or love itself has risen
from its squalor of neglect.
Everytime the kids turn their backs
I touch my wife's breasts
and when she checks the dinner
the unfriendly cat on the dishwasher
wants to rub heads, starts to speak
with his little motor and violin —
everything, everyone is intelligible

in the language of touch,
and we sit down to dinner inarticulate
as blood, all difficulties postponed
because the weather is so good.

STEPHEN DUNN
(1939–)

Born in New York City, Stephen Dunn was educated at Hofstra University, the New School for Social Research, and Syracuse University. He married Lois Kelly in 1964, and they have two daughters. He has worked as an editor, a teacher, and a semiprofessional basketball player. In 2001, he won the Pulitzer Prize for poetry.

At the San Francisco Airport

To My Daughter, 1954

This is the terminal: the light
Gives perfect vision, false and hard;
The metal glitters, deep and bright.
Great planes are waiting in the yard —
They are already in the night.

And you are here beside me, small,
Contained and fragile, and intent
On things that I but half recall —
Yet going whither you are bent.
I am the past, and that is all.

But you and I in part are one:
The frightened brain, the nervous will,
The knowledge of what must be done,
The passion to acquire the skill
To face that which you dare not shun.

The rain of matter upon sense
Destroys me momently. The score:
There comes what will come. The expense
Is what one thought, and something more —
One's being and intelligence.

This is the terminal, the break.
Beyond this point, on lines of air,
You take the way that you must take;
And I remain in light and stare —
In light, and nothing else, awake

YVOR WINTERS
(1900–1968)

Written for his daughter, Joanna, this was one of Winters's last poems.

Yvor Winters was born in Chicago, where his father became a grain and stock trader on the Chicago Stock Exchange. After a year at the University of Chicago, Winters was diagnosed with tuberculosis, and he spent the next three years in Sunmount Sanatorium in Santa Fe, New Mexico. He lived in New Mexico for two more years as a schoolteacher in coal camps. Eventually he earned degrees from the University of Colorado and Stanford. Winters married Janet Lewis in 1926 (she had also been a patient at Sunmount), and they had two children. He won a Bollingen Prize in 1961.

Hunting with My Brother

My brother blasts pigeons beneath the bridge
and lets them lie. *They're only flying rats,*
he says, and just like Daddy I snap, "Two wrongs
don't make a right." *But two rights make a left,*
he says. We laugh, and talk of how his wife
cooks squirrels with dumplings and black pepper
and how my garden's gone to seed.

He swings the shotgun to his shoulder. Two quick
squirrels scrabble, spiraling up a water oak.
Frustrated, Mike fires into the ragged nests.
"Hey, knock it off!" I yell. He shrugs,
twists up the choke, and fires again.
I grab the barrel and wrench it. His fist
clips my left ear. I cock my fist.
But we're already backing off,
apologizing — unlike when, younger,
we'd roll across the ground, kick, gouge,
and bite.

We hike two miles in silence.
Mike's wife looks from the kitchen window.
We hold up empty hands and shrug. She laughs.
We glare at her and, goddamn, she laughs louder.
Then slowly we laugh too. Who wouldn't laugh
at Cain and Abel coming home —
no meat, no beans, and both alive.

ANDREW HUDGINS
(1951–)

Andrew Hudgins was born in Killeen, Texas. Because his father was a career officer in the
U.S. Air Force, Hudgins grew up in Georgia, North Carolina, Ohio, California, England,
Paris, and Alabama. He studied at Huntington College and the universities of Alabama,
Syracuse, Iowa, and Stanford. After college, he taught elementary school for a year. Now
he and his wife, the fiction writer Erin McGraw, both teach at Ohio State University. For
another poem by Hudgins, see page 142.

To My Brothers

Small, busy flames play through the fresh laid coals,
And their faint cracklings o'er our silence creep
Like whispers of the household gods that keep
A gentle empire o'er fraternal souls.
And while, for rhymes, I search around the poles,
Your eyes are fix'd, as in poetic sleep,
Upon the lore so voluble and deep,
That aye at fall of night our care condoles.
This is your birth-day Tom, and I rejoice
That thus it passes smoothly, quietly.
Many such eves of gently whisp'ring noise
May we together pass, and calmly try
What are this world's true joys, — ere the great voice,
From its fair face, shall bid our spirits fly.

JOHN KEATS
(1795–1821)

aye — always

Written on November 18, 1816, at a time when the three orphaned boys, ages twenty-one (John), nineteen (George), and seventeen (Tom), were all sharing lodgings in London. Tom had by this time already contracted tuberculosis, the disease that would eventually kill both him and John.

John Keats was born in London as the son of a stable manager who was thrown from a horse and killed when the poet was eight. His mother died of tuberculosis about five years later. Though he was apprenticed to a surgeon, he gave up medicine for poetry, and as his poetry began to be published, he struggled to care for his younger siblings — two brothers and a sister. His brother Tom, who was ill with tuberculosis, needed particular attention before his death in 1818. Keats himself died of the disease three years later, at the age of twenty-six. He had been engaged to Fanny Brawne, but his poverty and illness prevented their marriage. He has been remarkably influential given that his career as a poet lasted only about five years.

Europe and America

My father brought the emigrant bundle
of desperation and worn threads,
that in anxiety as he stumbles
tumble out distractedly;
while I am bedded upon soft green money
that grows like grass.
Thus, between my father
who lives on bed of anguish for his daily bread,
and I who tear money at leisure by the roots,
where I lie in sun or shade,
a vast continent of breezes, storms to him,
shadows, darkness to him, small lakes, rough channels
to him, and hills, mountains to him, lie between us.

My father comes of a small hell
where bread and man have been kneaded and baked together.
You have heard the scream as the knife fell;
while I have slept
as guns pounded offshore.

DAVID IGNATOW
(1914–1983)

Ignatow's father, a Jewish Russian immigrant, came to the United States from Kiev in 1905.

For a biography, see page 20. For more poetry by Ignatow, see pages 20, 108, and 120.

Consolation

My wife, I dread to come and tell you
how we've failed. It is not our doing
wholly. What has gone out of us
is the impelling reason to succeed,
to set ourselves above others,
to live more perfectly. All this
has left us as though we too
had been possessed of a fever,
and our minds now turning cool
have revealed to us our arms
enclosed about each other.

DAVID IGNATOW
(1914–1983)

For a biography, see page 20. For more poetry by Ignatow, see pages 20, 108, and 119.

Our Wives

One rainy night that year we saw our wives
talking together in a barroom mirror.
And as our glasses drained I saw our lives

being lived, and saw that time deceives:
for we had thought of living as the Future,
yet here these lovely women were, our wives,

and we were happy. And yet who believes
that what he's living now *is* his adventure,
that the beer we're drinking is our lives?

Or think of all the pain that memory leaves,
things we got through we're glad we don't see clearer.
Think of our existence without wives,

our years in England — none of it survives.
It's over, fallen leaves, forgotten weather.
There was a time we thought we'd make our lives

into History. But history thrives
without us: what it leaves us is the future,
a barroom mirror lit up with our wives —
our wives who suddenly became our lives.

JONATHAN GALASSI
(1949–)

Born in Seattle, Washington, Jonathan Galassi was educated at Harvard and Cambridge.
He is married to Susan Grace, a museum curator; they have two daughters. He is the trans-
lator of several works by the Italian poet Eugenio Montale, and he has published two col-
lections of his own poetry, most recently *North Street and Other Poems* (2001). Galassi is
also the publisher of Farrar, Straus and Giroux, one the the world's foremost literary pub-
lishing houses. He currently serves as the chairman of the Academy of American Poets.

from Three Poems for a Twenty-Fifth Anniversary

1. Housecleaning

after returning
all the tools I borrowed
from neighbors and friends
and the books to the library

I am amazed to find
so many things around the house
like you
that really belong here

I had thought
you were on loan and overdue
the fines were mounting into millions
I could never pay them

so for twenty-five years
I looked everyone straight in the eyes
pretending you were mine
and I kept you

RICHARD SHELTON
(1933–)

Written in 1981 for his wife Lois.

Richard Shelton was born in Boise, Idaho, and educated at Abilene Christian College
and the University of Arizona. In 1956, he married Lois Bruce, and they have one child.
Shelton taught seventh- and eighth-grade English for two years before moving on to a
career at the University of Arizona.

Tell Me Now

"Tell me now, what should a man want
But to sit alone, sipping his cup of wine?"
I should like to have visitors come and discuss philosophy
And not to have the tax-collector coming to collect taxes:
My three sons married into good families
And my five daughters wedded to steady husbands.
Then I could jog through a happy five-score years
And, at the end, need no Paradise.

WANG CHI
(585–644)
Translated from the Chinese by Arthur Waley

Wang Chi was a native of Shansi Province; his two brothers were also scholars. He held several insignificant posts during the Sui dynasty, retired in the chaos of dynastic succession, and then took two minor positions in the early T'ang dynasty. For most of his life, however, he lived as a farmer-poet, modeling his life on that of T'ao Yüan-ming. (For a poem by T'ao, see page 100.) Wang's fondness for wine was legendary, even for a Chinese poet.

My Daughter and Apple Pie

She serves me a piece of it a few minutes
out of the oven. A little steam rises
from the slits on top. Sugar and spice —
cinnamon — burned into the crust.
But she's wearing these dark glasses
in the kitchen at ten o'clock
in the morning — everything nice —
as she watches me break off
a piece, bring it to my mouth,
and blow on it. My daughter's kitchen,
in winter. I fork the pie in
and tell myself to stay out of it.
She says she loves him. No way
could it be worse.

RAYMOND CARVER
(1938–1988)

Raymond Carver was born in Clatskanie, Oregon. At nineteen, he married the sixteen-year-old Maryann Burk, after which he began his education at Yakima Community College. He later attended Chico State College and Humboldt State College. The Carvers had a daughter and a son before two bankruptcies and alcoholism led to their divorce in 1982. He is best known as an author of short stories, and some of his books are dedicated to his second wife, the poet Tess Gallagher. He died of lung cancer at the age of fifty.

The Happiest Day

It was early May, I think
a moment of lilac or dogwood
when so many promises are made
it hardly matters if a few are broken.
My mother and father still hovered
in the background, part of the scenery
like the houses I had grown up in,
and if they would be torn down later
that was something I knew
but didn't believe. Our children were asleep
or playing, the youngest as new
as the new smell of the lilacs,
and how could I have guessed
their roots were shallow
and would be easily transplanted.
I didn't even guess that I was happy.
The small irritations that are like salt
on melon were what I dwelt on,
though in truth they simply
made the fruit taste sweeter.
So we sat on the porch
in the cold morning, sipping
hot coffee. Behind the news of the day —
strikes and small wars, a fire somewhere —

I could see the top of your dark head
and thought not of public conflagrations
but of how it would feel on my bare shoulder.
If someone could stop the camera then . . .
if someone could only stop the camera
and ask me: are you happy?
perhaps I would have noticed
how the morning shone in the reflected
color of lilac. Yes, I might have said
and offered a steaming cup of coffee.

LINDA PASTAN
(1932–)

For a biography, see page 24. For other poems by Pastan, see pages 23 and 71.

The Sunlight on the Garden

The sunlight on the garden
Hardens and grows cold,
We cannot cage the minute
Within its nets of gold,
When all is told
We cannot beg for pardon.

Our freedom as free lances
Advances towards its end;
The earth compels, upon it
Sonnets and birds descend;
And soon, my friend,
We shall have no time for dances.

The sky was good for flying
Defying the church bells
And every evil iron
Siren and what it tells:
The earth compels
We are dying, Egypt, dying

And not expecting pardon,
Hardened in heart anew,

But glad to have sat under
Thunder and rain with you,
And grateful too
For sunlight on the garden.

LOUIS MACNEICE
(1907–1963)

free lances — originally, soldiers available for hire
We are dying . . . — in Shakespeare's play, Antony exclaims to Cleopatra, "I am dying,
    Egypt, dying" (IV.xv.41).

Written as a farewell to his first wife, Mary, a few weeks after their divorce in 1936. She
had once been described as "the best dancer in Oxford."

Louis MacNeice was born in Belfast. His mother died of tuberculosis when he was seven,
and he was educated at Marlborough and Oxford. He married Mary Ezra in 1930, and they
had one son before she ran off with an American graduate student who was living with
them at the time. They divorced the next year, in 1936. He taught classics for a few years
and then in 1940 started working for the BBC, where he made a career as a feature writer
and producer. In 1942, he married Hedli Anderson, with whom he had one daughter.

Winter Verse for His Sister

Moonlight washes the west side of the house
As clean as bone, it carpets like a lawn
The stubbled field tilting eastward
Where there is no sign yet of dawn.
The moon is an angel with a bright light sent
To surprise me once before I die
With the real aspect of things.
It holds the light steady and makes no comment.

Practicing for death I have lately gone
To that other house
Where our parents did most of their dying,
Embracing and not embracing their conditions.
Our father built bookcases and little by little stopped reading,
Our mother cooked proud meals for common mouths.
Kindly, they raised two children. We raked their leaves
And cut their grass, we ate and drank with them.
Reconciliation was our long work, not all of it joyful.

Now outside my own house at a cold hour
I watch the noncommittal angel lower
The steady lantern that's worn these clapboards thin
In a wash of moonlight, while men slept within,

Accepting and not accepting their conditions,
And the fingers of trees plied a deep carpet of decay
On the gravel web underneath the field,
And the field tilting always toward day.

WILLIAM MEREDITH
(1919–)

Written for the poet's sister, Katherine Meredith Keast Goldenberg.

Born in New York City, William Meredith was raised in Connecticut and educated at Princeton. He served as a naval aviator during the Second World War and advanced to the rank of lieutenant. In 1952, he reenlisted to fly missions in the Korean War. He taught English at Connecticut College from 1955 until his retirement in 1983 and still lives in Connecticut with his partner Richard Harteis. Meredith was consultant in poetry to the Library of Congress from 1978 to 1980; he won a Pulitzer in 1988 and a National Book Award in 1997.

My Father in the Basement

Something had gone wrong down in the basement.
Something important needed rearranging
Or shaping up down there like the neat shadows
He kept in the coal bin and under the workbench.
But when he went to find it, he couldn't find it.

None of the fuses had blown as dark as storms
At their tiny portholes. Nothing was on fire
But the fire in the furnace, and nothing was frozen
But the humming freezer and the concrete floor
And the hands he'd poured it with, now cold and hard.

Had his mother sent him there to fetch crab apples,
Spicy and gold, or piccalilli for supper?
Was that his father shouting and then turning
A deaf ear to his answer? It was cold
And hard to remember why he wasn't working.

So he lay down on the floor, doing things right
The first time because nothing was worth doing
Unless he did it himself. There was no use
In calling strangers if something was out of order
Because if he couldn't fix it, nobody could.

DAVID WAGONER
(1926–)

---

piccalilli — a relish of chopped vegetables and spices

David Wagoner was born in Massillon, Ohio, as the son of a steelworker. He grew up in Whiting, Indiana, and was educated at Pennsylvania State and Indiana University. He served in the U.S. Navy from 1944 to 1946. At the encouragement of his teacher and friend Theodore Roethke (whose poems appear on pages 30 and 42), he moved to Washington State in 1954, where he taught at the University of Washington for the rest of his career. In 1982, he married Robin Seyfried (his third marriage), and they adopted two daughters when he was in his fifties. Wagoner has edited the journal *Poetry Northwest* since 1966.

Alzheimer's: The Husband

for Jean Mauger

He'd been a clod, he knew, yes, always aiming toward his vision of the
    good life, always acting on it.
He knew he'd been unconscionably self-centered, had indulged himself
    with his undreamed-of good fortune,
but he also knew that the single-mindedness with which he'd attended
    to his passions, needs and whims,
and which must have seemed to others the grossest sort of egotism, was
    also what was really at the base
of how he'd almost offhandedly worked out the intuitions and moves
    which had brought him here,
and this wasn't all that different: to spend his long-anticipated retirement
    learning to cook
clean house, dress her, even to apply her makeup, wasn't any sort of
    secular saintliness —
that would be belittling — it was just the next necessity he saw himself as
    being called to.

C. K. WILLIAMS
(1936–)

Written for the poet's father-in-law.

For a biography, see page 89. For other poems by Williams, see pages 88 and 140.

The Old Gray Couple (1)

They have only to look at each other to laugh —
no one knows why, not even they:
something back in the lives they've lived,
something they both remember but no words can say.

They go off at an evening's end to talk
but they don't, or to sleep but they lie awake —
hardly a word, just a touch, just near,
just listening but not to hear.

Everything they know they know together —
everything, that is, but one:
their lives they've learned like secrets from each other;
their deaths they think of in the nights alone.

ARCHIBALD MACLEISH
(1892–1982)

Raised in Glencoe, Illinois, Archibald MacLeish graduated from Yale in 1915 and then took a law degree from Harvard. He married Ada Hitchcock in 1916; they had three children. During World War I, he served as an officer in the field artillery, and later, at the age of thirty-one, he quit his job as a lawyer and took his family to Paris to devote himself to poetry. After his return to America five years later, he held positions as the editor of *Fortune*, the librarian of Congress, and assistant secretary of state (1944–1945). He was awarded Pulitzer Prizes in 1933 and in 1953, the same year he won a National Book Award and a Bollingen Prize. His play *J.B.*, a modernized version of the biblical story of Job, was produced on Broadway in 1958 (for which he won yet another Pulitzer, this time for drama).

A Mad Poem Addressed to My Nephews and Nieces

The World cheats those who cannot read;
I, happily, have mastered script and pen.
The World cheats those who hold no office;
I am blessed with high official rank.
   The old are often ill;
I, at this day have not an ache or pain.
   They are often burdened with ties;
But I have finished with marriage and giving in marriage.
No changes happen to disturb the quiet of my mind;
No business comes to impair the vigour of my limbs.
Hence it is that now for ten years
Body and soul have rested in hermit peace.
And all the more, in the last lingering years
What I shall need are very few things.
A single rug to warm me through the winter;
One meal to last me the whole day.
It does not matter that my house is rather small;
One cannot sleep in more than one room!
It does not matter that I have not many horses;
One cannot ride in two coaches at once!
As fortunate as me among the people of the world
Possibly one would find seven out of ten.
As contented as me among a hundred men
Look as you may, you will not find one.

In the affairs of others even fools are wise;
In their own business even sages err.
To no one else would I dare to speak my heart,
So my wild words are addressed to my nephews and nieces.

Po Chü-i
(772–846)
Translated from the Chinese by Arthur Waley

Written in 835, when Po was sixty-three. His only son, A-ts'ui, had been born six years earlier, but had died at the age of two. Since the Chinese family system dictated that daughters would be married into other family lines, Po knew that his line might come to an end with himself — and unless he could get another kinsman designated as an heir there would be no recognized descendants to make offerings to his spirit after his death. Hence this confiding poem to his nephews and nieces, expressing a contentment that would have seemed strange to many.

For a biography, see page 81. For more poetry by Po, see pages 81 and 94 and the next poem.

Half in the Family, Half Out

Comfortably fixed for clothing and food, young ones married off,
from now on family affairs are no concern of mine.
In nightly rest, I'm a bird who's found its way to the forest;
at morning meals, I'm one in heart with the monk who begs his food.
Clear-cries, several voices — cranes under the pines;
one spot of cold light — the lamp among the bamboo.
Late at night I practice meditation, sitting in lotus posture.
My daughter calls, my wife hoots — I don't answer either of them.

Po Chü-i
(772–846)
Translated from the Chinese by Burton Watson

Written around 840, when the poet was nearing seventy. To be "in the family" means to be a lay Buddhist believer; to be "out of the family" means to be a monk. His daughter, Summer Press, gave birth to a son that year. Two years later she became a widow, at age twenty-six, after seven years of marriage, and she moved back in with her parents.

⬧VI⬧
PARTING

....

from Last Days

"Dying is simple," she said.
"What's worst is . . . *the separation*."
When she no longer spoke,
they lay alone together, touching,
    and she fixed on him
her beautiful enormous round brown eyes,
    shining, unblinking,
and passionate with love and dread.

DONALD HALL
(1928–)

From *Without*, a volume of poems about the death of the poet's wife, Jane Kenyon, from cancer.

For a biography, see page 76. For a biography of Kenyon, see page 21.

Grace

Almost as good as her passion, I'll think, almost as good as her presence,
     her physical grace,
almost as good as making love with her, I'll think in my last aching
     breath before last,
my glimpse before last of the light, were her good will and good wit,
     the steadiness of her affections.

Almost, I'll think, sliding away on my sleigh of departure, the rind of
     my consciousness thinning,
the fear of losing myself, of — worse — losing her, subsiding as I think,
     hope it must,
almost as good as her beauty, her glow, was the music of her thought,
     her voice and laughter.

Almost as good as kissing her, being kissed back, I hope I'll have the strength
     still to think
was watching her as she worked or read, was beholding her selfless
     sympathy for son, friend, sister,
even was feeling her anger, sometimes, rarely, lift against me, then be
     forgotten, put aside.

Almost, I'll think, as good as our unlikely coming together, was our
     constant, mostly unspoken debate
as to whether good in the world was good in itself, or (my side) only
     the absence of evil:
no need to say how much how we lived was shaped by her bright spirit,
     her humor and hope.

Almost as good as living at all — improbable gift — was watching her once
     cross our room,
the reflections of night rain she'd risen to close the window against
     flaring across her,
doubling her light, then feeling her come back to bed, reaching to find
     and embrace me,

as I'll hope she'll be there to embrace me as I sail away on that last
    voyage out of myself,
that last, sorrowful passage out of her presence, though her presence,
    I'll think, will endure,
as firmly as ever, as good even now, I'll think in that lull before last,
    almost as ever.

C. K. WILLIAMS
(1936–)

For a biography, see page 89. For other poems by Williams, see pages 88 and 132.

Elegy for My Father, Who Is Not Dead

One day I'll lift the telephone
and be told my father's dead. He's ready.
In the sureness of his faith, he talks
about the world beyond this world
as though his reservations have
been made. I think he wants to go,
a little bit — a new desire
to travel building up, an itch
to see fresh worlds. Or older ones.
He thinks that when I follow him
he'll wrap me in his arms and laugh,
the way he did when I arrived
on earth. I do not think he's right.
He's ready. I am not. I can't
just say good-bye as cheerfully
as if he were embarking on a trip
to make my later trip go well.
I see myself on deck, convinced
his ship's gone down, while he's convinced
I'll see him standing on the dock
and waving, shouting, *Welcome back.*

ANDREW HUDGINS
(1951–)

For a biography, see page 117.

In the Nursing Home

She is like a horse grazing
a hill pasture that someone makes
smaller by coming every night
to pull the fences in and in.

She has stopped running wide loops,
stopped even the tight circles.
She drops her head to feed; grass
is dust, and the creekbed's dry.

Master, come with your light
halter. Come and bring her in.

JANE KENYON
(1947–1995)

For a biography, see page 21.

Mourning for My Son

His Baby Name Was Shih-shih

Traveling by boat, we rested at Fu-li.
There my son, little Shih, died.
I felt only astonishment looking down at him;
Strange, but the greatest sorrows bring no tears.
Not until my feelings settled did awareness come,
And searing fires seemed to mass inside.
His mother too I lost, not long before,
And I am still grieving for her.
Now mornings are passed in weeping for my wife —
Tears drop and moisten robe and sleeves.
Then nights are passed in weeping for my son;
The doubled pain sinks into my heart.
Let me ask of heaven above:
What is the reason for all this suffering?
I only have two sons;
Why so hasty in taking one away?
It is the birds of spring alone who thrive,
Feeding the thronging young in their nests.

MEI YAO-CH'EN
(1002–1060)
Translated from the Chinese by Jonathan Chaves

Written in 1045. Shih-shih's death followed that of his mother by less than a month.

For a biography, see page 92.

Two Haiku

Crawl, laugh
Do as you wish —
For you are two years old
This morning.

The world of dew
Is the world of dew,
And yet . . .
And yet . . .

Kobayashi Issa
(1763–1827)
Translated from the Japanese by Nobuyuki Yuasa

These poems, both referring to Kobayashi's daughter, Sato, appear in the midst of an autobiographical narrative. The second, on her sudden death from smallpox at age two and a half, comes immediately after this passage:

> Her mother embraced the cold body and cried bitterly. For myself — I knew well it was no use to cry, that water once flown past the bridge does not return, and blossoms that are scattered are gone beyond recall. Yet try as I would, I could not, simply could not cut the binding cord of human love.

The first son of a farmer in Nagano Prefecture, Kobayashi Issa lost his mother at the age of two. When he was seven his father remarried, and after she gave birth to a son of her own there was constant conflict between him and his stepmother. He was sent to Edo (modern Tokyo) at the age of thirteen, where he studied poetry and became a teacher, but he gave up the position for a life of travel, poverty, and poetry that lasted until he was fifty. That year he finally settled a ten-year inheritance dispute with his stepmother and half brother and moved back to his native village. He married a twenty-seven-year-old village woman named Kiku, who bore him four sons and a daughter, all of whom died in infancy. His wife died when he was sixty, and the next year he married again, only to divorce two months later. He married yet again at sixty-two, and his third wife, Yao, gave birth to a daughter shortly after his death.

On My First Son

Farewell, thou child of my right hand, and joy;
My sin was too much hope of thee, loved boy:
Seven years thou'wert lent to me, and I thee pay,
Exacted by thy fate, on the just day.
O could I lose all father now! for why
Will man lament the state he should envy
To have so soon 'scaped world's and flesh's rage,
And, if no other misery, yet age?
Rest in soft peace, and asked, say, "Here doth lie
Ben Jonson his best piece of poetry."
For whose sake henceforth all his vows be such
As what he loves may never like too much.

BEN JONSON
(1572–1637)

child of my right hand — a translation of the Hebrew name Benjamin
on the just day — he died on his seventh birthday
father — fatherly feelings

The boy was named Benjamin, for his father. He died of the plague in 1603.

The posthumous son of a London clergyman, Jonson worked as a bricklayer (his step-father's profession), a soldier, and an actor before becoming a successful playwright. He was as arrogant and quarrelsome as he was brilliant, and he was jailed many times (including once for killing a fellow actor in a duel). Many of the details of his personal life are uncertain, but he married Anne Lewis in 1594 (her name was only discovered in the 1930s) and they had at least four children, three of whom died in childhood. The fourth child, who was three when the plague struck their household and claimed his seven-year-old brother Benjamin, may very well have perished also. There is evidence that Jonson married again in 1623.

Mid-Term Break

I sat all morning in the college sick bay
Counting bells knelling classes to a close.
At two o'clock our neighbours drove me home.

In the porch I met my father crying —
He had always taken funerals in his stride —
And Big Jim Evans saying it was a hard blow.

The baby cooed and laughed and rocked the pram
When I came in, and I was embarrassed
By old men standing up to shake my hand

And tell me they were 'sorry for my trouble'.
Whispers informed strangers I was the eldest,
Away at school, as my mother held my hand

In hers and coughed out angry tearless sighs.
At ten o'clock the ambulance arrived
With the corpse, stanched and bandaged by the nurses.

Next morning I went up into the room. Snowdrops
And candles soothed the bedside; I saw him
For the first time in six weeks. Paler now,

Wearing a poppy bruise on his left temple,
He lay in the four-foot box as in his cot.
No gaudy scars, the bumper knocked him clear.

A four-foot box, a foot for every year.

SEAMUS HEANEY
(1939–)

In 1953, Heaney's four-year-old brother Christopher was hit by a car on the road near their house and killed. Fifteen years later, Heaney named his second son Christopher, in memory of his deceased brother.

For a biography, see page 27. For other poems by Heaney, see pages 27 and 41.

#101

Driven across many nations, across many oceans,
    I am here, my brother, for this final parting,
to offer at last those gifts which the dead are given
    and to speak in vain to your unspeaking ashes,
since bitter fortune forbids you to hear me or answer,
    O my wretched brother, so abruptly taken!
But now I must celebrate grief with funeral tributes
    offered the dead in the ancient way of the fathers,
accept these presents, wet with my brotherly tears, and
    now & forever, my brother, hail & farewell.

CATULLUS
(CA. 84–54 B.C.)
Translated from the Latin by Charles Martin

Catullus was a Roman poet, born in Verona to a wealthy family. He went to Rome in about 62 B.C. and seems to have lived there for most of the rest of his life. Unfortunately, we know very little about his life other than what we can surmise from his poems — he served as an aide to the governor of Bithynia for a year, he visited his brother's grave at Troy, and he had a love affair with a woman whom he called Lesbia.

My Sisters

Who whispered, souls have shapes?
So has the wind, I say.
But I don't know,
I only feel things blow.

I had two sisters once
with long black hair
who walked apart from me
and wrote the history of tears.
Their story's faded with their names,
but the candlelight they carried,
like dancers in a dream,
still flickers on their gowns
as they bend over me
to comfort my night-fears.

Let nothing grieve you,
Sarah and Sophia.
Shush, shush, my dears,
now and forever.

STANLEY KUNITZ
(1905–)

Written late in life in memory of Stanley Kunitz's two older sisters — his only siblings —
both of whom died while he was still young.

———

Stanley Kunitz was born in Worcester, Massachusetts, as the son of Lithuanian immi-
grants. His father committed suicide six weeks before his birth, and his mother thereafter
forbade any mention of her dead husband. He was educated at Harvard, but anti-
Semitism in the 1920s kept him from teaching there. He served in the U.S. Army from
1943 to 1945, and he has worked as a reporter, an editor, a translator, and a teacher. He
has been married three times and has one daughter. He won a Pulitzer Prize in 1959, a
Bollingen Prize in 1987, and a National Book Award in 1995 (at the age of ninety). In
2000 he was appointed poet laureate of the United States.

Thinking of My Wife

Alone in my sorrow, where do my thoughts go?
Man's life is like the morning dew.
Wandering in distant provinces,
fondly, tenderly I call up the past.
Your love follows me even here;
my heart too turns back in longing.
Though our bodies are parted and cannot touch,
our spirits join at journey's midpoint.
Have you never seen the hilltop pine,
how even in winter it keeps the same hue?
Have you never seen the knoll and valley cypresses,
in year-end cold, guarding their constant green?
Don't say it is my wish that parts us;
far away, my love grows stronger still.

P'AN YÜEH
(247–300)
Translated from the Chinese by Burton Watson

Born to a family of moderate wealth at a time when China was politically divided, P'an Yüeh became an official and held a number of positions before he retired from political life in 278. In 285, however, he resumed his career, attaching himself to a variety of statesmen and tying his fate with theirs. He was implicated in a plot to set up his patron Chia Mi as the crown prince and was executed in 300. Only about twenty of his poems survive.

My Dearest Dust

My dearest dust, could not thy hasty day
Afford thy drowsy patience leave to stay
One hour longer, so that we might either
Have sat up, or gone to bed together?
But since thy finished labor hath possessed
Thy weary limbs with early rest,
Enjoy it sweetly, and thy widow bride
Shall soon repose her by thy slumb'ring side.
Whose business, now, is only to prepare
My nightly dress, and call to prayer;
Mine eyes wax heavy and the day grows old.
The dew falls thick, my beloved grows cold.
Draw, draw ye closed curtains, and make room;
My dear, my dearest dust, I come, I come.

LADY CATHERINE DYER
(D. 1654)

Written in 1641 as an epitaph on the tomb of Lady Dyer's husband, Sir William Dyer;
Colmworth Church, Bedfordshire.

Except for the above epitaph, no other poems by Lady Dyer survive, and very little is
known of her life.

To My Father

You gathered incredible strength
in order to die
to seem calm and fully conscious
without complaint, without trembling
without a cry
so that I would not be afraid

Your wary hand
slowly grew cold in mine
and guided me carefully
beyond into the house of death
so I might come to know it

Thus in the past you used to take my hand
and guide me through the world
and show me life
so I would not fear

I will follow after you
confident as a child
toward the silent country
where you went first
so I would not feel a stranger there

And I will not be afraid.

BLAGA DMITROVA
(1922–)
*Translated from the Bulgarian into French by J. Bossolova
and Guillevic. English version by Joanna Bankier*

Born in Tirnovo, Bulgaria, Blaga Dmitrova studied Slavic philology in Sofia and attended
the Maxim Gorky Institute in Moscow. She has written novels and film scripts in addi-
tion to her poetry, and she has worked as an editor and a translator.

Holding On

Because the dead have no memory
we must always be remembering for them.
You learn now to live under water.
Even if you grow pale with longing
for sunlight and sunsets of violet,
you must float with the currents and be of them —

and it is comforting here without the treacherous,
shifting temperatures of the earth world.
Some would call it dark
but I say no: here shines
all the light I need. Here everything exists,
though it cannot grow.

CELIA GILBERT
(1932–)

From *An Ark of Sorts*, a sequence of poems about dealing with the loss of a child. These were written many years after the death of the Gilberts' youngest daughter (age six) from a brain tumor.

For a biography, see page 26. For other poems by Gilbert, see pages 26 and 103.

What the Living Do

Johnny, the kitchen sink has been clogged for days, some utensil
     probably fell down there.
And the Drano won't work but smells dangerous, and the crusty
     dishes have piled up

waiting for the plumber I still haven't called. This is the
     everyday we spoke of.
It's winter again: the sky's a deep headstrong blue, and the
     sunlight pours through

the open living room windows because the heat's on too high
     in here and I can't turn it off.
For weeks now, driving, or dropping a bag of groceries in the
     street, the bag breaking,

I've been thinking: This is what the living do. And yesterday,
     hurrying along those
wobbly bricks in the Cambridge sidewalk, spilling my coffee
     down my wrist and sleeve,

I thought it again, and again later, when buying a hairbrush:
     This is it.
Parking. Slamming the car door shut in the cold. What you
     called *that yearning.*

What you finally gave up. We want the spring to come and the
     winter to pass. We want
whoever to call or not to call, a letter, a kiss — we want more
     and more and then more of it.

But there are moments, walking, when I catch a glimpse of
    myself in the window glass,
say, the window of the corner video store, and I'm gripped by a
    cherishing so deep

for my own blowing hair, chapped face, and unbuttoned coat
    that I'm speechless:
I am living. I remember you.

MARIE HOWE
(1950–)

Written for her brother John who died, of AIDS, in 1989.

Marie Howe was born in Rochester, New York, and grew up as one of nine children. She received an MFA from Columbia University and is now a member of the writing faculty at Sarah Lawrence College. She lives in New York City.

Methought I Saw

Methought I saw my late espouséd saint
   Brought to me like Alcestis from the grave,
   Whom Jove's great son to her glad husband gave,
   Rescued from Death by force, though pale and faint.
Mine, as whom washed from spot of child-bed taint
   Purification in the Old Law did save,
   And such, as yet once more I trust to have
Full sight of her in heaven without restraint,
Came vested all in white, pure as her mind.
   Her face was veiled; yet to my fancied sight
   Love, sweetness, goodness, in her person shined
So clear as in no face with more delight.
   But O, as to embrace me she inclined,
   I waked, she fled, and day brought back my night.

JOHN MILTON
(1608–1674)

Jove's great son — Hercules
Purification . . . Old Law — Leviticus 12:1–8 prescribed a period of purification for
   women after childbirth. For sons, this was forty days; for daughters, eighty.

Written in memory of Milton's second wife. Since Milton had gone blind before the wedding, he probably had never actually seen her. In Euripides' play *Alcestis*, Admetus is promised by Apollo that he can escape death if he can find someone willing to go to Hades in his place. Friends and relatives all refuse, except for his wife Alcestis. When she dies, Admetus regrets making his request, and a sympathetic Hercules brings Alcestis back to him from the underworld, veiled.

A London native, John Milton studied at Cambridge University. In 1642, at the age of thirty-three, he married the seventeen-year-old Mary Powell, who shared neither his scholarly interests nor his politics. They separated, and he wrote four treatises arguing for the legalization of divorce. Eventually, however, they reunited. Milton's eyesight began to fail from the strain of reading and writing long hours by candlelight and he was completely blind by 1652. This was the year that Mary died in childbirth, leaving three daughters and a son, who died a few months later. Milton's second wife, Katherine Woodcock, died after two years of marriage, a few months after giving birth to her first child, a daughter, who also died. Milton continued to write and at this time he wrote his greatest work, the epic poem *Paradise Lost*. He married yet again, at the age of fifty-four, to Elizabeth Minshull.

Written to the Tune: "River Town"

Lost to one another, the living and the dead, these ten years.
I have not tried to remember
What is impossible to forget.
Your solitary grave is a thousand miles away,
No way to tell you my loneliness.
If we were to meet, you would not recognize me —
Face covered with dust,
Hair like frost.

Last night in a dark dream I was all at once back home.
You were combing your hair
At the little window.
We looked at one another without speaking
And could only weep streaming tears.
Year after year I expect it will go on breaking my heart —
The night of the full moon
The hill of low pines.

(The twentieth of the first month, 1075, to record a dream)

Su Tung-p'o
(1037–1101)
Translated from the Chinese by James Robert Hightower

The dream was of Su Tung-p'o's first wife, Wang Fu, whom he had married in an arranged marriage in 1054, when she was fifteen and he was seventeen. They lived together for eleven years before her death in 1065. The hill of low pines in the last line refers to her grave mound at the family cemetery in Szechwan. In the course of a busy career as an official, he was never able to visit the site again after her burial. This particular translation, by a longtime Harvard professor at the end of his career, would probably have been thrown away had it not been rescued from a pile of scattered, unpublished materials by the editor of an anthology of Chinese literature.

For a biography, see page 75.

✦VII✦
ℐNHERITING

from A Poet's Welcome to His Love-Begotten Daughter
The First Instance that Entitled Him to the Venerable Appellation of Father

Lord grant that thou may ay inherit
Thy Mither's looks an' gracefu' merit;
An' thy poor, worthless Daddie's spirit,
    Without his failins!
'Twad please me mair to see thee heir it
    Than stocked mailins!

For if thou be, what I wad hae thee,
And tak the counsel I shall gie thee,
I'll never rue my trouble wi' thee,
    The cost nor shame o't,
But be a loving Father to thee,
    And brag the name o't.

ROBERT BURNS
(1759–1796)

ay — always
mair — more
stocked mailins — well-stocked farms

The infant addressed here was Elizabeth, born May 22, 1785, the illegitimate daughter of Burns and Elizabeth Paton, who had once been a servant in his father's household. Burns manages a joyful welcome in an earlier stanza — "Welcome, my bonnie, sweet, wee dochter! / Tho' ye come here a wee unsought for" — and he took charge of the child until the time of his marriage, after which she stayed with his mother and brother. Burns and Elizabeth did public penance in Mauchline Church for their sins, and later Burns arranged for profits from his first book of poems to go to this daughter for her upkeep and education.

For a biography, see page 59.

To Willie and Henrietta

If two may read aright
These rhymes of old delight
And house and garden play,
You two, my cousins, and you only, may.

You in a garden green
With me were king and queen,
Were hunter, soldier, tar,
And all the thousand things that children are.

Now in the elders' seat
We rest with quiet feet,
And from the window-bay
We watch the children, our successors, play.

"Time was," the golden head
Irrevocably said;
But time which none can bind,
While flowing fast away, leaves love behind.

ROBERT LOUIS STEVENSON
(1850–1894)

tar — sailor

Written for Willie and Henrietta Traquair, two of his nearly fifty cousins. This poem appears toward the end of Stevenson's famous collection A Child's Garden of Verses — recollections of childhood that he wrote in his early thirties at a time when a serious lung hemorrhage forced him to lie still in bed for several weeks and write with his left hand.

Robert Louis Stevenson was born in Edinburgh, Scotland, as the son of a lighthouse engineer. An only child, he was often sickly and lonely, though at his grandfather's house he had the companionship of numerous cousins. He studied engineering, and then gave that up to pursue law, but by the time he finished his degree he had decided to devote his life to literature. Stevenson traveled widely in Europe seeking a cure for the chronic bronchial condition (perhaps tuberculosis) that on several occasions nearly took his life. While living in France he fell in love with Fanny Osbourne, a married American woman ten years his senior with two children. When, several years later, he heard that she was divorcing her husband, he sailed to America and married her in 1880. His first literary breakthrough — the novel Treasure Island — began as a story told to his young stepson Lloyd. His fame increased with novels such as Dr. Jekyll and Mr. Hyde and Kidnapped, but constant ill health finally led him to settle with his family in Samoa in 1890, where he lived for the rest of his life.

Those to Come

Will those who come after us
remember who we were except for
three or four generations of
family? Will there be a child
who amuses herself by going
through cartons of old letters
in the attic? Will she draw
crayon pictures of the people
she reads about, showing what
she imagines we were like?

I'd be a fool to hope that any
of my verses would remain in
print. I must value them by
the amusement I have in composing
them. Just that, nothing more.

But what happened to make me
grow old so soon? When I was
young I never thought of old
age, of what it would be like.
And why can I recall only part
of some scene I'd like to relive
now? Where have the lost fragments
gone? As I lie wakeful in bed
what I see is a long corridor
of closed doors.

JAMES LAUGHLIN
(1914–1997)

Born in Pittsburgh as the son of a steel magnate, James Laughlin was educated at
Harvard, though he took six months off after his freshman year to study poetry with Ezra
Pound in Italy. Pound thought him an unpromising student and finally advised him to go
back to Harvard and "do something useful," by which he meant publishing the poetry of
others. In 1936, while still an undergraduate, Laughlin founded the New Directions
Publishing Corporation, and today he is known less for his own poetry than for promot-
ing the work of some of the finest poets of the twentieth century. He had a son and
daughter from his first marriage, and two sons from his second.

To My Dear Children

This book by any yet unread,
I leave for you when I am dead,
That being gone, here you may find
What was your living mother's mind.
Make use of what I leave in love,
And God shall bless you from above.

ANNE BRADSTREET
(1612–1672)

Written as an epigraph at the beginning of a brief spiritual autobiography that Bradstreet
left for her children.

For a biography, see page 47. For other poems by Bradstreet, see pages 47 and 70.

Inscribed on the Doors of My Bookshelves

Mine was a trading family
Living in Nan-hao district for a hundred years.
I was the first to become a scholar,
Our house being without a single book.
Applying myself for a full decade,
I set my heart on building a collection.
Though not fully stocked with minor writings,
Of major works, I have nearly everything:
Classics, history, philosophy, belles-lettres —
Nothing lacking from the heritage of the past.
Binding up the volumes one by one in red covers,
I painstakingly sew them by hand.
When angry, I read and become happy;
When sick, I read and am cured.
Piled helter-skelter in front of me,
Books have become my life.
The people of the past who wrote these tomes,
If not sages, were certainly men of great wisdom.
Even without opening their pages,
Joy comes to me just fondling them.
As for my foolish family, they can't be helped;
Their hearts are set on money alone.
If a book falls on the floor, they don't pick it up;

What do they care if they get dirty or tattered?
I'll do my best by these books all my days,
And die not leaving a single one behind.
There are some readers among my friends —
To them I'll give them all away.
Better that than have my unworthy sons
Haul them off to turn into cash.

YANG HSÜN-CHI
(1456–1544)
Translated from the Chinese by John Timothy Wixted

classics, history, philosophy, belles-lettres — the four divisions of traditional Chinese
    libraries

Born into a merchant family that did not own a single book, Yang Hsün-chi became a
scholar and received his *chin-shih* degree in 1484. He served as an official for a few years,
and then feigned illness so that he could return to Soochow and devote himself to liter-
ature and scholarship.

from 2 Henry IV

This part of his conjoins with my disease,
And helps to end me. See, sons, what things you are!
How quickly nature falls into revolt
When gold becomes her object!
For this the foolish over-careful fathers
Have broke their sleep with thoughts, their brains with care,
Their bones with industry; for this they have
Engrosséd and piled up the cankered heaps
Of strange-achievéd gold; for this they have
Been thoughtful to invest their sons with arts
And martial exercises; when, like the bee
Culling from every flower the virtuous sweets,
Our thighs packed with wax, our mouths with honey,
We bring it to the hive, and, like the bees,
Are murdered for our pains. This bitter taste
Yields his engrossments to the ending father.

(Act 4, Scene 5)

WILLIAM SHAKESPEARE
(1564–1616)

part — act
conjoins — unites
engrosséd — accumulated
cankered — tarnished
strange-achievéd — through schemes or exertions or in foreign lands
thoughtful— careful

_____

When King Henry IV, very near death, awakens from a troubled sleep to find that his son
Prince Hal has taken his crown, he suspects the worst. Happily, this time he is mistaken,
though Hal's new sense of responsibility and propriety come as a shock to all who knew
him before. As King Henry V, Hal became one of Britain's most beloved monarchs.

_____

For a biography, see page 63.

A Poem for Emily

Small fact and fingers and farthest one from me,
a hand's width and two generations away,
in this still present I am fifty-three.
You are not yet a full day.

When I am sixty-three, when you are ten,
and you are neither closer nor as far,
your arms will fill with what you know by then,
the arithmetic and love we do and are.

When I by blood and luck am eighty-six
and you are someplace else and thirty-three
believing in sex and God and politics
with children who look not at all like me,

sometime I know you will have read them this
so they will know I love them and say so
and love their mother. Child, whatever is
is always or never was. Long ago

a day I watched awhile beside your bed,
I wrote this down, a thing that might be kept
awhile, to tell you what I would have said
when you were who knows what and I was dead
which is I stood and loved you while you slept.

MILLER WILLIAMS
(1930–)

Written at the birth of Miller Williams's first grandchild.

Miller Williams was born in Hoxie, Arkansas, and educated (in part) at Arkansas State University and the University of Arkansas. Indeed, he has lived in Arkansas for most of his life. He taught college biology before becoming a professor of English. He is married to Jordan Hall, and they have two daughters and a son, as well as three grandchildren and a great-granddaughter (whose mother is in fact the Emily of the above poem).

Grandfather

Your grandchildren
are climbing
the oak tree in the backyard
on the planks of wood
you nailed in its side
Soon they will not remember
who spaced them so evenly
Do you feel the weight
of a small foot on your heart,
and when they reach the top
will you grasp their hands
and hoist them up with you?

MOHJA KAHF
(1967–)

Written when the poet was fifteen. When this poem won first place in a contest, Kahf's father taught her a Bedouin saying: "The tribe rejoices on three occasions: the birth of a boy, the acquiring of a horse, and the emergence of a poet." Kahf comments, "He knew the first part was sexist. And we're not even Bedouin. My dad was just finding a way to say, 'Hey! You are emerging as a poet, and poetry is very important to Arab folk; let's rejoice.'"

Mohja Kahf, the oldest of eight children, was born in Damascus, Syria, and immigrated to the United States as a three-year-old. She was educated at Rutgers University and is now a professor at the University of Arkansas. She lives with her husband and two children in Fayetteville.

Perennials

I've betrayed them all:
columbine and daisy,
iris, day-lily,
even the rain barrel
that spoke to me in a dream.

I inherited this garden,
and miss my grandmother
in her big sun hat.
My inexperienced hands
don't know what to hope for.

Still, flowers come: yellow,
pink, and blue. Preoccupied,
I let them go
until weeds produce spikes
and seeds around them.

I never used the rain barrel.
Water froze in the bottom;
too late, I set it on its side.

Now lily-of-the-valley comes
with its shy bloom,
choked by a weed
I don't know the name of. One day,

too late, I'll weed around them,
and pull some lilies by mistake.

Next year we'll all be back,
struggling.

Just look at these flowers
I've done nothing to deserve:
and still, they won't abandon me.

KATHLEEN NORRIS
(1947–)

Though born in Washington, D.C., Norris spent much of her childhood in Hawaii. She
was educated at Bennington College, and then when she inherited her parents' house in
Lemmon, South Dakota, she and her husband, David Dwyer, moved there to manage a
farm and write. She has been an oblate (lay associate) of the Benedictine Order and is best
known for two spiritual memoirs — *Dakota: A Spiritual Geography* and *The Cloister Walk*.

Apology

Mother, I have taken your boots,
your good black gloves, your coat
from the closet in the hall, your prettiest things.
But the way you disposed of your life gives me leave.
The way you gave it away.
Even as I pillage your bedroom,
make off with your expensive, wonderful books,
your voice streams after me, level with sensible urgency.
And near to the margin of tears as I used to be,
I do what you say.

ANNE STEVENSON
(1933–)

Anne Stevenson was born in Cambridge, England, to American parents. She grew up in Vermont and was educated at the University of Michigan. Since 1954, however, she has lived in England. She has a daughter and two sons from four marriages, and has worked as a schoolteacher, a publisher, an editor, and a bookseller. She has also written a biography of Sylvia Plath (whose poem appears on page 72).

Eating Together

In the steamer is the trout
seasoned with slivers of ginger,
two sprigs of green onion, and sesame oil.
We shall eat it with rice for lunch,
brothers, sister, my mother who will
taste the sweetest meat of the head,
holding it between her fingers
deftly, the way my father did
weeks ago. Then he lay down
to sleep like a snow-covered road
winding through pines older than him,
without any travelers, and lonely for no one.

LI-YOUNG LEE
(1957–)

For a biography, see page 29.

Moments of Summer

The horizontal tugs me more and more.
Childhood hours spent reading with my father
rise in a kind procession once again.
Disparate gravities of our two ages
dissolve as we lie back and let the pages
take us, float us, sail us out to sea.

What special spell (not always narrative:
the winter we read *De Senectute*
I was fifteen; you had two years to live)
braided our endless differences to one?
Today a mother reading to my son,
I savor freshly that sweet nourishment,
especially if we are lying down.

RACHEL HADAS
(1948–)

De Senectute — "On Old Age," an essay by the Roman orator Cicero (106–43 B.C.)

The poet's father, the renowned classical scholar Moses Hadas, was sixty-three the summer they read Cicero together.

For a biography, see page 101.

from Psalm 78

Give ear, O my people, to my law;
    incline your ears to the words of my mouth.
I will open my mouth in a parable;
    I will utter dark sayings of old
which we have heard and known,
    and our fathers have told us.
We will not hide them from their children,
    showing to the generation to come
the praises of the Lord, and his strength,
    and his wonderful works that he hath done.
For he established a testimony in Jacob,
    and appointed a law in Israel,
which he commanded our fathers,
    that they should make them known to their children;
that the generation to come might know them,
    even the children which should be born;
who should arise and declare them to their children,
    that they might set their hope in God,
    and not forget the works of God,
    but keep his commandments.

THE HEBREW BIBLE
(NINTH–EIGHTH CENTURY B.C.)
King James Version (1610)

---

dark sayings — hidden things

These are the opening lines of a psalm that recounts the story of how God blessed the children of Israel from their deliverance in Egypt down to the reign of King David.

from The Iliad

Like leaves on trees the race of man is found,
Now green in youth, now withering on the ground;
Another race the following spring supplies;
They fall successive, and successive rise:
So generations in their course decay;
So flourish these, when those are passed away.

(Book VI, lines 145–150)

HOMER
(LATE EIGHTH CENTURY B.C.)
Translated from the ancient Greek by Alexander Pope (ca. 1716)

With these words, the Trojan Glaucus disparaged the importance of lineage when he was challenged by his aristocratic enemy Diomedes, but he nevertheless went on to tell the story of his forebears, a story that in the end saved his life.

The idea of the natural procession of generations recurs regularly in ancient texts. The comparison of people to leaves that drop in the fall and then grow again in the spring also appears in Ecclesiasticus 14:18 and Aristophanes' Birds. In fact, the second-century Christian writer Clement of Alexandria claimed that Homer had plagiarized the passage above from an even earlier poet named Musaeus.

Nothing for certain is known about the poet who composed the Iliad and the Odyssey, though evidence from the poems suggests that he was a bard who created these epics orally before the reinvention of writing in ancient Greece. His general topic was the Trojan War, usually dated to about 1200 B.C.

Heredity

I am the family face;
Flesh perishes, I live on,
Projecting trait and trace
Through time to times anon,
And leaping from place to place
Over oblivion.

The years-heired feature that can
In curve and voice and eye
Despise the human span
Of durance — that is I;
The eternal thing in man,
That heeds no call to die.

THOMAS HARDY
(1840–1928)

Thomas Hardy was born in Dorset, England. He was apprenticed to a local architect and then worked in that profession for five years in London. He published his first novel in 1871, the same year that he met his future wife Emma Lavinia Gifford, whom he married in 1874. He went on to write fourteen novels, including such classics as *Far from the Madding Crowd* and *Tess of the d'Urbervilles*. In 1885 he and Emma moved to Dorchester, where they lived until her death in 1912, despite increasing marital difficulties. After Emma's death, he wrote more than a hundred poems about their relationship (in fact, most of his poetry was published after he had given up writing novels). Two years later he married Florence Emily Dugdale. When he died, his heart was buried next to Emma in Dorset and his ashes were interred in Westminster Abbey.

A Timepiece

Of a pendulum's mildness, with her feet up
My sister lay expecting her third child.
Over the hammock's crescent spilled
Her flushed face, grazing clover and buttercup.

Her legs were troubling her, a vein had burst.
Even so, among partial fullnesses she lay
Of pecked damson, of daughters at play
Who in the shadow of the house rehearsed

Her gait, her gesture, unnatural to them,
But they would master it soon enough, grown tall
Trusting that out of themselves came all
That full grace, while she out of whom these came

Shall have thrust fullness from her, like a death.
Already, seeing the little girls listless
She righted herself in a new awkwardness.
It was not *her* life she was heavy with.

Let us each have some milk, my sister smiled
Meaning to muffle with the taste
Of unbuilt bone a striking in her breast,
For soon by what it tells the clock is stilled.

JAMES MERRILL
(1926–1995)

damson — an Asian plum

Written about the poet's older half sister, Doris.

For a biography, see page 12. For other poems by Merrill, see pages 12 and 57.

Notes on Poetic Forms

Poetry is a particularly deliberate, intensified mode of expression in which the authors rely on a wide array of techniques including allusion, imagery, metaphor, repetition, and wordplay. They are also generally concerned with the way their poems sound when spoken aloud. Often poetic forms play a role in how poets choose and arrange their words, and sometimes the form can be integral to what the poet is trying to accomplish. Because some background (or review) can be useful in discerning various patterns, I am including a few comments on the subject, with illustrations from the poems in this anthology. All of this, I suppose, is something of a demonstration that there is more to fine poetry than first meets the eye, and the poems included in this collection are well worth a second, a third, or even a fourth reading.

Rhythm and Meter

Poems are frequently characterized by regular rhythm or meter. In Greek, Latin, and Sanskrit, this was based on the length of vowels. In English, rhythm is often the result of regular patterns of stress. Metrical poetry starts with units of two or three syllables called *feet*:

    iamb: ˘ ´   okáy

    trochee: ´ ˘   spléndid

    anapest: ˘ ˘ ´ in a pínch

    dactyl: ´ ˘ ˘   wónderful

    spondee: ´ ´   góod jób

These feet, then, can be strung together into lines of regular length, the most common of which are:

    dimeter (two feet)   I síng the whíle[1]

[1] William Blake, page 77

⌣ ╱ | ⌣ ╱ | ⌣ ╱

trimeter (three feet)　　And hand in hand we'll go;[1]

╱ ⌣ | ⌣ ╱ | ⌣ ╱ | ⌣ ╱

tetrameter (four feet)　　Quiet and small and just astir,[2]

╱ ⌣ | ╱ ⌣ | ╱ ⌣ | ╱ ⌣ | ╱ ⌣

pentameter (five feet)　　Sundays too my father got up early[3]

As can be seen in the tetrameter example, different types of feet can be combined in a single line, and part of the pleasure of metrical poetry is seeing (or hearing) how poets set up regular rhythms and then vary them to add interest or play off our expectations. For instance, you can see how Howard Nemerov draws attention to the physical connection between parent and child with the spondee in the middle of the following line:

⌣ ╱ | ⌣ ╱| ╱ ╱ | ⌣ ⌣ ╱ | ⌣ ╱

My child and I hold hands on the way to school,[4]

It is especially noteworthy when the rhythm reinforces the content. The iambic trimeter in the Robert Burns example lends itself to a lilting recitation that reflects the folksong origins of the poem, and the heavier, slightly awkward trochees in Hayden's line help us feel the dutiful lethargy of dragging oneself out of bed on a weekend morning. W. B. Yeats's "A Cradle Song" consists nearly entirely of anapests, reminiscent of nursery rhymes like "To market, to market, to buy a fat pig":

⌣ ╱ | ⌣ ⌣ ╱ | ⌣ ⌣ ╱ | ⌣ ⌣ ╱

The angels are bending / above your white bed,

⌣ ╱ | ⌣ ⌣ ╱ | ⌣ ⌣ ╱ | ⌣ ⌣ ╱

They weary of tending / the souls of the dead.[5]

[1]Robert Burns, page 59
[2]Donald Hall, page 76
[3]Robert Hayden, page 31
[4]page 99
[5]page 80, Note to purists: This is not an exact scansion — I cheat by running the lines together — but the anapestic meter becomes quite clear when the lines are taken two at a time.

Rhymes and Slant Rhymes

Rhymes are common enough in English poetry that many readers look for them to signal the ends of lines. In Brad Leithauser's "Old Bachelor Brother" (page 38), for instance, every other line ends with a similar sound, and rhymes such as *square* and *there* are perfectly standard. Yet he also employs multisyllable rhymes (*rehearsal / Purcell* ; *so that / silhouette*) and slant rhymes, where the rhyme is partial rather than exact — *church / march* or *did / crowd*. In these cases, the final consonants stay the same though the vowel sounds are different. Leithauser's sheer delight in the sounds of words is manifest in his extravagant last rhyme — *to part the sea / anonymity.*

Poets may also make their phrases more interesting and memorable by choosing words with similar sounds. Within a line or two we might encounter repeated first letter sounds (*alliteration*), repeated consonants (*consonance*), repeated vowel sounds (*assonance*), and full or slant rhymes (*internal rhymes*) — all of which appear in just two short lines by Theodore Roethke:

> My lizard, my lively writher,
> May your limbs never wither,[1]

The last words in each line rhyme (sort of), but there are also repeated *l*'s in *lizard / lively / limbs* (alliteration) and *r*'s in *lizard / writher / your / never / wither* (consonance); repeated long *i*'s in *my / lively / writher* (assonance); a slant rhyme within the second line of *never* and *wither*, and another in the beginning words *my* and *may*. The preceding sentence may take a fair amount of concentration to follow, but even without the careful analysis, Roethke's words are simply fun to speak aloud, and he gets further credit for immortalizing "lizard" as a term of endearment.

Of course, not all poetry rhymes in a regular fashion. We usually expect the techniques of meter and rhyme to go together, but there are poems in traditional meters that do not rhyme — Andrew Hudgins's "Elegy for My Father, Who Is Not Dead" (page 142), for instance, is in unrhymed iambic tetrameter, and William Shakespeare's lines from 2 *Henry IV* (page 167) are unrhymed iambic pentameter. But this is somewhat rare. More common are poems that make no pretense at all to regular meters, standard line lengths, or recurrent rhyming patterns. These are characterized as *free verse*. There

[1]page 42

are many examples in this anthology, including striking poems by David
Ignatow and Linda Pastan.

Free verse is not, however, formless or unconcerned with the way it sounds
— alliteration, assonance, internal rhymes, and occasional end rhymes are
often in evidence. These can be seen in the following lines by Jacqueline
Osherow:

> There *is* life beyond our own. Gabriel
> Whispers, softly fluttering his wings,
> With every touch a hushed annunciation.[1]

Say these words aloud and listen for the rustling *s*-sounds and the soft *f*'s.
Hear how the short *i* repeats in "is," "whispers," and "with." Notice how
"touch" rhymes with "hushed" and the *sh* is picked up yet again in the final
syllable ("wings" also echoes the sound of "strings," which appeared four
lines above). The whole aural effect reinforces the meaning of the words;
Osherow's lines sound like an angelic murmer of affirmation.

Both rhyming, metered poems and free verse can employ the technique
of *enjambment*, in which a phrase or sentence keeps going despite a line
break. The quotation above provides an example in the transition from the
first to the second line; there the subject — Gabriel — is stranded apart from
the rest of his sentence. Poetic lines frequently consist of complete grammat-
ical units, with a pause of some kind at the end (often marked by a comma,
a semicolon, or a period), as can be seen in Seamus Heaney's lines:

> Ahead of us the sky's a geyser now.
> A calm voice talks of cloud yet we feel lost.
> Air-pockets jolt our fears and down we go.
> Travellers, at this point, can only trust.[2]

Contrast this with Emily Dickinson's

> She rose to His Requirement — dropt
> The Playthings of Her Life[3]

[1]page 68
[2]page 41
[3]page 49

or Jane Kenyon's conclusion to her lovely allegory "In the Nursing Home":

> Master, come with your light
> halter. Come and bring her in.[1]

A tension is created here between the pauses that we expect at the end of lines and the grammatical syntax that carries us forward. In the last example, Kenyon plays with this by letting us think, for a moment, that what the master brings is light (a noun that would complete the thought), when it is actually a light (adjective) halter.

The flexibility of free verse may also allow poets to experiment with the way the poem looks on the page. The irregular shape of Edward Hirsch's "Infertility" (page 64) immediately marks it as free verse, but to me, the uneven, randomly broken lines seem to reflect the theme; they can't quite come together to complete a pattern that seems so natural and easy for others.

The extremely short lines of Linda Pastan's "Only Child" (page 23) give the poem a thin, sparse appearance that can represent the lonely incompleteness that she describes, and the five lines of just two syllables highlight her image of twinning.

A Summary of Poetic Forms
What follows is a brief summary of conventional poetic forms, based primarily on stanza lengths and rhyme schemes. In standard notation, end rhymes are indicated by small italicized letters, so that *abab* is the form of Emily Brontë's poem:

> Upon her soothing breast   *a*
> She lulled her little child;   *b*
> A winter sunset in the west   *a*
> A dreary glory smiled.[2]   *b*

The meters are not specified and have to be figured out individually (in this case, Brontë uses iambic trimeters with an extra foot in the third line).

I have also included comments on non-English poetic forms, though the problem of translation adds another layer of complexity. Translators usually

[1]page 143
[2]page 78

concentrate on the meanings of the words, leaving behind the sounds and patterns of the original languages. In some types of poetry, such as Hebrew parallelism, the most important features of the poem are evident in translation, while the free verse renderings of most Chinese poems are quite misleading, at least with regard to the linguistic intricacies of the originals. Very rarely do translators attempt to put their versions into poetic forms — though Alexander Pope tries to give readers a sense of Homer's Greek dactylic hexameter by using English iambic pentameter couplets (page 176). In the entries below, comments about syllables and rhymes in non-English poems refer to the original languages rather than the translations — so even though every Japanese haiku needs exactly seventeen syllables, this is not the number of syllables in the English versions on page 145.

Blank verse — unrhymed lines of iambic pentameter. Seamus Heaney's "Mid-Term Break" (page 147) is an example of this, as is the excerpt from Shakespeare's *2 Henry IV* (page 167). Howard Nemerov's "September, the First Day of School" (page 99) is blank verse, though the last two lines form a rhyming couplet that sets them off as a summary statement.

Chōka — a Japanese form that originated in the first anthology of Japanese poetry, the *Man'yōshū* (mid–eighth century). Because of particularities of the language, Japanese poetry pays little attention to accent, stress, vowel length, or rhyme. Instead poetic forms are based on strict counting of syllables. The longest of the regular forms is the *chōka*, which consists of alternating lines of five and seven syllables, with an extra seven-syllable line at the end. There is no specified length, though the longest *chōka* in the *Man'yōshū* runs to about 150 lines. Frequently a *chōka*, is followed by a *hanka* (usually translated as "envoy"), which is a short, associated poem in the *tanka* style (five lines with syllables in a 5-7-5-7-7 pattern) that summarizes or supplements the main poem. There is one *chōka* in this collection: Lady Ōtomo of Sakanoé's "Sent to Her Elder Daughter from the Capital" (page 109).

Chüeh-chü — a shortened form of the Chinese *shih* employing four lines of either five or seven characters, with required rhymes at the end of lines two and four, and an optional rhyme at the end of line one. Each character in Chinese is pronounced a fixed pitch or tone (there are four in modern Mandarin), and there were complicated rules about where certain tones could or could not be used in a line. Li Shang-yin's "When Will I Be Home?" (page 53) is a *chüeh-chü* with seven-character lines (for more details, see pages 192–194).

Couplet — two adjacent lines whose last words rhyme: *aa*. Some poems consist entirely of couplets, such as D. H. Lawrence's "Piano" (page 28) or Anne Bradstreet's "Before the Birth of One of Her Children" (page 70). Other examples include Ben Johnson's "On My First Son" (page 146) and Robert Louis Stevenson's "To Willie and Henrietta" (page 162), in which each stanza ends with a slightly longer line.

Epic — a long, narrative poem in an exalted, heroic style. The archetypes are the two epics of Homer — the *Iliad* and the *Odyssey* — originally written in Greek in dactylic hexameter. This anthology includes an excerpt from Homer's *Iliad* (page 176).

Haiku — a short Japanese form that developed in the seventeenth century. It consists of the first three lines of the traditional *tanka*, that is, three lines of 5, 7, and 5 syllables. Kobayashi Issa is the author of the two haiku included here (page 145), the second of which ("The world of dew") can be transliterated as:

> *Tsuyu no yo wa*
> *tsuyu no yo nagara*
> *sari nagara*

Our translator breaks this into four lines for his English version.

Hebraic poetry — the style of the poetic sections of the Hebrew Bible, which is based on parallelism. Rather than employing rhyme or meter, poetry is arranged by parallel lines, where the second line restates the meaning of the first, but in different words. There is tremendous flexibility in this pattern, so that the second line might repeat the initial idea in negative terms, or it might complete the thought, and sometimes there are two responding lines. All of this can be seen in the excerpt from Psalm 78 (page 175).

Octet — a poem with eight-line stanzas. Fleur Adcock's "For a Five-Year-Old" (page 93) rhymes *abbccdda*.

Quatrain — the most popular of English stanzaic forms, this is a stanza consisting of four lines. Common rhyme schemes include *abcb* and *abab*. Theodore Roethke's "My Papa's Waltz" (page 30) is an outstanding example of the latter, in trimeter (three beats per line, as befits a waltz). Richard Wilbur's "A Wedding Toast" (page 40) is *abba*, its short trimeters in the third line of each stanza contrasting with the remaining pentameter lines. William Blake rhymes his "Infant Sorrow" *aabb* (page 77). Archibald MacLeish plays with the possibilities of this form in his "The Old Gray Couple" (page 133), where each of the three quatrains uses a different rhyme pattern: *abcb ddee fgfg*.

Quintet — a relatively rare form in English, with five-line stanzas. Brad Leithauser provides a striking example in his poem "A Honeymoon Conception (1952)" (page 66), with rhymes arranged into an *abcba* order (the shorter length of the third line underscores the pattern). This gentle pendulum motion gives way to something new — *abcbc* — in the last stanza, perhaps reflecting the way a new presence joins their marriage. Yvor Winters's "At the San Francisco Airport" (page 115) is written in strict *ababa* form.

Septet — also relatively rare, with stanzas of seven lines. James Merrill varied the line length in his "Upon a Second Marriage" (page 57), while keeping the regular rhyme scheme *abacbcb*.

Sestet — a stanza of six lines. Robert Burns wrote much of his poetry in sestets, which derived from a medieval form that survived in Scotland long after poetic fashion in England had turned to pentameter couplets. "A Poet's Welcome to His Love-Begotten Daughter" (page 161) follows this traditional pattern, rhyming *aaabab*, where lines 1, 2, 3, and 5 are tetrameter, while lines 4 and 6 are dimeter. Thomas Hardy's "Heredity" (page 177) has two sestets that rhyme *ababab*.

Sestina — the most complicated of traditional verse forms, it depends on the repetition of significant words. There are six unrhymed stanzas of six lines each, and each line must end with a particular word. The poem ends with an envoy of three lines, each of which must include two of the six key words:

stanza 1	A	B	C	D	E	F
stanza 2	F	A	E	B	D	C

stanza	3	C	F	D	A	B	E
stanza	4	E	C	B	F	A	D
stanza	5	D	E	A	C	F	B
stanza	6	B	D	F	E	C	A
Envoy

This sounds almost mathematical in its complexity, but Elizabeth Bishop meets all these requirements in her "Sestina" (page 17) and makes the repetitions seem gentle and lulling rather than rigidly artificial. In that poem the key words are:

A — house
B — grandmother
C — child
D — stove
E — almanac
F — tears

And the envoy has them in the order:

F E
B D
C A

Shih — An ancient Chinese form that dates back to the *Book of Odes* (ca. 1000 B.C.). In that collection, poems usually had lines of four characters, with rhymes at the end of even-numbered lines. P'an Yüeh's "Thinking of My Wife" (page 150) and T'ao Yüan-ming's "Blaming Sons" (page 100) are *shih* with five-character lines. In the T'ang dynasty (618–907), the rules for *shih* became stricter and more complicated. The standard form was an eight-line poem, with lines of either five or seven characters and rhymes at the end of even-numbered lines. Two main categories emerged: the "old style," which allowed occasional lines of irregular length, and the "new style," where lines had to be exact and meet additional requirements for grammatical parallelism and the placement of tones. Po Chü-i's "Half in the Family, Half Out" (page 136) and Ch'in T'ao-yü's "Poor Girls" (page 37) are examples of "new-style" (or regulated) *shih* poems with seven-character lines. Po Chü-i's "Children" (page 94) and

Yang Hsün-chi's "Inscribed on the Doors of My Bookshelves" (page 165) are examples of five-character old-style *shih*.

Sonnet — fourteen lines of iambic pentameter, generally arranged according to one of two rhyme schemes:

Italian: *abba abba cdcdcd* (often with a thematic break between lines eight and nine)

English: *abab cdcd efef gg* (again with a shift of thought after line eight, and with a summarizing ending couplet in addition)

Augusta Webster, John Keats, and John Milton all provide strict examples the former (pages 102, 118, and 156); Shakespeare's sonnets are the classic prototypes of the latter (page 63). As with any traditional form, poets have not been able to resist playing with the pattern, and they have found it to be unusually rich. George Barker's "Sonnet to My Mother" (page 25) only roughly follows the outline, with somewhat irregular line lengths and a rhyme scheme of *abcd abcd efg efh*, while Seamus Heaney's "Clearances" (page 27) is a blank sonnet, with no regular rhymes at all. George Meredith created a new form of metrically strict sixteen-line sonnets for his fifty-poem sequence "Modern Love," of which #17 is included in this anthology (page 56).

Tercet — a stanza of three lines, which may or may not rhyme. Sylvia Plath's "Morning Song" (page 72) and Alan Shapiro's "Night Terrors" (page 90) are unrhymed examples. John Ciardi's "Men Marry What They Need" (page 48) takes the special form of a *terza rima*, where the middle line of each stanza rhymes with the first and third lines of the next. This form was used by Dante in his *Divine Comedy*, of which Ciardi was a distinguished translator.

Tz'u — a Chinese form in which a poem is written to fit the rhymes, rhythms, and tonal sequence of a preexisting song. Line lengths are irregular, but specified according to the particular tune. After the original melodies were lost, poets continued to write *tz'u* using earlier examples as guides, and the titles of tunes usually have nothing to do with the content. The two *tz'u* in this anthology are Li Ch'ing-chao's "Written to the Tune: 'Song of Picking Mulberry'" (page 43) and Su Tung-p'o's "Written to the Tune: 'River Town'" (page 158), the second of which consists of eight-line stanzas of 7, 3, 3, 4, 5, 7, 3, and 3 syllables — the pattern of the original song. A Scottish counterpart can be seen in Robert Burns's "John Anderson My Jo" (page 59), where he wrote new words to fit an earlier, somewhat bawdy folksong of the same title in which a wife laments that her husband's abilities in bed are not what they once were.

Villanelle — a long form consisting of five tercets rhyming *aba* followed by a quatrain of *abaa*. In addition, entire lines are repeated, so that the first line of the poem occurs again at the ends of stanzas two and four, and the third line reappears to conclude stanzas three and five. The poem is brought to an end with one final repetition of the first and third lines in a concluding couplet. The complete form, then, would be:

stanza 1: A¹ b A²
stanza 2: a b A¹
stanza 3: a b A²
stanza 4: a b A¹
stanza 5: a b A²
stanza 6: a b A¹ A²

where A¹ and A² stand for whole lines. James Merrill's "The World and the Child" (page 12) is a fairly strict example of a villanelle (though the repeated lines vary slightly); Jonathan Galassi's "Our Wives" (page 121) is much freer, but still generally adheres to the pattern.

Additional Comments on a Few Specific Poems

Poets can do astonishing things with words, and this is often evident in the ways in which they play with form to add another level of meaning and memorability to their work. I offer here just a few examples from poems in this anthology. It may take some effort to follow what is happening line by line, but good poems will amply repay the time it takes to read closely. Generally, poets put more thought into each word than most readers can imagine, and the better one knows such poems, the better they become.

Louis MacNeice's "The Sunlight on the Garden" (page 127) has four stanzas of six lines that rhyme *abcbba*. The first stanza is:

The sunlight on the garden
Hardens and grows cold,

We cannot cage the minute
Within its nets of gold,
When all is told
We cannot beg for pardon.

The end rhymes are matched by an intricate system of initial rhymes, so that in every stanza the first word of the second line mirrors the a-rhyme (*hardens / garden*), and the fourth line begins with the c-rhyme (*within its / minute*). In addition, there is a nice interplay between the masculine rhymes (one stressed syllable) of *b* and the feminine rhymes (a stressed, rhyming syllable followed by an unstressed one) of *a* and *c*. Finally, the "sunlight on the garden" of the first line is balanced by the same phrase in the last line of the poem. So also "hardens" appears in lines 2 and 20, "pardon" in lines 6 and 19, and "the earth compels" in lines 9 and 17, giving the poem as a whole a chiastic feel (where the same elements return in reverse order). MacNeice's tight construction provides a sort of verbal cage, a hedge against the chaos and uncertainty that awaits, in this particular case, both the end of MacNeice's marriage and the political dissolution of 1930s Europe. The poem's strict form offers a reassurance that order is possible, even as it acknowledges that change is inevitable. And it ends with a nod toward tradition, suggesting that we can appreciate the good in the past even as we face an uncertain future.

In Miller Williams's poem on the birth of his granddaughter Emily (page 168), the breakdown of regularity reinforces the theme of the poem. Each of the stanzas consists of four lines that rhyme *abab*, except for the last stanza, which suddenly has five lines. The unwelcome intruder here is the fourth, the one that envisions the poet's death:

a day I watched awhile beside your bed,
I wrote this down, a thing that might be kept
awhile, to tell you what I would have said
when you were who knows what and I was dead
which is I stood and loved you while you slept.

The harsh word "dead" is not entirely unexpected — after all, the poem has been imaginatively forecasting the poet's advancing age from his fifties through his sixties and into his eighties — but I would guess that one's own expiration always comes as something of a shock. Yet it does not throw everything into complete disorder — the new rhyme scheme is *abaab*. We get an *a*-rhyme when we were expecting a *b*, and there is a moment of suspense and confusion until the poem settles back into a familiar, expected sound — suggesting that life's regularities are carried into the next generation despite the poet's absence (which to some degree is overcome by the existence of this written poem, conveying what he would have said had he been there).

Even poems that are not in prescribed patterns may demonstrate a desire to match form and meaning. Edna St. Vincent Millay, imagining Penelope's emotional state in the absence of her husband, Ulysses, writes:

> you can't keep weaving all day
> And undoing it all through the night;
> Your arms get tired, and the back of your neck gets tight;
> And along toward morning, when you think it will never be light,
> And your husband has been gone, and you don't know where, for years,
> Suddenly you burst into tears;
> There is simply nothing else to do.[1]

The tension increases as the lines get longer and longer (the rhymes help to emphasize this), and the phrases pile up in a way that literally makes one breathless, until the surprisingly short next-to-last line, like the tears it describes, comes as a release. Other poems set up expectations only to break them in interesting ways: James Tate cuts short his three-line stanzas in "Five Years Old" with an unexpected twist (page 15); the only word not in a regular line in Forrest Hamer's "Lesson" is the disturbing "noises" that keep him awake (page 33); and the one broken line of Andrew Hudgins's "Hunting with My Brother" describes a lapse into sullen silence (page 117).

Several other poems offer short lines where we would expect something longer, and the missing beat makes us pause just a bit to imagine the scene or reflect on the meaning of what we have just read. For instance, listen to how the very short line "and smile" breaks the general pattern of the longer, surrounding lines in Galway Kinnell's "After Making Love We Hear Footsteps" (page 82), but in a reassuring way that highlights the parents' unspoken understanding. Or how the last, foreshortened line in Marie

[1] page 55

Howe's "What the Living Do" (page 154) represents the speaker's reconciliation after a period of agitated mourning: "I am living. I remember you" (until this point, each stanza consisted of two extraordinarily long lines).

A poem that creates it own form, brilliantly, is C. K. Williams's "Grace" (page 140). The first four stanzas are single sentences of three long lines each. Each sentence begins with the word "almost," includes the verb "think," and mentions some "good" (actually, four "goods" in the first sentence). In addition, the word "hope" weaves into four of the five stanzas. Because the syntax is quite convoluted — there are three "almosts" and two "thinks" in the first sentence alone — it is much easier to follow the intricate grammar if you read the poem aloud. After a while, however, the meaning becomes clearer since each sentence basically covers the same territory — the poet imagines his death, and then tells himself that his very last thought in this life will be of his wife. But she has so many admirable qualities that it will be difficult to choose just one for that final remembering. To paraphrase his dilemma — "I'll think her X was good, but her Y was almost as fine." The poem thus becomes a list of the virtues of his beloved (one of the oldest of love-poem devices), but Williams gives it a novel, distinctive form. The fifth and last sentence also begins with "almost" and includes a "think" and a "good," but it expands into two stanzas as the poet stakes the goodness of life itself against one tender act by his wife on one particular night. And then he wraps it up in the last line with one more appearance of each of his three key words, thinking of how her presence will endure "as firmly as ever, as *good* even now, I'll *think* in that lull before last, *almost* as ever" (italics added).

At the opposite end of the spectrum, where the form is highly dependent on traditional models, is Li Shang-yin's ninth-century poem "When Will I Be Home?" (page 53). In translation, medieval Chinese poetry usually appears spontaneous and easygoing; in fact, it is almost always very tightly constructed in accordance with intricate rules. Here is Kenneth Rexroth's version:

When will I be home? I don't know.
In the mountains, in the rainy night,
The Autumn lake is flooded.
Someday we will be back together again.
We will sit in the candlelight by the West window,

And I will tell you how I remembered you
Tonight on the stormy mountain.

This is an accurate translation of the sense of the poem, but the free-verse
style obscures a great many parallels, patterns, and symmetries that are inte-
gral to what makes the poem so memorable in Chinese. Here is the original,
with each character's tone category indicated by a + or o and the end rhymes
underlined:

o + o o + + o
君問歸期未有期
o o + + + o o
巴山夜雨漲秋池
o o + + o o +
何當共剪西窗燭
+ + o o + + o
卻話巴山夜雨時

The first thing to notice is that the Chinese is much more concise and
ordered — just four lines of seven characters each (Rexroth splits lines two
through four in half). This is required by the particular form that Li uses —
a seven character *chüeh-chü*, which also requires the following:

1. Lines two and four must rhyme (with an option to rhyme the first
   line, as Li does here).
2. The lines should form grammatical units, with syntactic paral-
   lelism between the two lines of a couplet — which helps Chinese
   readers interpret ambiguous phrases.
3. Each of the two couplets ought to be a complete grammatical
   unit as well.
4. Chinese characters are always pronounced with a specified pitch
   or tone, and in this poetic form the tones must follow a fixed pat-
   tern. In medieval prosody, the possible tones were classified as
   either level (o) or deflected (+). The rules were complicated, but
   in general the second and sixth character of each line had the
   same tone, which was opposite that of the fourth character.

Similarly, the fifth and seventh characters had to have opposite tones. Finally, each couplet had to have opposite tones in these key positions — 2nd, 4th, 5th, and 7th (with two exceptions when the first line rhymed with lines two and four).

Part of the wonder of this poem is just seeing how Li meets the challenge of a very difficult form, yet there is more. (There is always more.) The basic idea is one of reversal:

> First couplet: Now I am alone, on a rainy night in the mountains, imagining talking to you — answering your question: "When are you coming home?"
> Second couplet: Someday I will actually be in your presence again, and it will be this long, rain-drenched night that is imagined, or recalled in our conversation.

The whole pattern of having two couplets that are complete thoughts in themselves, but are cast as opposites in tonal quality, reinforces the dramatic shift from imagination to actuality (and vice versa) at the heart of this poem. This comes through clearly enough in the translation, but it is even more striking in the original, where the image of a rainy night in the mountains quite literally returns — the first four characters in line two, "rainy night on Pa Mountain," are repeated exactly in the last line, but in places three through six. (You can see this if you look carefully.) A repeated four-character phrase is a large portion of a twenty-eight-word poem (the English translation has almost twice as many words), and seeing the old image in a new context further emphasizes the link between the two experiences, and also how much has changed. Both the form and content of this poem pivot around Pa Mountain, which of course stays solidly in Szechwan Province while the speaker's location at the end of the poem is markedly different from where he began. And amazingly, though the four-character phrase is shifted to a new place in a new line, it still fits the required tonal pattern. If in English Li Shang-yin's technical virtuosity doesn't take your breath away, Kenneth Rexroth still does an admirable job of capturing the poignant reversal at the center of Li's poem to his faraway wife.

As a final example of how form affects meaning, here is the music for Robert Burns's "John Anderson My Jo" (page 59). I knew this poem for many years before I realized that it was written to fit a particular tune, and it was even longer until I learned that the melody is still in existence. When I first heard the song it caught me by surprise, for this light, good-natured verse is set to a melody in a minor key, and this changed the way I thought about the poem as a whole. I still see it as a warmhearted celebration of a long and satisfying marriage ("lively" is the tempo marking), but it is more reflective than I had first assumed. It takes a certain maturity to rejoice in a minor key, similar perhaps to what is required to find delight in everyday interactions with family members, or to maintain a gracious faith despite inevitable partings.

John Anderſon my jo, John,
  We clamb the hill the gither;
And mony a canty day John,
  We've had wi' ane anither:
Now we maun totter down, John,
  And hand in hand we'll go;
And ſleep the gither at the foot.
  John Anderſon my Jo. [1]

---

[1] From James Johnson, ed., *The Scots Musical Museum*, volume 3 (Edinburgh, 1790; reprint, 1853).

ACKNOWLEDGMENTS

The generosity and cooperation of many individual poets and their publishers made this anthology possible. I am grateful to Lisa Holmstead for comments on an early draft, and to my colleagues Rick Chess and Sheryl Sawin for their encouragement and advice. My parents, the Ernest Mills Endowment, and UNCA's Humanities Program provided welcome financial assistance. And I owe a tremendous debt to the keen eye and astute literary sensibilities of my wife, Heather.

Gallagher. Editor's preface, commentary, and notes copyright © 1996 by William L. Stull. Used by permission of Alfred A. Knopf, a division of Random House, Inc.

Catullus, #101, from *The Poems of Catullus*, p. 138, translated by Charles Martin. Copyright © 1989 by the Johns Hopkins University Press. Reprinted by permission of the Johns Hopkins University Press.

John Ciardi, "Men Marry What They Need" from *Selected Poems*. Copyright © 1984 by John Ciardi. Reprinted by permission of the Ciardi Family Publishing Trust.

Stephen Corey, "The Tempest" from *All These Lands You Call One Country*. Copyright © 1992 by Stephen Corey. Reprinted by permission of the author.

Emily Dickinson, #723, "She rose to his requirement — dropt." Reprinted by permission of the publishers and the Trustees of Amherst College from *The Poems of Emily Dickinson*, Thomas H. Johnson, ed., Cambridge, Massachusetts: The Belknap Press of Harvard University Press. Copyright © 1951, 1955, 1979 by the President and Fellows of Harvard College.

Blaga Dmitrova, "To My Father," translated by Joanna Bankier, from *The Other Voice: Twentieth-Century Women's Poetry in Translation*, edited by Joanna Bankier, Carol Cosman, Doris Earnshaw, Joan Keefe, Deirdre Lashgari, and Kathleen Weaver. Used by permission of Joanna Bankier.

Rita Dove, "Daystar" from *Selected Poems*, Pantheon Books. Copyright © 1993 by Rita Dove. Reprinted by permission of the author.

Carlos Drummond de Andrade, "Childhood," translated by Dudley Poore, from *Anthology of Contemporary Latin-American Poetry*, edited by Dudley Fitts. Copyright © 1947 by New Directions Publishing Corp. Reprinted by permission of New Directions Publishing Corp. The excerpt from "Family Portrait," translated by Elizabeth Bishop, is from Bishop's *The Complete Poems 1927–1979*. Copyright © 1979, 1983 by Alice Helen Methfessel. Reprinted with permission of Farrar, Straus & Giroux.

Stephen Dunn, "I Come Home Wanting to Touch Everything" from *New and Selected Poems: 1974–1994*. Copyright © 1994 by Stephen Dunn. Used by permission of W. W. Norton & Company, Inc.

T. S. Eliot, "A Dedication to My Wife" from *Collected Poems 1909–1962*. Copyright © 1936 by Harcourt, Inc. Copyright © 1964, 1963 by T. S. Eliot. Reprinted by permission of the publisher.

Jonathan Galassi, "Our Wives." Copyright © 1988 by Jonathan Galassi. Used by permission of Jonathan Galassi.

Celia Gilbert, "Portrait of My Mother on Her Wedding Day" from *Bonfire*. Copyright © 1983 by Celia Gilbert. "Holding On" and "Maps" from *An Ark of Sorts*. Copyright © 1998 by Celia Gilbert. Reprinted by permission of Celia Gilbert.

Nikki Giovanni, "Nikki Rosa" from *The Selected Poems of Nikki Giovanni*. Compilation copyright © 1996 by Nikki Giovanni. Reprinted by permission of HarperCollins Publishers, Inc./Willam Morrow.

Rachel Hadas, "Twelfth Birthday" and "Moments of Summer" from *Halfway Down the Hall: New and Selected Poems*. Copyright © 1998 by Rachel Hadas. Reprinted by permission of Rachel Hadas and Wesleyan University Press.

Donald Hall, "My Son, My Executioner" from *Old and New Poems*. Copyright © 1990 by Donald Hall. Reprinted by permission of Donald Hall. Excerpt from "Last Days" from *Without*. Copyright © 1998 by Donald Hall. Reprinted by permission of Houghton Mifflin Company. All rights reserved.

Forrest Hamer, "Lesson" from *Call and Response*. Copyright © 1995 by Forrest Hamer. Reprinted by permission of Forrest Hamer.

Robert Hayden, "Those Winter Sundays." Copyright © 1966 by Robert Hayden, from *Angle of Ascent: New and Selected Poems by Robert Hayden*. Used by permission of Liveright Publishing Corporation.

Seamus Heaney, "Clearances, #3" and "Mid-Term Break" from *Opened Ground: Selected Poems 1966–1996*. Copyright © 1998 by Seamus Heaney. "Honeymoon Flight" from *Poems: 1965–1975*. Copyright © 1980 by Seamus Heaney. Reprinted by permission of Farrar, Straus and Giroux.

Edward Hirsch, "Infertility" and "My Grandmother's Bed" from *The Night Parade*. Copyright © 1989 by Edward Hirsch. Used by permission of Alfred A. Knopf, a division of Random House, Inc.

Marie Howe, "What the Living Do" from *What the Living Do*. Copyright © 1997 by Marie Howe. Used by permission of W. W. Norton & Company, Inc.

Andrew Hudgins, "Hunting with My Brother" and "Elegy for My Father, Who Is Not Dead" from *The Never-Ending*. Copyright © 1991 by Andrew Hudgins. Reprinted by permission of Houghton Mifflin Company. All rights reserved.

David Ignatow, "Consolation," "Europe and America," "In Limbo," and "The Journey" from *Poems: 1934–1969*. Copyright © 1970 by David Ignatow. Reprinted by permission of Yaedi Ignatow.

Mohja Kahf, "Grandfather." Used by permission of Mohja Kahf.

Jane Kenyon, "Drawing from the Past" and "In the Nursing Home" from *Otherwise: New and Selected Poems*. Copyright 1996 by the Estate of Jane Kenyon. Reprinted with the permission of Graywolf Press, St. Paul, Minnesota.

Galway Kinnell, "After Making Love We Hear Footsteps" from *Mortal Acts, Mortal Words*. Copyright © 1980 by Galway Kinnell. Reprinted by permission of Houghton Mifflin Company. All rights reserved.

James Merrill. "A Timepiece" and "Upon a Second Marriage" from *Collected Poems* by James Merrill and J. D. McClatchy and Stephen Yenser, editors. Copyright © 2001 by the Literary Estate of James Merrill at Washington University. Used by permission of Alfred A. Knopf, a division of Random House, Inc.

Edna St. Vincent Millay, "An Ancient Gesture" from *Collected Poems*, HarperCollins Publishers, Inc. Copyright © 1954, 1982 by Norma Millay Ellis. All rights reserved. Reprinted by permission of Elizabeth Barnett, literary executor.

Gabriela Mistral, "Rocking," translated by John Eric Gant. Used by permission of John Eric Gant.

Pat Mora, "Elena" from *Chants*. Copyright © 1985 by Pat Mora. Reprinted with permission from the publisher of *Chants* (Houston: Arte Publico Press — University of Houston, 1985).

Lisel Mueller, "Daughter" from *Alive Together: New and Selected Poems*. Copyright © 1996 by Lisel Mueller. Reprinted by permission of Lisel Mueller and Louisiana State University Press.

Howard Nemerov, "September, the First Day of School, #1" from *The Collected Poems of Howard Nemerov*. Copyright © 1997 by Howard Nemerov. Reprinted by permission of Margaret Nemerov.

Kathleen Norris, "Perennials" from *Journey*. Copyright © 2001 by Kathleen Norris. Reprinted by permission of the University of Pittsburgh Press.

Naomi Shihab Nye, "Grandfather's Heaven" from *Different Ways to Pray*. Copyright © 1980 by Naomi Shihab Nye. Reprinted by permission of the author, Naomi Shihab Nye, 2002.

Sharon Olds, "35/10" from *The Dead and the Living*. Copyright © 1987 by Sharon Olds. Used by permission of Alfred A. Knopf, a division of Random House, Inc.

Carole Simmons Oles, "To a Daughter at Fourteen Forsaking the Violin" from *The Deed*. Copyright © 1991 by Carole Simmons Oles. Reprinted by permission of Carole Simmons Oles.

Jacqueline Osherow, "After Midnight, the Fifth Month" and "Five A.M., the Ninth Month" from *Looking for Angels in New York*. Copyright © 1988 by Jacqueline Osherow. Reprinted by permission of Jacqueline Osherow.

Lady Ōtomo of Sakanoé, "Sent to Her Elder Daughter from the Capital," translated by the Nippon Gakujutsu Shinkōkai, from the *Manyōshū*. Copyright © 1965 Columbia University Press. Reprinted with the permission of the publisher.

P'an Yüeh, "Thinking of My Wife," translated by Burton Watson, from the *Columbia Book of Chinese Poetry*, edited by Burton Watson. Copyright © 1984 Columbia University Press. Reprinted with the permission of the publisher.

Linda Pastan, "Only Child" and "The Happiest Day" from *Heroes in Disguise*. Copyright © 1991 by Linda Pastan. Used by permission of W. W. Norton & Company, Inc. "Notes from the Delivery Room" from *Carnival Evening: New and Selected Poems 1968–1998*. Copyright © 1998 by Linda Pastan. Used by permission of W. W. Norton & Company, Inc.

Sylvia Plath, "Morning Song" from *Ariel*. Copyright © 1961 by Ted Hughes. Reprinted by permission of HarperCollins Publishers, Inc.

Po Chü-i, "Golden Bells' First Birthday," translated by Charles O. Hucker in *China's Imperial Past*. Copyright © 1975 by the Board of Trustees of the Leland Stanford Junior University. With the permission of Stanford University Press, www.sup.org. "Half in the Family, Half Out," translated by Burton Watson, from *Po Chü-i Selected Poems*. Copyright © 2000 Columbia University Press. Reprinted with the permission of the publisher.

Katha Pollitt, "Playground." Used by permission of Katha Pollitt.

Theodore Roethke, "My Papa's Waltz," copyright © 1942 by Hearst Magazines, Inc., "Wish for a Young Wife," copyright © 1963 by Beatrice Roethke, Administratrix of the Estate of Theodore Roethke, from *The Collected Poems of Theodore Roethke*. Used by permission of Doubleday, a division of Random House, Inc.

Sappho, "I Have a Beautiful Daughter," translated by Josephine Balmer in *Sappho: Poems and Fragments*. Copyright © 1984 by Josephine Balmer. Reprinted by permission of Josephine Balmer.

Alan Shapiro, "Night Terrors" from *Mixed Company*. Copyright © 1996 by the University of Chicago. Used by permission of the University of Chicago. All rights reserved.

Richard Shelton, "Three Poems for a Twenty-Fifth Anniversary: #1 Housecleaning" from *Selected Poems, 1961–1981*. Copyright © 1982 by Richard Shelton. Reprinted by permission of Richard Shelton.

Stephen Spender, "To My Daughter" from *Collected Poems, 1928–1985*. Copyright 1934 and renewed 1962 by Stephen Spender. Used by permission of Natasha Spender.

Anne Stevenson, "Apology" from *Reversals*. Copyright © 1969 by Anne Stevenson Elvin. Reprinted by permission of Wesleyan University Press.

Su Tung-p'o, "Written to the Tune: 'River Town,'" translated by James Robert Hightower, from *The Columbia Anthology of Chinese Literature*, edited by Victor H. Mair. Copyright © 1994 Columbia University Press. Reprinted with the permission of the publisher.

T'ao Yüan-ming, "Blaming Sons," translated by Burton Watson, from *The Columbia Book of Chinese Poetry*, edited by Burton Watson. Copyright © 1984 Columbia University Press. Reprinted with the permission of the publisher.

James Tate, "Five Years Old" from *Selected Poems*. Copyright © 1991 by James Tate. Reprinted by permission of James Tate and Wesleyan University Press.

David Wagoner, "My Father in the Basement" from *Traveling Light: Collected and New Poems*. Copyright © 1999 by David Wagoner. Used with permission of the poet and the University of Illinois Press.

Richard Wilbur, "A Wedding Toast" from *The Mind-Reader*. Copyright © 1972 by Richard Wilbur. Reprinted by permission of Harcourt, Inc.

C. K. Williams, "Alzheimer's: The Husband" and "Instinct" from *Selected Poems*. Copyright © 1994 by C. K. Williams. Reprinted by permission of Farrar, Straus and Giroux, LLC. "Grace" from *The Vigil*. Copyright © 1994 by C. K. Williams. Reprinted by permission of Farrar, Straus and Giroux, LLC.

Miller Williams, "A Poem for Emily" from *Some Jazz a While: Collected Poems*. Copyright © 1999 by Miller Williams. Reprinted by permission of Miller Williams and Louisiana State University Press.

Yvor Winters, "At the San Francisco Airport" from *The Selcted Poems of Yvor Winters*, edited by R. L. Barth. Reprinted with permission of Swallow Press/Ohio University Press, Athens, Ohio.

Yang Hsün-chi, "Inscribed on the Doors of My Bookshelves," from Yoshikawa Kojiro, *Five Hundred Years of Chinese Poetry*, translated by John Timothy Wixted. Copyright © 1989 by Princeton University Press. Reprinted by permission of Princeton University Press.

Note on the Cover

Vincent Van Gogh (1853–1890), the famously troubled impressionist, painted this domestic scene in January 1890. A largely self-taught artist, he is here copying a picture by Jean-François Millet which he knew from a black-and-white photograph that his younger brother Theo had taken and sent to him at the mental asylum where Vincent had voluntarily committed himself. Van Gogh kept most of the elements of the original, but added his own distinctive coloring and brushwork.

Happy family life eluded Van Gogh. His relations with his father were difficult, and the two women he courted spurned his attentions (a third tried to commit suicide when her parents objected to her interest in the artist). At one point he tried to form a family by moving in with a pregnant prostitute and her eleven-year-old daughter, but the relationship did not last long. Van Gogh never married and had no children. The strongest tie in his life was with Theo, who provided him with financial and emotional support during years of poverty, poor health, mental instability, and loneliness. Theo was a successful art dealer and when he and his new wife were expecting their first child, Van Gogh painted this picture as a gift for them. They named the baby Vincent, after his uncle. Seven months afterward, at the age of thirty-seven, Van Gogh shot himself in the chest and died two days later in Theo's arms. Theo survived his brother by less than half a year.

This painting depicts a common experience rather than a particular family, and the impressionist style seems to universalize it, or depict it through the vivid haze of memory. A child takes her first uncertain steps, and this new sensation — both frightening and exhilarating — is made possible by the security afforded by loving, attentive parents. They have put aside their own labors — the laundry hanging on the fence, the shovel and wheelbarrow standing idly by — to encourage this small beginning, which will eventually lead to maturity and independence. The golden sunlight, the budding fruitfulness, and verdant growth (the color extending even into the thatched roofing) make this a magical yet thoroughly ordinary moment.

Index of the Poems

As a senior in aeronautical engineering at Purdue, I taught aerodynamics to the Cadette Class of 1944. A few faculty members absolutely refused to teach "girls," but I found that among the Cadettes there was a normal distribution of those just "getting by" and those who were so capable at complex engineering details they could have pursued careers as graduate engineers. The Cadettes' contributions to the development of the Navy's Helldiver airplane — and their being let go at the conclusion of the war with no record or credit for having been there — is an important story. Jean-Vi's monumental effort to find, throughout the country, information that was largely suppressed, "unavailable," and in some cases destroyed, reads like a personal odyssey. I congratulate her on restoring this missing piece in the history of women in aviation.

GEORGE PALMER *(professor emeritus,*
Aeronautical Engineering, Purdue University)

Women Airforce Service Pilots (WASP) and Rosie the Riveter/Wanda the Welder (aircraft- and ship-assembly workers) during WWII have been recognized and honored for decades. Now we can add the Curtiss-Wright Cadettes, who also served their country but heretofore remained unknown.

GIACINTA BRADLEY KOONTZ *(aviation historian, author,* The Harriet Quimby
Scrapbook: The Life of America's First Birdwoman, 1875-1912)

Author Jean-Vi Lenthe has uncovered a little-known gem of women's aviation history. As she says in the foreword: "More than 900 Cadette engineers labored six days a week in five different Curtiss-Wright plants, including the company's research lab in Buffalo, New York. But at the end of the war, company management treated their vital contributions as a mere wartime aberration. Forgotten were all the promises of promoting the Cadettes and helping them upgrade to full 'graduate engineer' status…" Exhaustively researched and thoroughly documented, Lenthe, whose mother was one of the 900, honors all the unkept promises and unsung work. Poignant surprises await you in this long overdue history.

HENRY M. HOLDEN *(aviation historian/author,* History Channel
narrator, founder of Women in Aviation Resource Center)

Jean-Vi has captured the facts and flavor of my experience as a Curtiss-Wright Cadette during WWII. Her remarkable research efforts have paid off with a fascinating story of the history I was a part of but did not fully appreciate until this book. *Flying Into Yesterday* would be of interest to anyone interested in history, women's experiences during the war, or just a good read.

NOVA ANDERSON WELLER *(mechanical engineer, retired, Battelle Corporation, Columbus, Ohio; Cadette Class of 1945, Purdue University)*

Aviation History magazine glamorizes test pilots and they talk about airplanes, but hardly ever talk about people other than the pilots. As *Flying Into Yesterday* confirms, the work of the Cadettes was truly critical to the war effort because there was a shortage of engineers, who were needed to keep up with the demands of the military. I worked many hours on the SB2C aircraft, on the original design and on "change requests" that came from the Navy as soon as combat situations showed a need for changes in the aircraft components, and believe me, there were many requests. The arrival of the Cadettes may not have been revolutionary but was of tremendous help to a weary and depleted engineering department.

LES HALL *(aeronautical engineer, retired; assistant project engineer, SB2C Helldiver, 1942-44)*

You have given me a new feeling of value for my war effort. I am very grateful to you for that.

BETH BENSON WEHNER *(Cadette Class of 1943, Purdue University)*

I just wish your mother could see you now. She would be so proud of you.

PEGGY ADAMS UPHAM *(Cadette Class of 1943, Purdue University)*

*To my mother and all the other
Curtiss-Wright Cadettes who stepped forward on behalf
of their country in World War II.*

*My job was to uncover factual evidence, but by
no means am I an expert on aviation history. I believe I
have fulfilled my commitment to honor these
pioneering women engineers.*

My Search for the
Curtiss-Wright
Aeronautical
Engineering Cadettes

Flying Into Yesterday

Jean-Vi Lenthe

WILD HARE PRESS
El Prado, New Mexico

Flying Into Yesterday: My Search for the Curtiss-Wright Aeronautical Engineering Cadettes

Copyright ©2011 by Jean-Vi Lenthe

Cover: Curtiss-Wright Cadette Inspectors, January 1944
Sitting (left): Instructor Ken Herbert (right, unidentified engineer)
Standing (left to right): Instructor George Sailor, Libby Rumpf (Penney),
Joan Ryan (Volk), Helen Smith, Moree Worley, Flossie Mooring (McQuirk),
Jackie Warren (Davis), Louise Ratchford (Blaney), Lucille Ratchford (Hestir).
On wing: Corky McCorkle (Williams), Josephine Johnson (Jackson),
Betty Henson (Masket), Johnnie Hemphill (Coyner), Mary Ullrich (Sprow),
Adelyn Lipscomb (Richardson), Dorothy Hegdal (Beach)

Back cover: Author and Wild Bunch Cadettes, 2009
Photo by Ed Vesely, SB2C Pilot, Commemorative Air Force

Cover and Interior Design: Kathleen Munroe, www.starrdesign.biz
Copy Editing and Typography: Barbara Scott, www.finaleyes.net
Content Editing: David Pérez, www.davidperezwow.com

ISBN: 978-0-9724703-1-5

Subject Listings
1. Autobiography/Memoir
2. Social Science/Women's Studies
3. U.S. History/World War II
4. Transportation/Aviation History
5. Technology/Aeronautical Engineering
6. Curtiss-Wright Cadettes 1943–45
7. Women in Industry

Printed in the United States

Wild Hare Press
P.O. Box 1546 • El Prado, NM 87529
Website: www.wildharepress.com/flyingintoyesterday
Email: publisher@wildharepress.com

Table of Contents

Chapter Four: Angling in Archives

Chapter Five: Going Back to Bexley

Chapter Six: *Perdu* at Perdue

Chapter Seven: Ricki's Goodbye

Epilogue

Poem: "Henson, Benson, and Bond"

Author's Note

Bibliography

Personal Acknowledgments

Endnotes

You must tell your children
putting modesty aside
that without us, without women,
there would have been no spring in 1945.

Rosie the Riveter/
WWII Home Front
National Historic Park,
Richmond, California

Foreword

*I*n February of 1943, the Curtiss-Wright Airplane Company, then America's largest aircraft manufacturer, began training and employing women in aeronautical engineering. These "Sisters of Icarus,"[1] 918 women who were chosen to stay firmly on the ground perfecting planes while their brothers flew into combat (and all too frequently went down in flames), were known as the Curtiss-Wright Engineering Cadettes. My mother, Ricki Cruse Lenthe, was one of them.

This story is my attempt to assemble a clearer picture about her life as a Cadette, the lifelong friends she made during that time, and the door that opened during World War II, if only briefly, for women to co-create the shape of aviation.

After a diligent search for historical documents, three dozen interviews with surviving Cadettes and Curtiss-Wright male employees, and hours of discussion with some of my mother's closest Cadette friends, I know that what these female engineers accomplished — in the universities and in the airplane plants — contained the seeds of a bona fide revolution. In an amazingly short period of time (February 1943 through August 1945), they proved the capability of women in a field that had previously been labeled male-only territory. They also bailed out a company whose planes were vital to winning World War II. Without them, the war would have dragged on even longer.

Cadette engineers labored six days a week in five different Curtiss-Wright plants, as well as in the company's research lab in Buffalo, New York. But at the end of the war, company management treated their vital contributions as a mere wartime aberration. Forgotten were all the promises of promoting the Cadettes and helping them upgrade to full "graduate engineer" status "when the peace for which we are all fighting is won."[2] But the Cadettes knew their value. If they hadn't been forced to by law and company pressure, a great many of them would not have gone home after the war.

Like the skewed or minimized record of other thwarted revolutions (usually demoted to "revolts" by the writers of history), the pages describing the Cadette Program in detail were cut from Curtiss-Wright's WWII record with such a razor-sharp edge that you almost can't tell they were ever there. This aviation mega-company that the Cadettes helped salvage from its own engineering deficiencies in a time of national crisis retained no documentation of their impressive achievements. In fact, corporate memory of the Cadettes is now so well excised that a few years ago an employee at Curtiss-Wright corporate headquarters responded to an inquiry about the Cadettes with indignation: "We don't know who in the world you're talking about. It's certainly not *our* Curtiss-Wright."[3]

The military's "fog of amnesia" is almost as dense. Neither the Navy nor the Army remembers approving the training initially; nor do they recall that inspectors of naval aircraft (INAs) in the Columbus plant signed off on the work of Cadettes who had competently inspected both sub- and final airframe assemblies. You will certainly never see references to the Cadette Program in World War II history books. Only the women themselves and the universities that trained them retained any written documentation on the Cadette Program.

*I*ronically, in August 1983, forty years after my mother finished her aeronautical engineering training, I helped dump her personal records from the Cadette years. My father had enlisted me to help clean out the basement of our family home because they wanted to sell it. I spent a month in one of the worst heat waves Moorhead, Minnesota, has ever experienced trying to overcome my mother's resistance to looking back through the mementoes of her college years and her later career as a teacher of high-school English and drama. She hated going down into the basement where everything was stored, partly because a furnace malfunction had blanketed everything with a fine layer of soot. I finally just gave up and reserved a seat on a plane back to the West Coast.

Midway through dinner on the evening before I was scheduled to fly out, assuming that my efforts were at an end, my mother said casually,

Foreword

"Well, I suppose most of it will just have to go to the dump anyway."

My Dad and I rarely acted in concert on anything. But that night, we looked at each other, pushed aside our plates, and made a beeline to the basement. In five short hours, we tore through everything, leaving several boxes and piles that looked important but in our haste throwing away many things that probably should have been kept. For years to come, whenever my mother couldn't find an item from her glory days as a theater director, she blamed me — though she was never certain it was gone because she still couldn't stand to spend much time in the basement.

They never sold the house, and due to the legal agreement I signed to resolve the estate issues after my parents were incapacitated, I was never entitled to set foot in that basement again. I would only truly regret this when I discovered, in the course of researching this book, that what my mother had done in her college years was a story of far more interest to me than anything she had put on stage. And the details of her young adult life before marriage probably went into the trash on that last hot evening in August.

In its own perverse way, my lack of access to the basement was a gift. It got me to look everywhere else and rekindled the kind of intense curiosity that had led me to study journalism in college. It also helped me keep a certain amount of distance from the story until I could more objectively evaluate whatever I might find out about my young mother that I hadn't known or even guessed at before.

I'm sorry I did not investigate my mother's engineering experience while she was still breathing. I'm even sorrier she can't see me now making it my business to restore this potentially game-changing moment in aviation history to the official WWII record. She'd be amazed to see her poet-performer daughter returning to her early training in history and journalism to hunt down the facts.

This story is for Ricki. May she rejoin her Wild Bunch and finally claim her golden wings.

You never know, until it happens,
what you will owe the dead.[4]
— Zadie Smith

Chapter One
Ricki's Ride

Think Purple!

On the first day of October 2008, I was sitting in a Denver motel near the airport waiting for a shuttle when I noticed a woman wearing a t-shirt that screamed "Think Purple!" She was in her late 50s, with gray hair and inquisitive eyes that looked all around the lobby but never rested on me, even though I was wearing a turquoise felt derby that stood out among the drab business-gray crowd. I was on my way to New York to feed my muse, with plans to write a play about my family, and I had tickets to eight shows, both on and off (and way off) Broadway. I didn't want to risk being sidetracked by a strange woman using her chest to proclaim a message, but on the shuttle she was the last passenger to board, and the only available seat was next to mine.

So I bit. "What does 'Think Purple!' mean?" I asked politely.

She turned to me without hesitation.

"It's from a conference I was just at. We were helping women who have earned—or are about to earn—engineering degrees hook up with potential employers."

"Ah. Okay. But what's the purple part?"

"It's about parity for women in all the sciences and professions, especially engineering," she said. "Just think how completely different the world would be if fully half the engineers were female. Women have such different sensibilities than men. Imagine how the everyday world would look and feel with women contributing equally to all the designs and materials we live with. I mean, every last thing around us is designed by *somebody*, usually a man."

"Yeah, more women engineers. Great idea." I looked at the flat brown fields whizzing past, trying to decide whether to share a piece of information I knew would impress her, but knowing that if she wanted details, I couldn't supply any.

"My mother was an engineer, in aeronautics, during World War II."

"Really?" said my companion. "How'd that happen?"

"The Curtiss-Wright Company. They trained a whole bunch of women. They called them Cadettes, though they weren't really military. My mother studied at Purdue and then worked at the company's plant in Columbus."

"That's just amazing," said my shuttle companion. "You should write a book about it."

"No, no, no. I don't think so. My mother's dead. And she never really told me anything about it. She never had any connections with engineering after the war. Her only passion was theater."

"I see. But still, don't you think other women would be interested?"

"Oh maybe. But I don't write history. I write poetry and plays. That's why I'm going to New York."

She nodded and seemed to give up. We were already arriving at the airport, so I just shifted my gaze back out the window. We wished each other well as we got off the shuttle, and she said it again.

"Really—I think you should write that book."

I laughed and headed for my plane. I was so amped about returning to the Big Apple that I planned to spend the whole flight reviewing my elaborate theater-hopping itinerary. But after takeoff, staring past the silver wing at a cloudless blue sky, I started wondering what the hell my mother had really been doing at Curtiss-Wright. From everything I knew about her, aeronautical engineering was simply not in her nature. But maybe young Ricki had had talents she'd later felt compelled to hide. Something about this time in her life was really beginning to click.

Who's in a Name?

My mother was born Betty Lu Cruse in 1924 and grew up in East Texas during the Great Depression, the eldest of three children. The family moved through a succession of small dusty towns, following her father, a traveling paymaster for Gulf Oil Company. Even with all the dislocation, Betty Lu managed to graduate valedictorian from high school at age 16. A picture taken of her two years earlier shows her with one hand on her hip, her head cocked in defiance. "*Nothing* is going to keep *me* in podunk East Texas!" said those dancing dark eyes.

Straight out of high school, Betty Lu got her first big break: a scholarship to study at Stephens College, an exclusive women's school in Columbia, Missouri. She came home after just one year when the money ran out. But when she returned from Stephens in June 1941, she was no longer Betty Lu. There were five boldly printed letters on the box-shaped handbag she carried as she stepped down from the train: R-I-C-K-I. Where she got that name, nobody ever knew.

She spent the next year at a local junior college and then in the fall of 1942 she enrolled at the University of Texas in Austin. Midway through the quarter, she got her second big academic break: Curtiss-Wright Airplane Company recruited her to study aeronautical engineering at Purdue University in Indiana. She began the training on February 12, 1943, and graduated in mid-December. By early January 1944, she was working in the engineering department at Curtiss-Wright's airframe plant in Columbus, Ohio. A little over a year later, she left the company and then married my father on March 15, 1945. The war ended five months to the day after they took those vows.

Eleven years and four children later — as soon as I, her youngest, was old enough to be left with a sitter — my mother resumed her pursuit of a college degree and earned a Minnesota teaching credential for high school English and drama. Consequently, for most of the 18 years I spent under the same roof with her, I knew her only as someone who taught all day and directed small-town versions of Broadway musicals at night. Nothing like these glittery high-stepping shows had ever graced the stage of Moorhead High School before. Ricki and her musicals became legends.

During final rehearsals, I would spend interminable hours fidgeting at her side in the darkened theater, watching her work her magic, waiting for her to put down her wand and give me a ride home. Though my sister and brother both played key roles in her plays, either acting or stage-managing, I was too young to be in any of the productions. But just wait: *my* turn would come. When she suddenly abandoned teaching, just as I was finally old enough to be in her classes and shows, I was shocked. I had to set aside my dreams of finding my way into the footlights with her guiding hand. No other drama teacher at Moorhead High could compare. I switched my focus to a career in journalism instead.

Over the years, the few times I heard my mother speak of Curtiss-Wright I was mystified. I assumed her time as a Cadette had been a lark, something to feed her during the war and fulfill her patriotic duty. All she talked about was the wonderful friends she had made and how much fun they'd had. She never let on that she'd accomplished something rather amazing for a sassy, style-conscious 19-year-old with zero ambition in science or math. Nor did she mention the real reason she had jumped on the Curtiss-Wright recruitment offer: to leave Texas permanently in the dust.

All My Sons

After my encounter with "Ms. Think Purple!" on the Denver shuttle, I was surprised to discover that the second Broadway show I had selected took me straight back into my mother's young-adult territory: airplane manufacturing in WWII. First produced in 1947, *All My Sons* established Arthur Miller as a serious playwright. I had only picked the play because it featured three of my favorite actors: Dianne Wiest, John Lithgow, and Patrick Wilson (who portrayed a closeted Mormon lawyer in HBO's movie *Angels in America*).

At the heart of the play is a man named Joe Keller, co-owner of a company that made engine heads for military planes during the war. Joe, the story reveals, had received an urgent phone call one afternoon from his partner, Steve, who was also his neighbor and close friend. Steve alerted him that a batch of defective cylinder heads had just come off the line and he wanted to know what Joe thought they should do about it. Joe told him to just weld over the cracks and ship them off. If the heads were delayed, he reminded Steve, they might lose their government contract.

So the cracked cylinder heads went into P-40 Warhawk fighter planes —a big-selling Curtiss-Wright design—and caused the deaths of 21 pilots. When the partners were prosecuted, Joe claimed Steve had done the fix all on his own. Coincidentally, Joe's older son, Larry, a pilot, was reported missing in action soon after the newspapers reported that both men were being tried. Joe stuck to his story and eventually got off, but Steve was sent upriver to serve a long jail term.

When the play starts, two years after the war, Joe (John Lithgow) has successfully rebuilt his business with the help of his younger son, Chris (Patrick Wilson). His wife, Kate (Dianne Wiest), still holds out hope that their missing-in-action son will return. The plot revolves around the "sudden" appearance one day of Steve's daughter, Ann, who was, for a long time, Larry's fiancée. She has come at Chris's invitation because they have an important announcement to make: Ann and Chris have fallen in love and plan to marry.

This goes over like the lead balloon one would expect. After all the traumatic reactions have played out and the war guilt and ghosts have raised their ugly heads, it's clear that not only was Joe responsible for the faulty cylinder heads that were shipped out but that Larry deliberately crashed his plane in shame when he found out what his father had done. Joe eventually admits that his failure lay in not seeing that the young men fighting for America were "all his sons." However, rather than let Chris take him to jail, he runs back into the house and puts a gun to his head.

Seeing this revival was exhausting and disturbing, but it was an uncannily perfect lead-up to my next pit stop: I planned to visit one of my mother's Cadette buddies in Chevy Chase, Maryland, before heading back home to the Southwest.

For many years, my mother had insisted that I should meet Betty Masket. "You'll get along famously," she'd said, but I was too busy in my young life and couldn't be bothered to call her. Finally, in 1988, Betty tracked me down to a former chicken ranch in Petaluma, California, where

I'd taken up residence while finishing a master's degree in poetics down the road in San Francisco. From then on, she called me once a year when she came to the Bay Area on site visits for the National Institutes of Health's Heart, Lung, and Blood Institute. For the next 20 years, Betty tried to tell me about the Cadette Program and the Helldiver, the plane she and my mother had worked on. But my main reaction was that "Helldiver" sounded like an apt description of the downward spiral my mother's life had taken after she gave up teaching and directing plays at age 43.

On the train to Chevy Chase from New York, I asked myself why, if my mother had been given the secrets of flight, she hadn't just used them to fly out of Moorhead, which obviously never suited someone with her theatrical talents. Could she have been a technical genius who just happened to like Broadway musicals and thus became a theater director instead of an aeronautical engineer? I was counting on Betty to shed some light.

This was my third visit to Betty's home. I loved the 65 wind-up antique clocks ticking away on shelves, living room walls, and in all three bedrooms. She greeted me enthusiastically with her soft-spoken Appalachian accent and hugged me hard. Then she stowed my gear in the second bedroom, handed me a warm cup of tea, and sat me down to talk. We only had time for a short visit because she was driving to her childhood home in western North Carolina the next morning.

I told Betty about seeing *All My Sons* because I knew she'd relate. Even though she had minimal interest in theater, she'd had a successful career in science and math. I never had any trouble picturing her in the Cadette engineering program.

"Yeah, Betty, it was intense — this guy selling faulty engine heads and making all these pilots crash."

"Y'know, Jean-Vi," she said, "when I was doing inspections at the Columbus plant, I found a problem with one of the Helldivers one afternoon and made them shut down the line so it could be fixed."

"You shut down the whole line? Whoa. Then what happened?"

"Well, unfortunately, I had to leave — my shift was ending. When I came back the next day, they had moved that plane right on down the line. I never did find out if they fixed it." She lowered her voice. "I always felt a little bad that I didn't follow up."

"So what kind of problem did you find?"

"There wasn't enough clearance around one of the lines that came out of the fuselage. It was a hydraulic line to the dive brakes on the wings. It would be nearly impossible to control the plane during descent if one of those lines got cut."

"Betty, do you think there were many other problems that slipped through inspections?"

"Oh, I'm sure of it."

I looked at her with more curiosity about Curtiss-Wright than I'd ever felt before.

"How exactly did you wind up being an inspector? I thought you just worked on the pilot's handbook with my mother."

"No, that was later. First I did inspections. There was a small group of us from Purdue, not including your mother, who were assigned to the Louisville, Kentucky, plant. But after we'd taken the train all the way down there from Lafayette, they told us they didn't need us. So they said we could do quality control and let us choose between Buffalo and Columbus. Most of us chose Columbus, and the plant gave us three weeks of training in inspection — all phases. We just loved it. But after six months, they took us off the job."

"Why?"

"No reason I can remember."

"How big was this Helldiver, Betty?"

"Wait here. I'll show you. I just got a book on it from my great nephew." She went to retrieve it from her bedroom.

The book Betty brought back was a thick, glossy, oversized paperback titled *Curtiss SB2C Helldiver,* by an English naval historian named Peter C. Smith. I hardly slept that night I was so busy marveling at photos and technical details of the plane and reading stories of its trials and tribulations. For the first time, I really understood that the work my mother and her friends had done was substantially more sophisticated and technical than I'd ever dreamed them capable of doing.

"So who paid for this program?" I asked Betty excitedly over coffee the next morning. "Was it government sponsored?"

"No, I think Curtiss-Wright paid for it. We were employees of the company all during the training and in the plants. But the company *did* have a lot of government contracts, so maybe some federal money *did* go into our training."

"Where can I find out about this?"

"Well, you could check with the National Archives. They're downtown on the Capitol Mall. They have all the government records from the war."

"Good idea, Betty. I'll go down there right after you leave for North Carolina," I said.

"And you should talk to Peggy down in Dallas," Betty advised. She'll tell you a lot more about the program because she used her Curtiss-Wright drafting skills after the war."

The Wild Bunch

Betty Masket and Peggy Upham, along with my mother, were members of a group of six women who trained at Purdue and then shared a house in Columbus while working for Curtiss-Wright. They called it Casa Dingy and got along so well, even with only one bathroom, that they decided to pool their money and resources and live cooperatively. Though they all went separate ways after the war, they remained in close contact. By the early '80s, when their children had finally left home, they started having reunions every few years. They had such raucous, unmitigated fun at these get-togethers that one of their husbands started calling the group "The Wild Bunch." This was considerably better than their own name for themselves during the war: "The Dingies" (said with a hard g).

My father didn't really think much of my mother's continued association with her old war buddies, and overall he liked to keep her in sight. So whenever she went to Wild Bunch reunions, she just went quietly and came back quickly before he missed her too much. Altogether, she attended about six of their gatherings. I was already living on the West Coast by then and never appreciated how much this group meant to her. Besides

Betty, I had only met one other Cadette — Beth Wehner. Like my mother, Beth had been at the University of Texas when Curtiss-Wright recruited her. Also like my mother, she later became a schoolteacher. In 1987, at my mother's urging, I had stopped by Beth's house on Lake Austin for a quick lunch, but we'd had no further contact since then.

On my way to the National Archives and Research Administration (NARA) from Chevy Chase, I had just emerged from the subway at Dupont Circle when I received a return call on my cell phone from Peggy Upham in Dallas. She had a powerful, throaty voice and was very excited that I had expressed interest in the Cadette Program. She poured out a steady stream of enthusiastic memories about their days as Cadettes. She also assured me that Betty was right: the program was paid for by Curtiss-Wright, not by the government.

It was a typically sunny mid-October day, and as I talked to her I strolled up and down the sidewalk in front of a block of Georgian row houses, developing an image in my mind of a woman who would probably tower over me but also be a formidable, strong-minded ally in my quest for information. My curiosity and conviction were growing stronger with every word she spoke. After we hung up, I strode on toward the National Archives with a wide smile and a spring in my step. This whole thing might just turn out to be a grand adventure.

No such luck. After proving I was an American citizen (and not a security risk), sitting through a dry orientation slide show on how to use the Archives, and storing everything except my clothes and ID in a locker, I discovered that enormous barriers still stood between me and the World War II materials. It would take days (and probably weeks) to even begin to penetrate the veil of protection surrounding official American documents; I had only a few hours.

It wasn't time entirely wasted, though: I found out that World War II records were unhandily split into two locations. The one on Capitol Mall contains documents up through the end of 1942. The other branch, an hour away in College Park, Maryland, covers 1943 to the end of the war. Since the Cadette Program had begun in 1943, I seemed to be in the wrong location. The friendly archivist who helped me found no records at all listed under the name "Curtiss-Wright Cadettes." He did, however, show me how to do an online request. I took my official researcher badge and went home to New Mexico, planning to plot my next steps from a secure base.

However, as autumn in Taos grew darker, colder, and more solemn, it cast a gloom over my initial excitement about investigating the Cadettes. Even though this quest would take me deep into uncharted territory, it would also throw me back on the doorstep of unresolved family issues. The Sangre de Cristos to the north loomed large and forbidding, creating a dense wall between me and the cold Minnesota winters. But even after 39 years of keeping my distance from the frigid landscape of my youth, its emotional weather was leaking through this surprisingly flimsy geological barrier.

Moon Over Man

In late March 1974, I agreed to go to Hawaii with my mother. She had called one morning to tell me that, due to business demands, my father couldn't go on the trip they'd planned. She invited me to go in his place.

I said sure, though I didn't know how in the world I could travel with her. We hadn't seen eye to eye since I'd gone off to journalism school at Northwestern University five years earlier. For one, I had betrayed my family's loyalty to the Republican Party and become staunchly opposed to the Vietnam War.

For another, I had lived "in sin" with a guy whose politics ruffled my parents' feathers even more than my defection from "the Party." The final affront was that I had left him *and* journalism school in the fall of my senior year—right before finals. Since then, I'd been dipping into hippie culture, traveling hither and yon, writing poetry, living on a farm with other Northwestern dropouts, and sampling Eastern spiritual religions. I had no long-term life plan.

My mother, I think, hoped to retrieve me. But she was still trying to keep a safe distance from the lifestyle changes going on all over the country in the early seventies. We made an unspoken agreement not to talk about anything controversial, and after Hawaii's Big Island had worked its warming magic on our frozen Midwestern bodies for a few days, we just relaxed and shared companionable space.

Arriving on Maui, our second island, we drove the long and tortuous coastal road to the eastern end and stayed three nights at a ranch resort near Hana. All the guests had separate cottages, and Mom and I shared one on a cliff above the beach.

This end of Maui seemed to be a magnet for flyers who'd been downed against their wills. For example, just up the beach was a two-story A-frame with lava-rock walls belonging to the world's most famous flyer, Charles Lindbergh, who called the place "Argonauta." We didn't know that he was dying of cancer and would be buried in a local church cemetery five months later.

On our second day on Maui, we toured private gardens that belonged to another downed flyer. Sam Pryor had been executive vice president of Pan American Airlines for 28 years, enabling him to fly all over the world collecting exotic plant specimens. It was his wife, however, who led the tour, because age and senility had taken their toll on Sam. Without saying a word, he followed along after us, one of his beloved Gibbons monkeys riding on his shoulder, trying to pick invisible nits off Sam's bald head. When we came to a small gazebo above a steep drop, his wife gestured gracefully down over the edge into a dense grove of coconut palms. She didn't mention that Lindbergh's house was hidden deep within. It was Sam, one of Lindbergh's best friends, who had persuaded Lindy to buy the property years earlier.

Our third and most intimate encounter with downed flyers began that evening back on the ranch. Sitting poolside after dinner, we struck up a conversation with a retired Air Force general. He told us he was resting from an exhaustive, worldwide search for his youngest son. Said son had apparently become as antiwar as I was, so he was hiding from his dad. The general, however, was gruffly certain he would find the errant lad. As he listened to me describe my spiritual quest and spur-of-the-moment traveling since dropping out of journalism school, he developed a dark gleam in his eye.

"So, you'd go anywhere, anytime," he said, with a hint of malice. "And where on earth do you think you'd like to go next?"

"Japan," I said, grabbing the first destination that came to mind. Back on the farm outside Evanston, I had practiced Zen Buddhism for seven months before moving back into town and taking up with an Indian guru. But Maharaj-ji's influence was fast fading with every hour I basked in this Hawaiian sun. Though I might not be cut out for Zen stoicism, I still found Japanese culture and art intriguing. I could visualize myself trotting from one temple to the next and letting their spiritual refinement seep gradually into my bones.

"Then I'll pay your way," he said, "airfare *and* expenses for a month—on one condition."

"What's that?"

"You have to leave tomorrow."

"Right."

"What—are you afraid?" he challenged.

"No, I just don't have a current passport."

"I still have military connections," he said. "I can get one for you overnight. So, do we have a deal?"

I looked at him for a long, long moment before answering. "Sure. You bet."

"Okay, I'll make some phone calls right now." He got up and left the table.

My mother had listened quietly as the general reeled out his offer. But once he was gone, she started gently questioning me. Having just reestablished a relationship with me after five years of estrangement, she was reluctant to interfere.

"You don't think he'd try to follow you, do you?" my mother asked.

"Oh," I said. "What an awful idea."

"You don't really know him, and you can see he's very upset about not finding his son."

I was surprised. It wasn't like my mother to so boldly question the virtue of a high-ranking military man. Like most of "the Greatest Generation," she'd experienced an unprecedented sense of American solidarity in World War II.

"Yeah, he's definitely not offering me this out of the goodness of his heart. Maybe I could just use the ticket, take the cash, and disappear among the temples until he gets tired of looking for me."

My mother shook her head.

"You're right," I acknowledged. "That probably won't work — the man's a complete control freak. I could probably never lose him."

We went back to our cottage and continued to debate his motives until long after midnight. Finally, we agreed that I should reject his offer.

In the breakfast buffet line the next morning, weary from late-night deliberations, I told the general I wasn't going.

"I knew you wouldn't," he crowed. "Great world traveler. Anywhere, anytime. Hah."

I walked away, my pride smarting, determined to put some distance between him and me. But that evening at a luau on the beach, while my mother was down the beach talking to another guest, the general continued hammering at me. I'd fended off this kind of verbal assault from my own father any number of times, but this guy was playing all my hot buttons and he clearly wasn't going to quit.

"I called your bluff," he sneered. "You're really just a baby, a youngster."

As I listened to the general's unending stream of jeers, the pressure inside my head started to boil. I thought my brain was going to explode right out of its skull. Finally, I just turned and walked away, but his taunting voice dogged my heels.

"Yeah, go have a good think on the beach."

I picked up speed, running faster and faster down the beach, furious at him, furious at myself. When the soft white sand ended in lava rock, I saw a path leading up a slope to a cliff and kept running until I reached the top. Over the edge I saw whitecaps on the breakers below. One small step and those sharp rocks and boiling waves would put an end to my misery. Teetering on the brink of desperate escape, I suddenly felt the tropical night air brushing my exposed skin.

"Oh man, what the hell am I doing!" I thought, jerking back from the edge. Kneeling down on the spongy grass, I turned over on my back and listened to the waves making night music far below, the ocean mist salting my skin. The moon had risen, gold and full. It was hovering right over me, pressing warmly on my chest. I felt like some kind of torpid sea creature, stranded high above the water, sinking lower and lower under a blanket of humidity.

"Enough of this," I said, jumping to my feet. Removing my clothes, I let gravity pull me down the opposite side of the cliff to a crescent of sandy beach, where I eased down into the foamy surge along its edge. Like a giant hand, the seawater started washing me side to side, retreating with audible sighs and returning with renewed strength, until my bones and muscles felt like jelly. With some effort, laughing gently to myself, I managed to drag myself upright and began turning slow dervish circles on the sand as the warm wind blew the moisture from my skin.

Coming gradually to a stop, dizzy *and* exalted, I told myself: "My mother got me here, but this is *my* body, *my* life. I just have to find my own current and move with it, like these waves — in and out, in and out."

I strode back to the top of the cliff, dressed, and then strolled casually back down the other side, past the general and on toward the cottage, waving at my mother as I passed. She rose and followed me to the cottage.

"Are you okay?" she asked once we were inside. "I heard the general going on at you."

"He just wants revenge for his son's disloyalty. It's too bad, y'know — I really *would* like to see Japan."

"Oh, you'll get there some day — on your own."

"Yeah. Maybe." I paused, with my hand on the light switch. "Mom?"

"Yes, dear?"

"Thanks for inviting me. This is an amazing place."

She smiled. "I'm glad you came. It was great having you along." Then this Texas belle, who'd never strayed far from my dad in 29 years of marriage, sighed and said: "I'm just sorry we have to leave."

When my mother got home, my father saw the look of relaxed well-being she wore and became furious she'd gone to Paradise without him. He forbade the mention of Hawaii (the "H-word") in his presence again. Because my father could pound away at pet subjects (or peeves) until you went insane, my mother obeyed this taboo for the rest of her life. She never even attempted to visit the Hawaiian Islands again.

But for me, the memory of that tropical night and the maternal current that had washed away my distress on the beach stayed with me. I never stopped longing to submerge myself in it again — and bring her along.

Rohatsu

On the morning of December 8, 2003, less than two years after my father passed away, I received a call that my mother was desperately ill. Flu symptoms had turned into pneumonia, and the previous day she had been taken by ambulance from the nursing home in Moorhead, Minnesota, to a hospital across the river in Fargo. At the time, I was living in the California Bay Area, 1,500 miles away. When I called her room, I was told she couldn't breathe well enough to speak on the phone. I started making frantic calls to find out if I needed to fly out immediately.

I finally managed to get through to the head nurse on her ward. I asked whether she thought my mother was close to death, but she refused to speculate.

I lost it. "Just tell me!" I screamed. "Do I need to get on a goddamn plane?"

She paused briefly and then responded coolly, "None of us knows when God will summon us home."

"Just forget it," I said, banging down the phone, furious at this woman's need to put a religious curtain around my mother.

Three hours later, my mother died in that hospital room, with none of her children at her side. Both my Moorhead siblings had gone home for lunch, not realizing she was so close to the end.

For several years after her death, I was stranded on the back side of the moon. I didn't understand why Mom hadn't given us more warning. What was her hot urgency to leave *right then?* Though she had never really accepted my independent lifestyle or my artistic efforts, she was my closest connection in the family. Even if I couldn't get her blessing, I wanted her back — I needed some kind of final goodbye.

Finally, on the sixth anniversary of her death, after I'd already been tracking down the missing history of the Cadettes for a year, I found a good explanation for why my mother had departed *right then.*

I was lying on a surgeon's table, my arm raised above my head, having a benign lump removed from under my arm. I told the surgeon, a soft-spoken, practicing Buddhist, that my mother had died on this date. He raised his eyebrows.

"Ah," he said, with an enigmatic smile, "Rohatsu."

"What?" I said.

"Yes, December 8th is called Rohatsu in Japan. It honors the day the Buddha achieved enlightenment."

The doctor's gnomish voice was so calming I almost forgot he was carving away at my armpit.

"Huh," I said. "I wonder if my mother knew about Rohatsu." She had loved Asian art but never talked about Buddhism or any other spiritual path.

"Few people know this," he said, "but Japan's military timed the bombing of Pearl Harbor to be right on Rohatsu because they thought they would have Buddha's blessing."

"How could they think Buddha would bless such violence?"

"Good question, especially since Hawaii is on the other side of the International Dateline, so it was still only December 7th on Oahu when they attacked."

"So, basically, they were 'flying into yesterday' to try to knock out our Pacific fleet."

"Yes. You could say that," he confirmed.

I'd spent the last two years struggling to master sitting meditation again, the first time since my brief Zen trial on the Illinois farm. I couldn't imagine how such a militant tyranny as Japan's WWII government could have embraced Buddha's precepts, even for a moment, while executing a bloodthirsty campaign in the Pacific. I'd long despised the hypocrisy of Western states, supposedly built on Christian ethics, waging war in spite of the First Commandment. But hearing that the other side was doing the same thing while huddling under a Buddhist umbrella made me even more uncomfortable.

I let the good doctor finish sewing me up and got off the table, my head swimming with possibilities. Did my mother *choose* Rohatsu to pass over? Or did the roulette wheel for her mortality simply stop spinning *right then*?

How ironic that the plane she helped engineer at Curtiss-Wright, the Helldiver, had helped deliver the deathblow to Japan's Navy.

It made sense that my mother would escape her physical body the same way she had left East Texas: with a blast of self-willed determination. For the Texas caper, she had hitched a ride on the "Curtiss-Wright Starlight Express." And now it looked like, for her final departure, she had latched onto the Buddha's moment of enlightenment to escape a pneumonia-stricken body — pretty stellar stuff.

When all the stardust had cleared, I could see that my quest for the lost history of the Curtiss-Wright Cadette Program — and my mother's participation in it — is my own version of "flying into yesterday." But unlike the Japanese planes zipping over the international date line to pulverize Pearl Harbor, I was taking the risk of never returning to the present moment. Sixty-six years after the Japanese signed the surrender papers, fascination with World War II — especially our deadly use of airpower to defeat the Germans and the Japanese — is a fog so dense and captivating that some people who go wandering in it never come back.

But to find young Ricki and get my final goodbye, it was a risk I had to take.

Chapter Two

All My Daughters

Cadettes Invade Campus[5]

Forty years after Orville and Wilbur first took to the air in the Wright Flyer 1, there was a blizzard in progress in West Lafayette, Indiana, with almost six inches of snow already on the ground. It was February 12, 1943, and 98 young women were arriving by train from schools all over the South, the Midwest, the Northeast, and Appalachia. They had each completed at least a year of college and were ranked in the top third of their math classes and the top half in everything else. Somewhere in that gaggle of courageous young women lugging suitcases across the campus was my mother, picking her way carefully through this cold white stuff she'd never seen firsthand.

Wood Women's Residential Hall, the three-story stone fortress that would house the Cadettes on the campus of Purdue University, was a 15-minute walk from the engineering buildings where their courses would be taught. The airport — with its hangars, machine shop, engine test cells, and wind tunnel — was 25 minutes in the other direction. Members of the Cadette Engineering Society, with chapters on each of the seven participating campuses, would have the opportunity to "practice tearing down and rebuilding airplane engines, and discuss topics such as high-altitude flying."[6]

Most of the males on campus were servicemen enrolled in short-term, federally funded training programs. They were preparing for technical jobs to aid the war effort. Of the men who would have been enrolled in the standard aero-engineering track, a great many had enlisted or been drafted before they could complete the four-year "graduate engineer" course. With enrollment numbers so reduced, most aero teaching staff were happy about the Cadettes' arrival: they had a group of bright-eyed females to keep them busy. And though they had never imagined teaching this material to "girls" (as they were always called on campus), they had hammered out a common curriculum with engineers at Curtiss-Wright and representatives from engineering departments at the other universities participating in the program.

The course of study was equivalent to two and a half years of the upper-division graduate engineering curriculum. For 44 weeks (or about ten months), with one week of vacation in the middle, the women would study engineering mathematics, theory of flight, aerodynamics, properties and processing of aircraft materials, job terminology and specifications, stress analysis and strength of materials, and applied descriptive geometry and aircraft drawing. When they emerged from this training, they would be equipped to function in a variety of engineering capacities in the various Curtiss-Wright plants, thus freeing the male "graduate engineers" to do more complex engineering assignments.

A sense of female "invasion" of male-dominated engineering departments was playing out at all seven of the universities that had contracted with Curtiss-Wright to train women as "assistant" or "primary" aeronautical engineers. Trainees were required to be at least 18 years of age, and most of them had leapt at the chance to become Curtiss-Wright Cadettes. The program, which had only been authorized in late 1942, would give them free tuition, room, board, transportation expenses, and an opportunity to study aeronautical engineering, a technical field women had been denied access to, with few exceptions, since it had been added to a handful of mechanical-engineering departments in major American universities in the mid-'30s. As employees of Curtiss-Wright, they would be paid $10 a week for supplies and other expenses. By today's value, about $120, this was a great deal of spending money for young women in post-Depression America.

Curtiss-Wright recruiters (nine women and three men) told the applicants that the plant they picked to work in would determine which school they would be sent to, even though management retained final authority to change their plant assignment after they graduated. For the most part, though, they would try to match them with their first or, at the very least, second choice of plant location. If a Cadette chose to work in the Columbus or Louisville plants, she would be sent to either the University of Minnesota or to Purdue. Those who chose the Buffalo plant would train at Cornell or Penn State, and Cadettes who selected the St. Louis plant would study at the University of Texas or Iowa State. All four of these were airframe plants. The Propeller Division, whose main plant was in Caldwell, New Jersey, trained its Cadettes at Rensselaer Polytechnic Institute (RPI) in Troy, New York.

The curriculum was the same for all seven universities for the first 22 weeks. In the second half, RPI Cadettes would focus on propellers, while the six other groups zeroed in on airframe structure and design. It was a given that, for all seven groups, the initial emphasis when they arrived at the plants would be on technical drawing. Cadettes could look forward to hours and hours at the drafting table drawing the constant changes to the aircraft designs or copying complete sets of drawings for use by subcontracting firms. But unlike people who worked as mere "tracers," the Cadettes would be using their technical expertise to translate complex engineering descriptions into clear graphic form. Their accuracy would enable Curtiss-Wright's various fabrication departments to produce exact structural components for the planes being designed — and redesigned — by senior engineers.

So really, the fact that women aero-engineers were finally allowed to participate in aviation design resembled dominoes falling back the other way: without the Cadette "invasion" of previously male-only engineering sanctuaries, U.S. military leaders would have had insufficient airpower to use in *their* invasion of lands that had previously been seized in yet another invasion — by the Germans and Japanese. Essentially, if there had been no tide of American women pushing back against the Axis surge, there would indeed have been no spring, as Western democracies knew it, in 1945.[7]

But the Cadettes weren't focused on where their work entered this larger historic picture. They were just showing up to do a technically sophisticated job, slide rules at the ready and ten months of upper-division aeronautical engineering foremost in their minds. It's doubtful that very many of them even knew about the genesis of this manufacturing giant that had decided to grant them access to aviation's hallowed halls.

The Death of Icarus and the Birth of Curtiss-Wright

According to Greek mythology, Daedalus, a brilliant Greek inventor, was imprisoned, along with his son Icarus, on King Minos's island (today's Crete). To liberate himself and Icarus, Daedalus invented wings of feathers and wax. Unfortunately, Icarus flew too high and the sun melted the wax holding his wings together, plunging him to a watery death.

After young Icarus went down, the human flying project took a very long while to get off the ground again. For more than 2,500 years, there were no airborne men. Other than da Vinci's designs (which, as far as we know, were never tested), the first flying vehicles in the 19th century — hot-air balloons, zeppelins, and dirigibles — proved either unmanageable in strong winds or draggingly slow in calmer conditions.

So aviation designers at the turn of the 20th century returned to the bird-wing design Icarus had modeled. This time, they made it out of paper and wood instead of feathers and wax. They also added a power train, so the vehicle was less at the mercy of the winds. And voilà! — modern aviation was born. These new "heavier-than-air" vehicles were designed to fly (more or less) where they were directed with the ease of a bird and usually more speed. But no sooner had the designers achieved this aerodynamic competence than their counterparts in industry and government realized these winged vehicles could be armed and made deadly. Significant numbers of lethal new designs were created and tested in preparation for the next big war.

Though World War I was waged partly in the air, most of the fighting was still done on the ground. Everyone in the trenches fervently wished they'd been "up there" instead. Twenty years later, when the next big war began, aviation technology had advanced so much that heavily armed "warbirds" were clearly the weapons of choice. By that time, the company that dominated aircraft manufacturing in the United States was the Curtiss-Wright Airplane Company.

Almost no one today, apart from aviation history buffs and World War II pilots associations, knows about Curtiss-Wright. When I started down this path in October 2008, with the Wall Street banking disaster in the headlines, I had no idea that the company had been formed right on the cusp of another great financial disaster: the stock market crash of 1929. As far back as the unfortunate Icarus, there seems to have been a link between men trying to become airborne and some kind of awesome crash.

That a company was ever created bearing both the names Curtiss and Wright was a definite fluke. Orville and Wilbur Wright, who flew the first American-made airplane in 1903, were involved in seemingly unending patent lawsuits with aviator, airplane manufacturer, and engine-designer Glenn H. Curtiss. Curtiss had successfully flown his first plane at roughly the same time as the Wrights. But because he had posted a public announcement before he demonstrated his plane, which the Wrights had failed to do, some people felt his performance qualified as the first powered flight.

The antagonism and exchanges of legal vitriol between the parties continued until all three of the original combatants withdrew from the conflict because they fell ill (Curtis, who later succumbed to complications from an appendectomy), died (Wilbur Wright, of typhoid fever), or tired of running the business (Orville Wright). There was no longer any reason not to unite the warring airplane tribes. With the power of one small hyphen, the twelve Wright- and Curtiss-affiliated companies merged into Curtiss-Wright. The date was July 5, 1929. The company began trading publicly on the New York Stock Exchange on August 22, and the stock market crashed a scant two months later.

The new company managed, through diversification and sales to Latin and South America, to stay afloat during the troubled times. By the late '30s, Curtiss-Wright had grown into the most influential aviation company in America, with cushy corporate offices at Rockefeller Plaza in New York and a company representative stationed in Washington to go after government funding.

With World War II revving up in Europe and a growing number of Americans clamoring for us to join the fray, federal tax dollars poured into Curtiss-Wright coffers as never before. The company had become the golden boy among American aircraft manufacturers and could more or less write its own contracts.

So why do so few people know about the Curtiss-Wright Airplane Company today? And what made them decide to train women as aeronautical engineers? The Helldiver, I was to discover, was a big part of the answer to both questions.

The Curtiss SB2C Helldiver

My body lies under the ocean
My body lies under the sea
My body lies under the ocean
Wrapped up in an SB2C
    — Helldivers Drivers Song[8]

In May 1939, more than two years before America entered World War II, Curtiss-Wright won a Navy design competition and signed a contract to build a large folding-wing, carrier-based bomber of unusual capabilities and dimensions. The Navy's specifications were challenging: it needed to fly longer distances and carry more tonnage than the smaller, fixed-wing Douglas SBD Dauntless, which until then had been the dive-bomber of choice. An added requirement made the task almost impossible: two of these bigger, badder planes had to fit side by side in the ship elevators to speed their delivery from a below-decks hangar to the flight deck.

And so was born the SB2C (Scout Bomber 2nd Series Curtiss) Helldiver. It would be a full four and a half years before the company managed to fulfill its contract and produce a reliable version of the plane. Among pilots it was known as the Big-Tailed Beast (or the Son of a Bitch 2nd Class) because it was so unwieldy with its heavier, bigger tail on a short, squat fuselage. Redesigned versions of the Helldiver continued to fail flight tests and carrier takeoff and landing trials. Even without a mission-worthy plane, the Navy was so desperate for dive bombers that the number of Helldivers they ordered just kept going up.

To throw an even worse wrench into the machinery of production, more and more company engineers were being drafted into the military. The seemingly endless design changes the chief engineers came up with to try to solve the plane's problems couldn't be drawn fast enough by the dwindling engineering staff. An unbelievable 889 major and minor design changes[9] were ordered between January 1942 and January 1946.

Curtiss-Wright's airplane division was also falling behind in its production commitments in two other plants (Buffalo, New York, and St. Louis, Missouri), where they made planes for the U.S. Army, again due largely to engineering personnel losses. But the problems with the Helldiver were so severe that Curtiss-Wright risked losing its valuable Navy contract. In late summer of 1942, management finally decided there was no choice: women had to be trained in aeronautical engineering and drafting to take up the slack.

Between February 1943 and the end of March 1945, 918 women began the Cadette training in the basics of aerodynamics and airplane design. Of the 766 Cadettes who graduated and actually reported for work, 365 were assigned to the Columbus plant. Together with the male engineers in the plant, these women helped Curtiss-Wright fulfill its commitment to produce a dive bomber that could help destroy Japan's navy and bring the war closer to an end.

Thus the Helldiver, with its mythical name and its beastly reputation, opened a place for women in aeronautical engineering. And my mother, as an editor of the pilot's handbook, had played her part in making the operations of the plane comprehensible to young recruits. So why didn't she ever tell me about that plane and her training? Had she faked her way through it? Or had she just endured it, moving on toward her real interests after she left the plant? Either way, I knew she had graduated from the intensive training program and worked in their Columbus plant, so she must have known something about aeronautical engineering. I just wanted to see proof.

Texas Calling

In January 2009, I decided the best way to further my Cadette research was to stage a reunion for my mother's surviving Wild Bunch friends. I wanted them to tell their stories on video and then take them to see a Helldiver in flight. Of the more than 7,000 built during the war, I'd found out there was one that could still fly. This Helldiver is owned and maintained by the Commemorative Air Force (CAF), a national organization of World War II airplane buffs headquartered in Midland, Texas. CAF had originally stood for Confederate Air Force, but in 2001 the membership finally voted to change the name. Good thing, because I wouldn't have gone near it with that moniker.

In late January, when my partner, Barbara Sheppard, returned from a Buddhist retreat feeling quite mellow, I had big news for her.

"Barbara, dear, I'm going to get the Cadettes together for a reunion. They haven't had one in six years."

"And where will you be doing this?"

"I'm not sure. I'm thinking Dallas."

"But you hate Texas, Jean-Vi! On our last trip home from the East Coast, you made us drive all the way across the Panhandle without stopping just to avoid setting foot on Texas soil."

"Yes, my bladder remembers quite well."

"You must want this bad."

"I do," I admitted. "I do."

"You planning to wear your cowboy boots?"

"No, this is aviation history. I'm thinking goggles and a white scarf."

It didn't take long for me to decide that I should spend the $200 annual membership fee to join CAF. This would give me access to pilot phone numbers and insider information about when and where the Helldiver would next be flown. I also wanted to support the organization that was keeping my mother's warbird aloft.

I called Peggy Upham to tell her that the only flyable Helldiver reputedly lived in a hangar in Graham, Texas, west of Dallas about two hours.

"Let's go see it," she replied.

"I was hoping you'd say that. I just want you to know that I've joined the Commemorative Air Force, Peggy. Members instantly become Colonels. So maybe I can get them to give us a ride in the Helldiver."

She laughed. "Now that is definitely something I would want to do."

Peggy had already seen a Helldiver on static display at the Naval Aviation Museum in Pensacola, Florida. But to see one in flight would be far better.

I kept a watchful eye on the CAF website for listings of scheduled Helldiver flights and soon saw a posting that said they'd be flying at the Air Fiesta in Brownsville, Texas, in mid-March. I phoned Peggy again.

"Let's have the reunion in Dallas, Peggy, and then go down to Brownsville to see the Helldiver fly."

She said, "Yes. Absolutely."

I started making plans.

I'd spent almost a month in Texas 22 years earlier when I was heading toward the Caribbean for another, far wilder, venture. On that trip I'd done genealogy research into my maternal grandfather's family in East Texas and heard stories from second cousins that made the hair on my neck bristle.

The Cruse Boys, as they were known, were a wild and woolly gang with a penchant for massive alcohol consumption, gambling, and what appeared to be suicidal impulsivity. Not that they were hicks. They included a doctor, a lawyer, a dentist, and a couple of businessmen. But just to illustrate what they were capable of, I'd heard that my Great Uncle Pat, a lawyer, had accepted a dare that he wouldn't drink down an entire bottle of bisulfide of mercury, a "hangover cure" he had just purchased in the local drugstore. He drank it down and dropped dead on the spot. His brother Sam, a dentist, didn't just drill teeth; he also drilled bullet holes into a man, served time, then died of alcoholism at age 60. Sam's son told me his father's demise had been the ugliest death imaginable.

These irrational, unruly, and addictive "Cruse traits" didn't set well with Genevieve Peck, my refined, St. Louis-bred grandmother. Even though she'd married one of the more mild-mannered Cruse boys, Buck (real name: Elmer), she kept her children at a distance from Cruse male relatives as best she could. She also raised her eldest daughter, my mother, to be a lady and never take a second look at the coarse oilfield workers who showed up in their kitchen at Buck's invitation. But none of the East Texas relatives had anything to do with Dallas, so I felt fairly safe visiting there. Besides, Peggy Upham would house me and guide me around, so I knew I'd be alright.

I wanted to videotape the Cadette stories in an aviation-history setting, so I contacted several museums in Dallas and the women's studies programs at a couple of local colleges. Everyone I called or emailed helped spread the word, and I finally made solid contact at the Frontiers of Flight Museum at Love Field, Dallas's original, smaller airport, with help promised by their education director, Dr. Sharon Spalding.

After word got around that I was looking for a video cameraman to shoot oral history, I got an unsolicited email from Austin. A man named William McWhorter, who worked for the Texas Historical Commission, was volunteering to travel with his broadcast-quality video camera from Austin to Dallas to shoot the ladies at the museum — at no charge. William specializes in Texans with World War II stories, and he promised to give me the videotapes afterward. To make sure we got clean copies, he would first download them to his computer then burn them to DVDs. This, too, would be done for free. The Texas warmth and hospitality aimed at my project was beginning to wear down my long-standing distaste. I might feel at home in the Lone Star State after all.

Now that I had such a good start on the Big Reunion in Dallas, I just had to time it so we could go on to Brownsville and see the Helldiver fly. The one surviving Wild Bunch Cadette who could not join us, Mary Sprow, had been disabled by a stroke a few weeks before I began my quest. But her daughter Cindy, who'd always loved hearing her mother talk about her Cadette experience, agreed to come from New Orleans to stand in for her. The sixth member of the group, Ruthe Mellott, had died in 2002, a year before my mother.[10] Since she had no children, there was no one to represent her. But having five out of six members of the Wild Bunch at the Reunion — either in the flesh or in their daughter's flesh — was a tremendously energetic force field. It seemed like nothing could stop us now. We'd get the Cadette story told, or at least the Wild Bunch version, and we'd see the Helldiver fly.

Muckraking 101

While waiting to go to Texas, I began contacting other aviation museums, starting with the Glenn H. Curtiss Museum in Hammondsport, New York. I struck gold immediately with an articulate, well-informed curator named Rick Leisenring. He told me they'd once had a Cadette on their volunteer staff who had donated various documents about the program. He promised to copy them for me, and within less than a week I got a small stack.

It included copies of propaganda used by Curtiss-Wright for recruiting that glamorized the nature of the training program and the "higher level technical work" the women would be performing. Besides a patriotic pitch, the brochure spoke in grand terms of how, after the war, the aeronautics field would be welcoming all men and women, evaluating them only on the basis of capabilities and performance on the job. "Men and women with vision see our war planes converted to a greatly expanded air commerce when the peace for which we are all fighting is won. To the men and women of the aircraft industry the future is bright, the visibility and the opportunities unlimited."[11]

I could just picture the young coeds in student advising offices at various universities seeing this brochure for the first time and feeling their hearts beat faster with excitement and hope. They might not have believed every word of it, but there it was in black and white: this training could very well lead to an actual career in aeronautical engineering. The aviation door was wide open to women at last, and it would not close after the war. Such were the promises, only to be countermanded by a bill that would pass Congress in two years requiring industries to give returning vets their jobs back — including those in aircraft manufacturers' engineering departments.

On the phone, Rick gave me a short history of America's aviation pioneers, starting with how far ahead of the pack Glenn Curtiss had been and what a shame it was he had died at the relatively young age of 52. "People don't know much about Curtiss," he said, "so they give all the early aviation credit to the Wrights."

The Curtiss Museum, Rick told me, is located close to where Curtiss had his first production facility; he encouraged me to visit. Then he gave me a parting piece of advice.

"Call Curtiss-Wright, see what they say. Just be aware that they've changed direction radically since the war, and the younger employees probably won't know much about their old airplane division *or* the Cadettes."

"Yes, I was thinking I'd call them."

"If you don't get anywhere at Curtiss-Wright, call the Boeing archives. With all the corporate mergers, they wound up owning patents for Curtiss-Wright's World War II designs, so they might have inherited some of the records related to the Cadettes."

"Great idea, Rick. Thanks so much."

"No problem. Call anytime."

I crossed my fingers that everyone I spoke to — or most of them — would be this congenial and well-informed. It would make my job so much easier.

I looked up the current incarnation of Curtiss-Wright, whose corporate headquarters are in Parsippany, New Jersey, and discovered that they make products to support the aerospace, defense, and nuclear-power industries. However, they *don't* make airplanes, engines, or propellers — their three big moneymakers during the war. Airframes had been the first to go. The company continued to do well with engines and propellers for a number of years after the war, but then jet engines replaced the old reciprocating engines, and there went the demand for the other Curtiss-Wright standbys as well. Nothing my mother and her pals had been trained to draw or test or weigh or inspect was in production at Curtiss-Wright anymore.

When I felt I had a clear sense of Curtiss-Wright's modern mission, I picked up the phone. The man who answered had never heard of the Cadettes. He told me that a great many of their World War II records had been damaged in a flood. "We sent off whatever we could salvage to the Smithsonian. But a lot of paper documents were so water-damaged they were just shredded."

"Oh. I see. Thanks anyway," I said. I hung up and tried to shake the feeling that he just wanted me to give up and go away. Instead I called a number that was supposed to connect me to the historical archives of Boeing. After listening to a dizzying rondelet of "I-don't-know, let-me-transfer-you-to…" performed by a variety of young female receptionists, I gave up and started looking through staff listings for the Museum of Flight at Boeing Field. The second number I called rang through to an assistant curator at the research facility nearby, and bingo, I found my second pot of informational gold: John Little absolutely *loved* talking about Curtiss-Wright, and he had some very righteous energy about it.

For starters, he was appalled that Curtiss-Wright's president during World War II, Burdette Wright (no relation to Wilbur and Orville), had gotten off with no jail time in spite of the company's overly free spending of government funds and their production of unflyable planes. He was specifically referring to the Helldiver.

"Do you know that Curtiss-Wright made the government pay in advance for every change they made to the Helldiver?" he railed.

He compared the Helldiver to the Brewster Company's Buccaneer, a lemon from start to finish.

"Brewster's top guys were way more obvious," he clarified. "They were paying themselves four different paychecks under different accounts. They did some major time. But they were small potatoes compared to Curtiss-Wright. Burdette should have gone down, too."

John was so hot under the collar about Curtiss-Wright that I got pretty stirred up myself and made a mental note to look him up the next time I went to Seattle. If this company had been so bold-faced and unrepentantly greedy while repeatedly failing to produce a battle-worthy Helldiver for the Navy, what might I find out about their treatment of the Cadettes? Would they have paid them fairly or just used them as cheap, technically skilled labor, never training them for or promoting them to higher-paying, upgraded jobs?

Other reviews of the company I found online reinforced this picture of Curtiss-Wright. When it came time to assemble a packet of information to send to the Wild Bunch and the Frontiers of Flight museum staff, I included the propaganda pamphlets, photos, and other materials I had received from a professor in the aeronautics and aerospace department at Purdue, but I also inserted two samples of the negative press. I didn't want Curtiss-Wright to pass as all sweetness and light, just doing their patriotic duty cranking out airplanes during the war.

During this initial search, I read about a Congressional Committee headed by Harry Truman that investigated misuse of government funds in the war-production industry. In fact, Truman had become so famous while trying to nab companies wasting government money or committing outright fraud that Roosevelt chose Truman as his running mate for his fourth term. I later spoke to Cadettes who'd been an arm's distance away from Truman as his entourage drove down the middle of Curtiss-Wright's plants in open cars during his inspections. Apparently, company management, in Columbus at least, had been less than cordial. The grandson of one of the plant managers blames the demise of the airplane division on Truman's grudge against the company. When Truman made the tour, no one at Curtiss-Wright imagined he would be president by the end of the war — with contract-canceling power.

In July of 1943, the Truman Committee released its main report. One of the biggest culprits they identified was Curtiss-Wright's engine plant in Lockland, Ohio, just north of Cincinnati.[12] They had evidence that the plant had made a quantity of substandard engines, orally changing tolerances at the last minute — similar to the too-narrow clearance around hydraulic lines to the dive brakes that Betty had found. They'd also, the report alleged, falsified inspection reports outright. For some reason, however, the criminal investigations eventually faded away and Curtiss-Wright was never legally held to account.

Arthur Miller's ghost started chortling behind me. I looked again at the Playbill notes on "All My Sons." Miller's inspiration for the play, it said, had been a newspaper article from somewhere in Ohio about a daughter who ratted on her dad for the same dishonest behavior attributed to Joe Keller in the play. Curtiss-Wright was a much bigger company than the fictional subcontracting plant Keller ran, but since the company's airplane division had not yet gone under when Miller published the play in 1947, he undoubtedly felt it wise not to point at them directly, if indeed the Curtiss-Wright malfeasance had been his inspiration.

By the time our entry into World War II seemed certain, Curtiss-Wright's connections in Washington, D.C., really began to pay off. Beginning in 1941, government dollars helped them create millions of square feet of additional airplane- and engine-production space in Buffalo, Columbus, St. Louis, and Wood-Ridge, New Jersey. The buildings used as airframe plants were officially the property of the U.S. government, but Curtiss-Wright had unfettered use of the space. With all that money flowing in their direction, even if they had been as bad as they were beginning to look after the Truman Committee Report, they would not have been brought down by a gentle tug at the ankle.

Other than passing along those few media snippets about Curtiss-Wright's unsavory reputation, I was careful not to demonize the company. My mother and her Cadette buddies had been honest and worked hard, no matter what shenanigans corporate management may have pulled. It was clear that with all the possibilities of litigation lingering over Curtiss-Wright's old configuration, I was never going to get a straight story about their activities in World War II—including the Cadette Program. The modern Curtiss-Wright was just another corporate entity with a whole chunk of memory surgically extracted from its unaccountable brain.

Next I contacted a few engineering deans' offices, libraries, and archives at universities that had trained the Cadettes, starting with Iowa State because their listings kept coming up first on all Internet searches. They had been conscientiously collecting everything they could about the program, and their archivist, Tanya Zanish-Belcher, offered me copies of several documents, including an article in the *Iowa Engineer* about women "invading the campus," which is how the male-dominated engineering departments' publications initially characterized the arrival of the Cadettes.

I also tried to get my hands on a copy of a master's thesis at the University of Minnesota that focused primarily on U of M's Cadettes. The library's archivists balked about copyrights and permissions, but I had a friend who worked on campus. She went right over, made a copy in the library, and mailed it to me. While she was at it, she copied the table of contents from another, harder to obtain report by a man named Warren Bruner, the Cadette Program's main coordinator. Bruner had overseen the second and third rounds of training, which the company reduced to six months and conducted at Purdue only. His sure-to-be-revelatory report summarized the Cadette Program from its inception through the end of December 1944.

When the master's thesis arrived, I was really jazzed. The author explained how the program was initiated and the dates on which the Army and Navy had each signed an agreement that would open the gates to government funding. The thesis, however, focused almost exclusively on the Minnesota Cadettes and repeatedly referenced the Bruner Report, which I still hadn't seen. The author didn't dig deeply into whether the Cadettes' salaries were anywhere near those of the company's male engineers whom they had replaced. She did, however, cite the estimated amount for training each Cadette for ten months, which, according to Chief Engineer R.C. Blaylock, was "not to exceed $1,220 per student."[13]

The one golden nugget I found in the thesis was a fact from the Bruner Report: Curtiss-Wright received $2 million from the U.S. government for the first round of the Cadette training program. This is the equivalent of about $75 million in today's currency. Training approximately 700 women, drawing on $2 million in government funds, comes to about $2,857 per student. If these figures are accurate, Curtiss-Wright netted $1,637 on each Cadette.[14] Truman, I'll warrant, would have been interested in this tidy little factoid if it had ever come to his attention.

Curtiss-Wright conveyed the impression that it paid for the entire Cadette Training Program, though every last dime came from Uncle Sam. Paying the Cadettes $10 a week made the Cadettes appear to be normal employees of the company, but in fact they were participants in a government-funded, though corporate-managed, war training program. Putting the women on the company payroll was an attempt to persuade the Cadettes that, considering "the company's largesse," they should feel obligated to work in Curtiss-Wright plants when they finished their training and not allow other companies to lure them away. From talking to various Cadettes, I found out that when they were recruited, their contracts did not commit them to work at Curtiss-Wright. The great majority, however, were so conscientious (and/or unsuspecting) that they just reported directly to the company's plants.

As mentioned, ten dollars a week was pretty big money in 1943. I've never heard a Cadette complain about the salary or how it essentially wedded her to the airplane manufacturing giant. Curtiss-Wright, if challenged, would no doubt have protested that it was simply trying to protect its investment. People, money, and goods were moving so fast in the rush to arm the country that corporate ethics and accountability — especially regarding personnel, not products — were low on the list for government scrutiny. If the Cadettes thought Curtiss-Wright was ponying up for this program, it was probably not a big enough issue for the War Production Board to make the company correct the impression.

When I requested a copy of the Bruner Report from the University of Minnesota's special collections, I was barraged with murmurings and mutterings from the guardians at the gates of protected information. "We'll have to look into copyright and royalties issues," said an anonymous, rather pompous-sounding archivist when I asked about it.

I couldn't understand how anyone could be so uptight about a 65-year-old document on a discontinued women's engineering program from a now defunct division of the Curtiss-Wright Corporation, so I just kept asking. They finally agreed to scan the report and email me six PDF files, the accessibility of which would supposedly time-out after I printed one copy of each. This was their effort to guarantee that I would not have a ready-made digital copy for unlimited reproduction. I said, "Fine, whatever," and got the file within 24 hours, thrilled to finally see something that had been generated directly from within Curtiss-Wright.

The Bruner Report was released on December 30, 1944, when the first group of Cadettes had only been in the plants for one year and the women in shorter, six-month trainings were either close to finishing or halfway through. Created for in-house review, the report was never intended for public circulation. Someone, however, had donated a copy to the University of Minnesota. At 140 pages, including a subject index and an appendix, it promised huge satisfaction to my investigative taste buds. But what it delivered was a watered-down gruel that wouldn't satisfy a toad. Though it's full of enticing references to reports, correspondence, and supplementary files, none of these were archived with the summary. Every time I thought I might get some juicy details and statistics, the trail dropped off a cliff.

For example, Curtiss-Wright's Cadette Training Office in Buffalo (at 1100 Main Street) kept academic report cards on each Cadette. They also had copies of the performance reports on the Cadettes generated by each of the plant managers and memos between the plants and the Training Office about how to deal with the Cadettes. Also retained, from numerous meetings attended by university and corporate representatives, were pages and pages of notes about how they had designed the program. Everything, in short, that would tell exactly how the program was set up, how the money was spent, and how the plant managers, engineers, and corporate managers viewed the Cadettes' work and design contributions was contained in those ancillary materials. And they're simply not there.

I pictured myself tracking down Warren Bruner to shake the rest of the story (and documents) out of him. But after months of asking various Cadettes, I ascertained from the few who remembered seeing him in the Columbus plant that he was middle-aged then, so he was definitely not among the living now.

Hatching the Cadette Egg

Though Bruner's "official report" — without the supporting files — was sketchy, several months later I acquired a professional engineering paper by a key player at Curtiss-Wright. Between the two documents, I pieced together a clearer picture of exactly how the Cadette Program came into being.

On September 21, 1942, a man named C. Wilson Cole,[15] supervisor of the Engineering Personnel Bureau (EPB) for Curtiss-Wright, unveiled his radical idea that women could be trained to replace company engineers who'd been drafted into the war. Cole polled the different Curtiss-Wright plants to find out how many additional engineers they each needed and came up with the figure of 750 total. Only the engine division chose not to participate in the program, which was a tad odd because Cole himself had been its chief engineer before taking over the EPB.

After rejecting the idea of training women on-site in the plants, Cole drew up a plan that included eight different universities with respected engineering schools who had shown an interest in the program. He then presented his plan to the Army and the Navy in early November. According to Bruner, both branches of the military signed off on it by December 7, 1942. With typical World War II exigency, the Curtiss-Wright Engineering Cadette Program went from conception to fully funded (and recruited) program in under five months.

The program was originally slated to begin in early January of 1943, but since the recruiting process took a little longer, training started in mid-February instead. Curtiss-Wright planned to assign a little over 100 Cadettes to each of the seven universities that finally agreed to participate (as mentioned earlier, this included the Universities of Minnesota and Texas, Cornell, Iowa State, Penn State, Rensselaer Polytechnic Institute, and Purdue). On each campus, a core group of engineering faculty were assigned to the teaching, and each school designated one professor to coordinate the effort. These coordinators attended the curriculum-planning meetings at corporate headquarters in New York City.

In June 1943, in the middle of the first round of Cadette training, Cole delivered his paper on "The Training of Women in Engineering" at the 51st Annual Meeting of the Society for the Promotion of Engineering Education (SPEE). In it, he explained that Curtiss-Wright, in order to give faculty an appreciation for the working methods of the company's engineering departments, had arranged for instructors to visit the plants and consult with company technicians. Curtiss-Wright also sent some of its engineers to the universities to give special lectures, conduct seminars, and explain the applications of subjects being taught. In addition, the company's engineering manual was studied and utilized by the engineering faculty at each of the seven participating universities.

The official requirements for admission to the initial 10-month Cadette Program, as noted earlier, were that students be at least 18 years of age with a year of college under their belts and good aptitude in math. But the unwritten requirements, if you look at all the pictures and the lists of recruit names, were that Cadette candidates had to be single and white (and preferably Christian). Over 2,000 colleges, mostly east of the Rockies, were contacted for likely candidates, and 3,000 interviews were conducted. One of my mother's friends remembers that the interview took exactly fifteen minutes.

Curtiss-Wright made offers to 1,000 women for the initial round of training, and 719 accepted, with recruits coming from 261 different schools. Recruitment was limited to only a few students per college: enrollment was down during the war, so schools did not easily part with paying students. The recruits were not allowed to train at the same college where they'd been enrolled at the time of recruitment. The idea was that they'd be more inclined to focus on their engineering studies if transplanted to a different campus. Or, as Bruner's report more delicately phrased it, they were sent to other schools for training so that "personal ties that might interfere with their seriousness of purpose would be stretched." Thus my mother, a student at the University of Texas when they recruited her, could not attend the training there.

Initially, Curtiss-Wright made a point of hiding from the Cadettes the fact that they were being graded during their training. Participating colleges were instructed to send the grades directly to the Cadette Training Office, at that time located in Passaic, New Jersey. Most of the Cadettes never knew if they were succeeding or failing or just doing average work until their on-campus Curtiss-Wright supervisor, as directed by Buffalo, would show up to tell them they needed to work harder in certain courses. The bottom line, revealed to them only after they'd completed the first half of their engineering studies, was: "Do a halfway decent job in the training and you are guaranteed a job at one of our plants." This had a somewhat dispiriting effect on the Cadettes, and some of them slackened their efforts. But, as I later discovered, the majority still achieved an overall mastery of the subjects offered to them, which made them invaluable in the plants.

In the initial training, Curtiss-Wright supervisors were responsible for overseeing the Cadettes' housing and dealing with personal problems, as well as distributing their weekly paychecks. They were also the ones who sent reports on the Cadettes (including the surreptitiously gathered grades) to the Cadette Training Office, which then forwarded them to personnel managers at the plants where they would be working.

Some of the students dropped or were asked to leave. Of the initial 719 recruits, 617 graduated. But according to Bruner, "the enormous scope of the undertaking, the speed with which it was launched, and the lack of precedents for predicting success resulted in some poor selections [of Cadettes]. There is reason to believe, however, that the number who could not make the grade was no greater than would have been the case in a corresponding group of boys."

He adds: "With regard to the girls who finished … there is unanimity of opinion to the effect that the girls were outstanding. In one college, after they had been gone for six months, they were still acclaimed the 'best group of students that had ever been on the campus, men or women.' A professor at another college said, 'In twenty-two years of teaching mechanics, I have never had a class like my Division A.' At a third institution: 'A few of the girls in this program could, if further trained, compete with the best men in the business if prejudices were barred.'"[16]

Bruner states that professors who had never taught women students before were surprised. For example, at Rensselaer Polytechnic Institute (RPI), one faculty member reported that "Cadettes catch on in a hurry, ask more questions than do the boys, take the detail better, and therefore learn their subjects more thoroughly."

At Purdue, faculty were concerned that male and female engineering students should be visually segregated. Several different Cadettes told me that to keep a clear distinction between men and women in Purdue's engineering department, males wore only beige (and usually very dirty) corduroy pants, while Cadettes were forbidden to wear beige slacks of any material, even for shop.

The difficulty of keeping the genders separated academically presented an even more interesting challenge. One Cadette from the Purdue class of '43 told me that the Cadettes were deliberately kept one step (or course) ahead of the male engineering students so that the males could not help them. I later asked a Cadette I met in Columbus about this, and she responded indignantly: "We didn't need any help." This was confirmed by a final comprehensive test—including mathematics, applied mechanics, and aerodynamics—given to Purdue Cadettes (the ten-month, first-round curriculum) and to 18 male students who had been pursuing aeronautical engineering degrees for three or three and a half years. The three highest marks were scored by Cadettes. On top of that, 50 of the 83 graduating Purdue Cadettes surpassed the male student with the lowest marks. Bruner also noted that at Penn State a third of the Cadettes regularly made the dean's list, compared with a usual class percentage of less than ten percent.

Since they never saw Bruner's report, their grades, or (for the Purdue class of '43) their outstanding test results as measured against advanced-standing male engineering students, when the Cadettes emerged from the 10-month program they had no idea just how remarkable their academic achievements had been. However, according to Bruner, "Whatever the contributing causes, an esprit de corps developed that could not be matched."

Chapter Three
The Wild Bunch in Texas

Legally Margaret

Shortly before I left for Dallas, Barbara expressed concern about the trip I had planned. As a retired social worker with all the right genes for anticipating obstacles and disasters, she thought I might be going in blind.

"You're going off with three women in their mid-80s," she said, "and you've set up meetings and events for them all over Dallas and southern Texas. What happens if one of them has a medical crisis?"

"These women are quite sound, Barbara. I've talked to them a lot and I know they are up to it. Besides, I have a gut feeling it's going to work out."

"I hope you're right," she said, still dubious.

I tried to ignore her. I had spent long, satisfying hours setting up the Dallas portion of the reunion, thrilled to find us all being taken quite seriously by the Frontiers of Flight Museum staff. Once I received confirmation that the Helldiver would indeed be flying in Brownsville, I booked lodgings for myself and the Cadettes at a B&B in Harlingen, a nearby town. Harlingen, as it turned out, is only a stone's throw from a small retirement community where one of my mother's dearest friends from Minnesota spends her winters, and I knew the Cadettes would love to meet her. She'd recently had a mild stroke, but she was still ambulatory and occasionally articulate. Her son Marc, who keeps her company in Texas, told me he'd make sure we got together. Her daughter Kate would also be in town during our visit and promised to help, too.

Everything was falling into place. Mary Sprow's daughter Cindy was flying in from New Orleans to join us in Harlingen and help with driving, freeing me to attend to other details about the Air Fiesta and the Helldiver.

When I finally pulled up behind Peggy Upham's four-story senior apartments, I got my first glimpse of her as she walked toward me from the building. I was amazed to see a woman leaner and shorter than me, probably five feet tall, with a slightly wobbly but exceedingly determined walk. She was very thin and hunched over from spinal curvature. But she had a deep throaty laugh, and her twinkly eyes reminded me of exaggerated drawings of elegant cats, slanting upward steeply. Her careful makeup and professional attire matched the businesslike speed and precision with which she moved me and my stuff out of the car and up to her apartment on the fourth floor. When we sat down for a bite of lunch at her kitchen table, I was so busy appreciating her warm glow and friendly smile, I could barely remember how I'd gotten there.

Peggy's husband had died a number of years earlier, so she'd downsized and moved to a location closer to her only son's family. The two-bedroom apartment was crammed with her plants and possessions — especially her collection of butterflies, made from every imaginable material, frozen in mid-flutter on every wall and table. One bedroom was full of office furniture and business files. That left the master bedroom and bath, which she surrendered to me, announcing that she planned to sleep on the couch.

"Peggy," I demurred, "I can't take your bed."

"No, no, it's fine. I'm very comfortable on the couch," she said, steering me into her room and depositing one of my bags in a corner.

I hated putting her out, yet I was in desperate need of a good night's sleep because I'd been awake most of the previous night in a motel with fever and coughing from the cold I'd caught en route. I accepted her generosity and arranged the rest of my bags and video gear off to one side. When I rejoined her, she was fluttering like one of her butterflies, rustling through photos and old documents, getting ready to show me everything she possessed that related to the Cadettes.

I had barely eaten a spoonful of soup before Peggy, too excited to relax, placed the photo-and-memento collection she'd assembled in front of me on the table. One of the pictures featured my folks holding their first baby, my older brother. My parents looked radiant, and my mother, the famously slender belle from East Texas, had just a hint of added flesh in her midsection and on her cheeks. Her long, wavy auburn hair and vibrant dark eyes were exactly as penetrating as in another shot taken two years earlier, right after the Cadettes completed their training at Purdue and before they reported to the plant.

"I want you to have these," said Peggy, handing me both originals.

"Are you sure?" I said, totally floored.

"Yes. Absolutely."

I accepted them gratefully. I had no photos from those years of my mother as a Cadette or of my newlywed parents, other than the sepia-toned wedding picture on the back of my mother's funeral program.

After lunch, Peggy and I spent the afternoon at a print shop arranging for the red t-shirts I'd brought to be printed with white letters proclaiming "Curtiss Engineering Cadettes, Purdue Class of '43." (Peggy used the airplane division's shorter name; the SB2C was often called the "Curtiss Helldiver.") While the friendly man who ran the shop and designed our t-shirts was watching Peggy sign the credit card slip, he said, "Thank you for your business, Peggy." (He'd heard me call her that several times.) Peggy stopped signing, looked him dead in the eye, and with a mischievous twinkle replied, "I'm really legally Margaret."

He and I exchanged a wink. "Okay," he said. "Then thank you, 'Legally Margaret.'" And that's what I called her for the next few days. Only later, as we were trying to board our plane out of Harlingen, would this special designation come back to haunt us.

The Flying Pancake

The next morning, Peggy and I drove off to preview the museum where we'd be doing the interviews. On the edge of Dallas's Love Field, the Frontiers of Flight is a fairly new museum with plenty of glass, a spacious main exhibit hall with an open balcony on the second level, children's exhibits and play areas, a bookstore, and plenty of airplanes and other aviation memorabilia, all staffed by a group of people who take their educational mission quite seriously. Museum volunteers take turns dressing up as famous aviation characters to give "firsthand accounts" of historical episodes that they (fictitiously) participated in to schoolchildren and other visitors.

It turned out we had picked "Women in Aviation" month. Just inside the entry was a large glass display case featuring women pilots' gear, as well as books about other women who'd been pioneers in aviation, from Amelia Earhart to the Women Airforce Service Pilots (WASP), the young females in World War II who had ferried huge numbers of planes from the manufacturing plants to military bases.

There was, of course, one grave omission from the display: the Curtiss-Wright Engineering Cadettes. This would have to be corrected.

Dr. Sharon Spalding, the Education Coordinator with whom I'd set this up, was a tall blond wearing a fur vest. She welcomed us exuberantly and then escorted us to the model shop she'd reserved for our interviews. The room was just past the main-entry area and had windows on three sides. Inside were at least two dozen model airplanes hanging from the ceiling or resting on worktables and shelves. As she led the way, she stopped to introduce us to other museum staff, graciously explaining why we were such honored guests.

As Sharon was whisking us out of the model shop, something bright yellow caught my eye, an airborne vehicle unlike anything I'd ever seen except in grainy sci-fi movies. The model, flat and almost completely round like the famous UFO discs, was equipped with an array of armaments. Three old geezer aviation buffs were bent over it in hushed earnestness, discussing its details.

"What's that?" I asked one of the men.

"It's the Flying Pancake," he said, lifting his head from the model just long enough to look at us and then turning back to his work.

I thought he was joking.

"Are you serious?"

"Yeah. It's a design from WWII."

He explained that the Flying Flapjack, as it's also called, had two engines and was able to take off and land in a very short space. (This, I later read, is referred to as VSTOL, Vertical and Short Take Off and Landing.) The plane was first tested in the early '40s and combined elements of both a traditional airplane and the newly developed helicopter. It could go so slow it almost hovered, flying between 40 and 425 mph. Technically labeled the V-173, the Zimmer Skimmer (after its inventor Charles Zimmerman) had done so well in test flights, including one by Charles Lindbergh, that the Navy decided to make a bigger and much-improved prototype, the XF5U-1. The new plane was scheduled to go to Muroc Dry Lake (later renamed Edwards Air Force Base) in California for testing, but before it could get there, the government decided jet engines were the design of the future and cancelled contracts for planes with propellers and reciprocating engines. So the beautiful XF5U-1 was stripped of usable parts and scrapped. The first model (the V-173), however, miraculously survived and was housed at the Smithsonian, though it was not in very good shape. Or so I was told by the model builders at the Frontiers of Flight.

If I hadn't seen that model and then looked into its remarkable history, I might have been content to let my revival of the Curtiss-Wright Cadettes story rest with the interviews we taped in Dallas and a few notes on what I'd heard from museum curators. But having seen the Flying Pancake, I doubt I'll ever stop hovering over the idea of how aviation might look today if long, bullet-shaped planes had not trumped other flatter or rounder designs.

Something about the Pancake reminded me of chic Parisian hats from the '50s, the kind with a round, super-wide brim and a low dome, made briefly popular by fashion icons like Audrey Hepburn or Grace Kelly. Imagine what women aero-engineers could do if given this shape to work with, instead of consigning it to the graphic archives, filing it under "Whacked-

Out UFO Sightings." This design could have been "the beginning of a beautiful relationship" (à la Humphrey Bogart to the French inspector at the end of *Casablanca*) between women, fashion, and flight.

In fact, Barbara and I had a perfect "Pancake Landing Pad" outside our house in Taos, right on the edge of a deep arroyo. We had been planning to make a stone labyrinth, but the pad was really too small for the grandiose design we had in mind. It would be perfect, however, for petite VSTOL vehicles. (I had a feeling Barbara was going to resist this idea, and I was right. She talked me into covering the whole area with small, coral pink stones and laying out a peace symbol with large white rocks. Not that a Flying Pancake can't set down on a Peace Pad.)

After scoping out the Frontiers of Flight, Peggy and I met Beth Wehner at the airport, flying in from Austin. She was just about as fast moving as Peggy, and between them I started wondering how I'd ever keep up. Silverblonde, with a sweet Southern voice, Beth was very much my mother's counterpart, with laughing flirtatious eyes. As I said, I had met her on my previous trip to Texas in 1987, but I hadn't known what to make of her then. At that point, I had been distracted by my hunt for the Cruse family history, so I was pretty blind to everything (and everyone) else. I did, however, have a clear memory of Beth's righteously independent spirit.

Beth had been known at Purdue as Beni because her maiden name was Benson. She was still feisty and free and getting around quite well, but during the next few days she made sure she had places to take a load off when she needed to so she could always keep up. She carried a light suitcase with her and had been very enthusiastic about the reunion. Every time she heard what Peggy and I were considering doing, she'd say, "Count me in. I don't want to be left out of any of it." I was hard pressed to remember anyone so vivacious *and* feisty among my mother's later friends.

In Columbus, Beth had been the only one of the Wild Bunch with a husband. He'd gone away to New York on military duty soon after they were married, and she took the train to be with him some weekends. She hated being the only married gal while her roommates (and most of the Cadettes) were all fancy free and footloose. When he finally came home after the war, they moved to Texas and had five children, all boys. She'd always loved flirting and being around men, so she got her wish many times over. But after 30-plus years of marriage, she realized she needed more freedom than her husband could tolerate, so she went off on her own. She got her college degree, became a math teacher, found a new male partner, lived alone, and enjoyed an independent life just within reach of those five boys and ex-husband. Over the long run, Beth's ex became such a good friend that she and her partner spent important holidays with him and the boys.

Peggy, Beth, and I drank coffee and ate pastries until it was time to go back to Love Field to retrieve Betty, who strode off the plane with that same "so, where are we off to now?" look I'd always loved about her. For a girl from a small North Carolina town (Cullowhee) who'd never left home before she joined the Cadette Program in 1943, she'd traveled the farthest, back then *and* now, to be part of the action. She had raised two children with a physicist husband who died when the girls were in their teens. As I said, my mother had never stopped telling me that Betty was someone I must meet. It might have been because of Betty's easy-going temperament and liberal politics. But now that my mother is gone, I think of Betty as my second mom.

Betty had had any number of medical challenges in the last few years, most of them relatively small, and several of them involved her feet. But she refused to let any of it hold her back. She got off that plane walking just as fast as ever and never lagged the entire trip. This put to rest any of Barbara's anticipatory concern that the Cadettes might need medical intervention. As for me, it seemed likely I'd get an extra shot of longevity juice just from being around them.

When everyone was collected, we made our way across Dallas to the hotel where we were staying, the same one where the Wild Bunch (including my mom) had stayed in 1991. That evening after dinner, in our side-by-side suites, the atmosphere was perfect for relaxed talks. I set up my home video camera on a tripod and recorded the Cadettes answering my pre-interview warm-up questions. The more I probed, the more they seemed to see that their short but brave experience as aero-engineers really might be a story worth capturing. When the clock struck twelve, I was the only one who wanted to call it a night.

Dallas Interviews

The next morning, we'd just convened for the interviews at the Frontiers of Flight Museum when William McWhorter, the Texas Historical Commission's cameraman, called to say he was driving through torrential rain and would be a little late. So we took our time settling in at the model shop and figuring out where the interviewee should be seated to include a good sampling of all the model airplanes hanging from the ceiling. William finally arrived, shaking rain off his hat and coat, and rapidly set up his equipment.

I had chosen Betty to start. I knew her time at Purdue had not been difficult because she'd been so good in math and had already set her sights on a career in science before she signed up with Curtiss-Wright. So I zeroed in on her experience at the plant.

"When you were at Columbus, where were the senior engineers who were giving you orders, Betty?"

"I have no idea. I never saw them after our first three weeks of instruction on how to do inspections. The person in charge of inspections, our boss, sat in his little office. He would come down on the line and talk with us now and then. I don't recall his name. But he was nice to us. I remember he had a sort of bewildered look on his face when he saw all these young ladies down there ready to do inspections. And we *were* ladies. The workers on the line were a little bit protective because they felt they should make sure we were treated properly. There weren't any women working this far down the line when we got there, other than three who did inspections. They'd all been trained on the job."

Peggy had a similar memory of working with minimal supervision in the drafting department.

"Do you remember seeing any senior engineers?" I asked Peggy.

"All I remember is the head of the checking department, Mr. Crumb. He was sitting at a board right there close to us. But not looking over your shoulder."

"Did the number of women in engineering positions outnumber the men?"

"Oh gosh, yes. The drafting department was huge, and there were very few men in there that I can remember."

"What exactly did you do in drafting?"

"We took the original working drawings of these airplanes and incorporated the engineering orders, EOs. Then we sent them to the checking department to make sure the EOs had been properly drawn. Like, if part of the assembly had been cut off four inches, you had to draw it to be sure it was four inches. Our rivets had to be in the exact right spot. I worked on the tail hook and the cockpit assembly. But we weren't limited to one particular part of the plane. It was just overall."

"So how do you think your work contributed to the war effort, Peggy?"

"The U.S. needed planes desperately. They couldn't wait two years. For that reason, I think we did help out, to a point, yes."

After Beth got moved out of drafting into the Handbooks Group with my mother, she was working on the maintenance manual for a trainer plane for Navy pilots.

"I would go down on the line and talk to the people who were doing it and see if the things I was putting in the manual were really true and were what they needed. I got some good help down there, although it was somewhat condescending. But I took it any way I could get it, the information. And they did answer my questions."

I asked Beth if she thought her work had had a positive impact on the outcome of the war.

"At the time I didn't think what we did was impressive. But if Curtiss-Wright made a difference in the war, then we made a difference in Curtiss-Wright, so we made a difference in the war. If we hadn't been there it would have been a lot harder, if not impossible, for Curtiss-Wright to operate all of their plants.

"It took everybody in America working together to win that war. On the home front, we gave up an awful lot without ever thinking anything about it or feeling at all deprived. We didn't have meat. We didn't have shoes. But nobody fussed about it. You just did your job and did the best you could.

"It was a pretty amazing time. It was a safe time. People all liked each other. When we had to work overtime, we were on our own to find a way home because our regular carpool would have left. So I had to go around and find somebody I didn't know from Adam. Ask them if they were going out the way I lived and if they would drop me off. Get me close to home. And sometimes they'd do just that. They'd drop me five blocks from home, and I'd trudge through the snow in the dark of night. You couldn't do that now. You wouldn't feel safe. People were trustworthy, especially the soldiers. Nowadays they have a bad reputation. But in those days it was your brother and your neighbor. Everybody was in the army."

When I finished interviewing Betty, Peggy, and Beth, William shot three minutes of me explaining how I started this project. I choked up the moment I started giving basic biographical data on my mother. Her absence was all the more painful among these dear friends who were still walking and talking, laughing and sharing their memories of World War II. When I signed off, I said I was doing this to restore the Cadette story to history and "to honor my mother," which made me completely tear up again.

"I wish she'd been here," I said after the camera stopped rolling. "She would have felt the deeper purpose of her service to Curtiss-Wright as much as you guys do now."

They all nodded and Peggy put her arm around my shoulder until my tears dried.

Afterward, we lingered so William could shoot stills of us bent over the worktable, poring over brochures from Curtiss-Wright and a well-worn engineering book Peggy had used in the Cadette Program. It was written by Professor E.F. Bruhn, who had taught them about airplane structures at Purdue. We packed up, left a note for Dr. Spalding thanking her for hosting us, and made our way toward the exit, satisfied with the job we'd done. William promised to deliver the finished DVDs and original tapes to our hotel early the next day.

The Wild Bunch in Texas

In the morning, after William dropped everything off, we celebrated by going to Neiman Marcus. Neiman's was my mother's favorite place to shop. When I went to Texas with her while I was in high school, I endured many long hours there as she went from one department to the next, chatting with every salesperson she met. Back in Minnesota, when Neiman catalogs came in the mail, she'd call and talk to department managers. They were always very eager to speak to Mrs. Lenthe. She'd listen to their recommendations and then say, "Oh yes, I'd like one of those, and one of those, and one of those. And charge it, please," sounding just like a grown-up version of Kay Thompson's "Eloise."

The irony of this is that the one and only time my mother coached me in dramatic interpretation, she talked me into performing an excerpt from "Eloise." Despite her best efforts to get me to slow down, I read the piece at a mile a minute because I was so embarrassed, at age 13, to be acting the part of a six-year-old. Whether this age disparity never occurred to my mother or whether she was herself permanently stuck in a younger, "give me whatever I ask for" frame of mind, I've never been sure.

But here I was in the company of her World War II friends, and I wanted to see if my adult eyes could detect what Neiman's sold that could so enthrall my mother. We hadn't gone far in the store before the Cadettes became paralyzed by the unbelievably high-priced — and basically unwearable — "art shoes" for women. We spent an hour, with the aid of a saleswoman who loved these 85-year-olds in their comfortable flats, ogling and pawing her wares. She seemed genuinely fascinated by their Cadette story and showed no impatience that we were clearly non-buyers.

"That was so fun," said Beth as we moved on to the store's restaurant. "It reminded me of how I splurged all my shoe ration coupons during the war on a pair of high-heeled red sandals with platform soles and an ankle strap."

The other Cadettes told me, with some wonderment, that when they shopped with my mother, she routinely picked up whatever she liked, walked to the counter, and pulled out her credit card without looking at the price. Nor did she waste time looking at the receipt when it was handed to her for a signature. I had no doubt they were telling the truth.

I hadn't shopped with my mother in years, but the last time I'd allowed her to buy me presents (in the late '80s in Seattle), she'd casually dropped $650 worth of items into my lap in less than 20 minutes. Being at that time a fringe-dwelling Bohemian with almost no furniture or other household possessions to bog me down, I could have lived on $650 for close to two months. But now, more than 20 years later, I was overlooking all my mother's consumerism, trying instead to prove the importance of what she had done in World War II.

After lunch, Betty bought dark-chocolate-coated potato chips for Barbara, whom she absolutely adores because Barbara's been such a solid, loving partner. But that was our only purchase.

Walking out of Neiman's without any packages under my arm, I turned to the Cadettes and laughed merrily. "I'd say this throws some doubt on whether I'm really my mother's daughter."

That night after dinner, we went back to our suites to pack, then spent another evening jabbering about Cadette life at Purdue and Columbus.

"Do you remember when Peggy's mom sent us a crate of live chickens at Casa Dingy?" asked Beth.

Betty laughed. "Yes—Mary would pick them up and twirl them around to break their necks."

"And somebody sent us a ham, and butter," said Beth. "Homemade."

"Yes, but it was Ricki," said Peggy, "who brought home that smoked turkey on Thanksgiving."

"Right," said Beth. "She was the one who went to all the parties. We knew we weren't going to get to go home for Christmas, so we hung that turkey on a rope outside the upstairs window until Christmas. Remember how frigid it was that winter?"

"Yes," said Betty. "And I especially remember how Mary, even tall as she was, loved to wear heels. Which she did, very nicely, but she was not too well coordinated. And she *hated* ice. I remember one time we were walking along the sidewalk, it was just a sheet of ice. I was trying to keep her up, but she did a complete twirl around me and landed on her face on the ice."

"All the way around behind you?" I asked.

Betty nodded, laughing until she cried. "Yes, I was trying to catch her. Oh, she provided some good stuff."

Peggy added, "All in all, it was a great, *great* bunch of ladies. I think everybody contributed. It was just a good time. We had our little petty problems occasionally, but that was it."

"I don't remember *any* problems," countered Beth. "Seemed to me like it just flowed so smoothly. And Betty took care of the furnace, so we always had heat."

"Yes," said Betty. "When it broke the first time, the guy came and crawled under the furnace and fixed it. I watched him, and I thought, what the hell, I can do that."

"Mary did practically all the cooking and ordering the food," Beth chimed in,

"But I had to go to the store with Mary because she couldn't add very well," said Betty.

"I thought you had to have a solid math background to get into this program," I said in consternation.

"It was sketchy in some cases," laughed Beth.

"Ruthe and I did most of the dishes and seeing to the linens," offered Peggy.

"Well, I did dishes, too — a lot," corrected Beth.

"And Ricki sat in the living room and looked pretty," said Betty. "I don't remember that she ever did anything."

"Right," said Beth, "Ricki had no household duties at Casa Dingy. She never lifted a finger to cook, shop, or clean. The servicemen in Columbus all succumbed to her charm. We were just very grateful for what she brought home!"

"Like what — besides a smoked turkey?" I pressed.

"Oh, you know, commodities that were only available to the military, like cigarettes or extra gasoline stamps and meat rations," answered Beth.

Once again it was almost midnight by the time we hit the sack. But the next morning we made it to the airport with time to spare, parked the car, ate breakfast, and boarded our flight for Harlingen. Mary Sprow's daughter, a tall, attractive blond with an easygoing manner and a ready smile, boarded our plane at Houston's Hobby Airport, and we all flew on to Harlingen. The Dallas segment had been a resounding success. Next stop: to see the Helldiver fly.

Air Fiesta in Brownsville

Brownsville is the farthest point south in Texas, where the Rio Grande empties into the Gulf of Mexico. The weather's usually warm enough all year for growing the plentiful produce for which the Texas section of the Rio Grande Valley is famous. But it was overcast and chilly when we disembarked in Harlingen, a half-hour drive north of Brownsville. We hustled into our rental van and drove to the local museum at a former Army Air Corps base. Here, I had read, pilots had once trained in Helldivers. This seemed like good juju to me.

The museum's curator greeted us and led us to a conference room for an impromptu group interview with the local library's oral historian, whom he'd invited without telling me. But we were being treated like historical celebrities, so we gladly gave them our time and attention.

The main museum building was made of stately stone and was once rather grand. However, the aviation collection itself, in decaying temporary Army buildings, was dusty and sparse, a rank disappointment after the Frontiers of Flight. After the interviews, we took a quick tour and moved on to our B&B.

Casa Rama, the former home of a man who'd made his fortune refrigerating all the valley's produce, was filled with beautiful antiques and was now owned by a gracious surgeon and his warm-hearted, hardworking wife, both of whom came from the Philippines. Cindy, Peggy, Beth, and I had rooms with private baths on the second floor, and Betty settled into a plush room with a canopied bed on the main level just past the library/ piano room. They'd given us great rates because it was so cold and wintry — and getting icier by the minute. We were grateful to have such a warm and accommodating place to hunker down.

The long group gab on camera that evening in front of the rose marble fireplace, sitting in our circle of Italian silk embroidered chairs, included a segment just for Mary, Cindy's stroke-debilitated Mom back in New Orleans. We assumed she'd want to feel included in our good fortune at having found Casa Rama. Peggy and Beth, the two Texans in the group, both told me I'd done "real good" finding the house. Betty assured me I really was my mother's daughter, because Ricki had been the one to procure their group house in Columbus and always found great accommodations for their reunions.

We climbed gratefully into soft warm beds a little earlier than the previous two nights, fingers crossed that the Helldiver would fly in Brownsville. Earlier in the day, I'd called the number I had in Houston for the pilot and left a message, asking if he was definitely going to be bringing the Helldiver down. There was nothing for it but to see what the weather would bring.

As forecasted, it just grew colder. No one remembered Harlingen or Brownsville ever being so icy in mid-March. The next morning, we drove down to the airfield where the show was supposed to be and found rows upon rows of cars parked around its perimeter, all trying to nab a good viewing spot without paying the entrance fee. It was so overcast, numbingly cold, and windy, it seemed unlikely anything at all could fly. All I saw in the air were three kites dancing fancifully over the entrance gate to the airfield. That might be all the air show anyone would get.

We pulled off on a side road, and I got out to speak with a Hispanic woman who was standing on the shoulder. Her family was huddled in the car farther down the road. She said nobody knew if any planes would fly, but everyone was still hoping. They'd all brought food and drink and were watching from the comfort of their warm cars and trucks. I stood outside, looking skyward hopefully, my cheeks turning numb, and finally came back to our van. "Let's go," I said. "I don't think this is gonna happen today."

When we returned to the B&B I finally got a call from the pilot. He and the Helldiver were still in Houston. He couldn't bring the plane down unless the cloud ceiling rose higher, because rain would wipe off the paint job they had just applied, which had taken three months to complete.

"It's the first time we've done it in 20 years," he explained.

I sympathized and said I hoped the weather would clear so he could fly down the next day.

"I'll certainly try," he said.

The next morning, the nasty cold was even nastier, with more rain and clouds than the previous day. I got on the phone again and the pilot said, nope, he couldn't come. But he had an idea.

"When you come back to Houston tomorrow, I'll come get you at the airport and take you to the hangar where the Helldiver is. It's not far and I think I can fit all of you in my SUV. Just call when you get in. My office is right at the airport."

For the rest of the morning we all got on the horn and made flight changes. Then we took a quick tour of antique row, the formerly prosperous heart of downtown Harlingen, and shopped at a grocery store to buy special items to serve my mom's friend Lucy and her daughter Kate, who had agreed to join us for afternoon tea.

Lucy had gone back for her teaching credential at the same time as my mother, both of them with four young children in school. The two of them drove three days a week through all kinds of weather, including blinding winter storms, to two different colleges in Moorhead, which was an hour north of the small river town where both our families lived at the time.

I'd always treasured Lucy for her wit and humor, but due to the stroke, she didn't say much during the tea. Kate spoke in her stead and gently watched over her. (Lucy later recovered a fair bit of her mental alacrity and told her children how delighted she'd been to spend an afternoon with my mom's Cadette buddies.)

We also had a guest named Dolores, who'd become friends with the doctor and his wife after his surgery skills saved her life. They had invited her to the tea because she too had worked in the war industry.

Betty asked her how she found her job.

"I just showed up at one of the factories, watched a demonstration of a machine they used to smooth burrs off a metal part, and then went to work removing burrs," Dolores explained.

"And how much did you make?" I inquired.

"$130 per month," she answered.

I shoved my fist down my throat to keep from commenting. Fresh off the street, Dolores had made exactly the same amount for her work as Curtiss-Wright had paid incoming Cadettes after their ten grueling months of aeronautical-engineering studies.

But the Cadettes were unfazed by the unfairness of this. All the war production veterans went on excitedly describing how they had survived the war and telling stories of resourceful women they knew who had managed to get war industries to provide childcare and basic medical necessities. They saw no need at this late date to quibble over wage disparities. I was the only one having a cow.

The weekend in Harlingen was a wonderful convergence of some of the bright female stars my mother had associated with, even though we didn't get to see the Helldiver fly. At least the next day we'd see it up close on the ground. The only downer was that Cindy couldn't stay to see the plane: she had job responsibilities back in New Orleans — plus her Cadette mother to care for.

Leaving Harlingen entailed just the one previously intimated snag. The young TSA official who checked our IDs against our boarding passes noticed that someone whose ID read Margaret was trying to board using a pass issued to someone named Peggy. I had procured the pass for her and listed her as Peggy. The security guard asked her to step aside while he summoned a senior TSA official. I stepped aside with her.

"Everybody knows that Peggy and Margaret are the same name," I told the guard, hoping to speed things up.

He wasn't having any of it. He was young, and no one in his acquaintance was named Margaret/Peggy. When his superior finally appeared, she was also too young to recognize the names as interchangeable. The plane was due to leave in ten minutes. Peggy decided to just go back to the ticket counter and get a boarding pass in her "Legally Margaret" name. In a few minutes, her composure completely unruffled, she came back through the security line and led the way past me onto the plane.

Caressing "The Big-Tailed Beast"

Most air shows are so crowded that if you get to be anywhere near one of the featured planes, you'll have about 15 seconds to look inside the cockpit as you move lockstep, in a long line of impatient people, up a ladder onto the wing, across it, then down another ladder on the far side. It was actually the best of all possible scenarios that the Cadettes and I got to visit the Helldiver in her lair at Pearland, a small regional airport 20 minutes from Houston's Hobby Airport.

Ed Vesely, the pilot, was as good as his word. He showed up within minutes after I called to tell him we'd arrived. He was so polite and efficient getting us loaded into his car that we were out of the passenger pickup zone in record time and headed to the Helldiver's hangar, passing green fields and pastures down tree-lined country roads, excitedly filling him in on who his distinguished passengers were.

I got out my video camera for the grand opening of the hangar's wide door and filmed the first thing I saw, which happened to be an authentic Japanese Zero, arch enemy of both the Curtiss P-40 *and* the Helldiver in World War II. I realized pretty quickly that my camera was aimed at the wrong target, but then I spotted the Helldiver behind her, wearing a gleaming new coat of cobalt and pale blue, colors the Navy had assigned her in the latter part of the war.

Ed immediately drew our attention to a small table near the side wall of the hangar. On top was a thick volume in a hard cardboard protective case. It looked a bit like the expensive, libraries-only version of the Oxford English Dictionary.

"This," he said, "is the Helldiver handbook."

I was psyched: sitting in front of me (I thought) was the handbook my mother had worked on, editing and re-editing its pages as the constant stream of paper describing engineering changes to the Helldiver flowed through.

I looked inside for the publishing date: February 1945. Since my mother had worked in the Handbooks Group through the end of December 1944, I figured she'd definitely had a hand in this particular edition.

Only much later did I find out that what we were looking at that day was actually *not* the pilot's operating handbook. In my excitement, I had not looked closely. If I had, I would have seen that it was the SB2C maintenance manual, which explained why it was so incredibly thick. The pilot's handbook was much slimmer and far simpler: it had to be easily accessed while flying the plane. I have yet to see an original copy, but I doubt I'll ever find my mother's name as editor or assistant editor on it. Or Betty's. Or Beth's. All three worked in Service Engineering, the department that handled publications. But only the engineers and some of the women in drafting would have put their names or initials on anything, and usually that would have been on the drawings, not the handbooks.

My mother was placed in the Handbooks Group immediately upon "induction" into the plant (quasi-military jargon abounded in private industry during WWII). How she was able to bypass the drafting department, where the majority of newly arrived Cadettes were assigned, and go directly to Service Engineering is a total mystery. But she seems to have had a magnetic, even hypnotizing, power in those years, because doors opened and smoked turkeys (and other commodities) just materialized out of nowhere. This talent exempted her from having to draw the seemingly endless changes to the Helldiver or copy the plane's designs for the two plants in Canada that were also producing them.

Only two members of the Wild Bunch performed drafting work with absolutely no complaint — Peggy Upham and Ruthe Mellott. After the war, Peggy parlayed her Curtiss-Wright drafting skills into a lucrative career, working for petroleum companies engaged in geological exploration. Later, she created an independent drafting business that lasted 22 years. She only closed it down when computer-assisted drafting (CAD) finally became equal and then better to the quality of drawings she could produce by hand. "I refused to sit in front of a computer all day," she told me. "But I miss the people. Badly."

Betty Masket, on the other hand, groaned nonstop about having to do drafting when she was transferred to that department after the Cadettes were taken off inspections.

"I managed to spill a bottle of ink on a drawing, so they moved me to the Handbooks Group with your mom."

Beth also managed to get a transfer to Service Engineering because, as she frequently reminded us, she was "just miserable" at drafting.

Here at last, I thought, as we stood in front of this bulky Curtiss-Wright tome, totally transfixed, is evidence of their editing work. They proudly posed for pictures with the manual, none of us noticing that it was just a little bit south of what they had actually done at Curtiss-Wright.

We moved on to examine the plane. Peggy had talked so much about the design of the tail hook, it was amazing to finally see one. The tail hook is a thin bar of striped red and white metal about six feet long that was supposed to stop the plane during landing by catching a cable stretched across the aircraft carrier. In the original design, it had been retractable, but this proved to be unreliable. So they decided to let it hang at a slight angle below the fuselage. Dangling there under the enormous body of the plane, it looked quite vulnerable, but Ed assured me it really does work, though he has never had to use it: he lands the Beast on dry land runways, not on aircraft carriers.

The Cadettes all walked up close to the Helldiver, stroked it lightly (the paint was still soft), and admired its dive brakes, the perforated flaps on the rear outer edge of the wings that tilt up and down, alternating from one wing to the other to help control the plane during descent. Betty regaled Ed with a much more graphic version of Mary's accident than she'd offered me back in Chevy Chase.

"When we were doing inspections, Mary almost lost her arm because one of these dive brakes was activated by a woman in the cockpit — who was *not* a Cadette. She was supposed to wait for spotters to give her the okay, but she didn't even look at them. Mary was leaning on the dive brake, talking to someone, and suddenly it just jerked up, slicing right into her arm. I was on another plane looking back and I saw her being helped off the line toward first aid, with this thick trail of blood behind her. I got down quick as I could and ran after her to see what was going on. They were getting her ready to go to the hospital, and she didn't seem to be too out of it. But I almost passed out from seeing so much blood, so they gave me an aspirin. They let me go to the hospital in the ambulance with her. We kept saying, 'Go faster. Turn on the siren.' But Mary was so lucid, the driver didn't think it was that serious. They sewed her arm back together so well she didn't even lose any function in her fingers. I know her mom was happy about how good those surgeons were. But Mary sure gave us a big scare."

"And didn't you tell me it was the hydraulic line to the dive brakes where you found the problem during inspections?" I said.

"Yep. When it works, it works really fast. Nothing to fool around with."

Ed offered to let us walk up over the wing and sit in the cockpit. Both Beth and Peggy took him up on it immediately, and I snapped their pictures with thumbs up. I decided I'd rather be in the gunner's seat, facing backward. I climbed in and took hold of the two machine-gun handles, trying to swivel them around and aim them at the ceiling. They were so heavy I couldn't budge them. I was just getting an intimation of how it must feel to spray bullets into the sky at an enemy airplane when Ed arrived at my side. I assumed he would tell me to take my hands off the guns, but he just looked down at me and smiled. "They still work, you know. And those are real bullets."

I asked Ed about the possibility of our getting to ride in the gunner/navigator's seat, any of us who wanted to, during a future Helldiver flight.

"You wouldn't want to," he assured me. "It's so noisy that even with noise-blocking headphones, you feel like you're gonna go deaf. And trust me, these cockpits are anything but warm."

Beth had brought a book with an old photo of the Helldiver that showed a detail of the original color scheme on an apparatus under the fuselage. Ed thanked her because he'd been asking about it while they were painting the Beast and no one knew, so he had just guessed. Now he had confirmation that he'd chosen the right colors.

We walked around oohing and ahhing for a solid 40 minutes, and then it was time to go. We didn't get to see how the wings folded because if you activated them at all, they had to be folded the rest of the way up before they could be straightened again, and the hangar ceiling wasn't high enough. We also couldn't ask Ed to taxi the plane out of the hangar because the Zero was parked in its way. Nonetheless, we had had intimate quality time with "the Big-Tailed Beast."

As Ed was driving us back to the airport, with everyone talking away, he exceeded a school-zone speed limit. A motorcycle cop nabbed us and a solo woman driver just ahead of us. The officer who strode up to Ed's window was a good-looking young man with dark mustache and muscular build. He told Ed to get out his license and registration, and he'd come back after he dealt with the other driver.

As soon as he left, Ed started rummaging through his glove compartment, muttering that he was pretty sure he didn't have his current registration. In the time it took the officer to write a ticket for the lady ahead of us, Ed figured out what to do. As the officer walked back toward us, Ed jumped out to talk to him a short distance from the car. We waited apprehensively. After all he'd done for us, we hated to see him get a ticket.

In a couple of minutes they both came back to the car. Ed was smiling. He told us the officer was absolutely dying to meet the Cadettes.

"Good afternoon, ladies," said the cop. "It's true: I have an incredibly soft heart for World War II vets." The quasi-military jargon had worked its spell on him.

He asked for their autographs, which the Cadettes gladly gave him, and he waxed so sentimental I thought we might need to get out and hug him — or at least take his picture with the Cadettes. But that would have broken too many police-conduct rules. We just laughed and enjoyed being celebrities again. Ed got off without a fine or a ticket.

Traveling with the Cadettes seemed to guarantee cheerful social encounters. I wanted to take them home with me so they could help with the rest of my research. Barbara wouldn't be thrilled to have them take up residence in our house, but she'd surely see the historical necessity of it. The Cadettes, however, all had active lives to get back to. It would just be Peggy and me flying back to Dallas after Betty and Beth caught their flights. We ate a late lunch at the airport and reluctantly went our separate ways.

The goodwill we were summoning by giving long-overdue recognition to the engineering war work of the Cadettes was a charm that kept me smiling all the way home to Taos, especially when I remembered Beth's parting comment: "Jean-Vi, your mother would be so proud of you."

Chapter Four
Angling in Archives

Tangled Up in Taos

When I returned from Dallas, Barbara congratulated me and heaved a sigh of relief. She thought I had done what I set out to do and now life could return to normal. We would plan our various summer outings and visit family and friends on the West Coast and just generally enjoy the good weather. Not wanting to alarm her, I didn't tell her that my research had barely started.

The videotaped interviews of the Wild Bunch in Dallas gave only a tiny part of the picture. I thought if I could only master video editing, I might make something from the tapes to show just how amazing and bright these Cadettes still were. Once people saw the video, they'd jump to help me in my quest.

After pulling my hair out for four weeks, I realized that video editing was a whole new career. My iMac had an allergy to the taped material I fed into it. Even after running it from the camera through two different video-editing software programs to make it "manageable," I kept losing synchronization between video and audio, resulting in deeply annoying silences, hiccups, and bleeps.

I finally decided to let it rest and look for more of the 65-year-old dirt with which to continue sculpting this "Mudwoman of Curtiss-Wright," the female golem[17] who had worked enough magic, in the Columbus plant in particular, to get the company over its engineering humps and help advance Helldiver production.

By the time the Cadettes arrived in January 1944, even though Helldivers had finally joined the Pacific fleet, production had been lagging behind schedule for a good portion of the previous two years. "Finished" Helldivers were routinely parked in an area called "the bone yard" immediately after they exited Building 3's main production line. They were then fed through the modification building for the latest design changes. The first Helldivers approved for combat had flown against the Japanese on November 11, 1943, at Rabaul, in Papua New Guinea. Those missions, however, produced a whole new spate of EOs for Helldiver changes. So by the time my mother's class of '43 reported for work in January 1944, there was still plenty of testing, redesign, and drafting work awaiting the Cadettes.

With only the sketchy summary provided by Warren Bruner to back me up, I couldn't yet assert without a shadow of a doubt that the Cadettes' work was a deciding factor in the timely production of the Helldiver. But after talking for so many days with my mother's friends and other Cadettes from the Purdue class of '43, I felt certain there was more to find about their actual contributions at the plant.

Before the Dallas/Harlingen trip, I had contacted the engineering department at the University of Texas to ask about their files on the Cadettes. The secretary in the engineering dean's office begged off, referring me to their library and archives. Three different librarians tried to scrounge something up, but all they found was a brief mention of the Cadette Program in their archival database. They referred me back to the engineering department. After further inquiry, it appeared that engineering had no official memory of having taught them. They also didn't seem to care that they couldn't find their own records on the program. I was aghast but couldn't persuade anyone to look more closely.

I also couldn't find any University of Texas Cadettes in the list of over 100 women who had attended the 50th National Cadette Reunion in Columbus in October of 1994. I found this very strange. Texas was the only one of the seven participating schools that wasn't represented. The

Texas-trained Cadettes, who had mostly been assigned to work in Curtiss-Wright's St. Louis plant, seemed to be missing in action.

I knew the Cadettes had been at Texas (95 of them in fact) because the Bruner Report confirmed it. I also had copies of "The Cadetter," a monthly mimeo of cartoons and writing produced during their training, with contributions by Cadettes on all seven campuses. That's where I found the names of five different Texas Cadettes. So I Googled the one with the most unusual name and found a picture of her doing her work for Curtiss-Wright St. Louis on the website of Rosie the Riveter/WWII Home Front National Historic Park in Richmond, California.

This park had been created ten years earlier, but I'd never heard of it, even though I'd lived in the Bay Area for 18 years. They were gathering histories and artifacts from every type of work people had done during the war (especially from women and blacks and other minorities). Visiting Barbara's family on the West Coast in June began to seem like a very good plan indeed.

Dorothy (Not in Kansas)

After I first saw a copy of the program for the Cadettes' 50th reunion, I called the main organizer of the event, Dorothy Wurster Rout. Dorothy graduated with the Purdue class of '44 and lives in Columbus. She would turn out to be a tremendously important connection, although subject to occasional short- and long-term memory lapses. She had kept regular contact with the engineering department at Purdue, including two professors I later spoke with who immediately asked about her when they heard I was researching the Cadette Program. In some kind of poetic justice, they remembered her, even as she was becoming more vague about them.

Dorothy also referred me to the long-term keeper (and updater) of the Purdue '43 Cadette address list, Lois Neff Haynes, who lives in Waco, Texas. Her memory is sharp as a tack, but she has become too physically disabled to get around freely any more. Her tongue, however, is quite mobile and gave me some fairly horrifying details of how the Cadettes had been "released" at the end of the war.

Lois told me she'd been called into the office to discuss whether she'd like to stay or leave and was reminded that if she stayed she would be preventing someone who "really needed a job" from getting one — as if the Cadettes themselves, most of whom were still single, had no need of employment.

I'd already heard from Betty that "the minute the war ended [on Victory in Japan/V-J Day, August 15, 1945], they fired us all." But Dorothy gave me an even more damning picture of how Curtiss-Wright parted company with "those women engineers": "They gave the Cadettes notification of termination on the radio. They ran an announcement telling us not to come in to work."

Glad as they were to have the war ended, the Cadettes were gravely wounded to find out how disposable they were.

"Yeah," Dorothy said. "I got a 'radio pink slip.'"

A small number of Cadettes, including Peggy and Ruthe from my mother's group, were retained for a couple of weeks to finish the drawings of the Helldiver, which the company continued to manufacture after the war.[18] The other four "Dingies," who'd lost their jobs at the plant, hung a large banner over the door expressing their sincere appreciation to their roomies, "the breadwinners and bacon-fetchers."

Like Rosie the Riveter, Wanda the Welder, Women Airforce Service Pilots (WASP), and American women in all fields of industrial and other war-related work, the Curtiss-Wright Cadettes were expected to go home. Make babies. Clean house. And (in the Cadettes' case) leave aeronautical engineering to the men.

This was true for all but a few. A handful of Cadettes received letters within a week or two requesting them to return to the Columbus engineering department to perform rudimentary tasks, including elementary drafting and basic computations. A couple of other Cadettes who worked at the Research Department in Buffalo were asked to stay on assisting senior engineers who were still trying to come up with experimental designs that would keep the airplane division viable.

But overall, Curtiss-Wright happily hid behind Congress's law requiring companies to give returning servicemen their old jobs back. The company assigned some of their Cadette re-hires to retrain vets who had worked in Curtiss-Wright engineering departments before the war, updating them on new designs and procedures, and then move aside. None of the Cadettes were offered additional training.

Some of the Cadette re-hires lasted until November 1950, when the airplane division declared bankruptcy. How the airplane division was able to declare bankruptcy is a mystery: the company had amassed $175 million in war production profits (today's value: about $10 billion). These funds, which could have been used to fulfill Curtiss-Wright's oft-repeated pledge to "upgrade" the women engineers and help them advance into full-time careers in aviation after the war, were plowed back into the company or deposited in the pockets of shareholders instead.

Curtiss-Wright was not alone in this: most of the engineering departments in aviation companies around the country reverted to male exclusivity. With little prospect of engineering work, Cadettes who didn't immediately marry and start families went back to school in fields that would guarantee them employment; a great number of them found they could use their advanced math skills for teaching in the public schools and in colleges. But it would be several decades before female aero-engineers began to emerge in significant numbers from university programs. By then the design and direction of aviation would be so advanced that these women would no longer learn how to build a flying vehicle from the ground up as the Curtiss-Wright Cadettes had.

One of the most promising informants that Dorothy referred me to was a good buddy of hers named Nolan Leatherman, an engineer who had gone to work in 1957 for North American Aviation, the company that took control of the plant in Columbus after Curtiss-Wright left. Nolan had been the head of contracts for many years, and he stayed on after North American merged with Rockwell International in 1980. He finally left when that company was bought by McDonnell Douglas in 1988.

Nolan knew a great deal about the physical layout of the plant and considerable detail about Curtiss-Wright's years there. He sent me in-house magazines, including the *Fly Leaf*, which was basically the corporation's brag sheet about their great plans and accomplishments. Their other regular publication during the war, the *Curtiss-Wright-er*, was a morale booster for employees and reported personal stories (including combat deaths) of those who had worked in the plant before they enlisted or were drafted.

One issue, November 1943, sported a color picture on the cover of a stunningly beautiful Cadette working at a drafting table. Inside was a three-page article about the training the "girls" were receiving, with pictures of them in the machine shop at one of the universities. The rest of the shots showed them in classrooms, studying in their dorm rooms, or in front of an engineering building. This was apparently Warren Bruner's first contribution to the *Fly Leaf*, as his name did not appear in earlier issues. He had recently been hired as the Cadette Training Program coordinator, working out of new offices in Buffalo.

According to Warren, they had planned to start a second program in January 1944, in which 400 more women would be trained, but that program had to be cancelled. The next one didn't start until July 1944, and by then the training had been compressed from 10 months to just six. This article in the November '43 *Fly Leaf* was Warren's announcement to the plants that these well-trained women engineers would be arriving, ready to work, in the new year. But the *Fly Leaf* never printed another article about the Cadettes.

This kind of grand trumpet blast about their impending arrival, I discovered, was as far as the propaganda department of Curtiss-Wright would ever go. Even the local newspapers in the cities where the plants were located exhausted all their interest in the Cadettes after blowing their "Here come the Cadettes!" horns. Not one paper, in or out of the Columbus plant, published profiles or interviews with the Cadettes describing their actual performance in the plants. Apparently, because the enormous engineering departments were scrambling to crank out drawings and designs (especially in Columbus, which had such difficulties with its key product), the Cadettes at work were not deemed newsworthy.

As Bruner said in his December '44 summary, "It is probably true that during their schooling the Cadettes had been made too much of.

It is equally true that after induction into the plants they were made very little of."

When I heard Cadettes describe the gargantuan size of the plants they worked in and the difficulty they had finding their way down to the production line (for engineering liaison or fact-checking against the planes on the line) and then retracing their steps back to the engineering department, I could see how they might disappear. Plus, there were tight security rules about where they could go. War-production factories checked employees' purses and other personal belongings as the workers entered and left to make sure no one had designs of the products or pictures taken inside the plant. None of the women could even bring home photos of each other working. Overall this gives the impression that the Cadettes were never really there. If there *were* pictures of them at work, the official propaganda office might not have kept them after the program ended.

In all this time, I have found only one picture of the Cadettes inside the Curtiss–Columbus plant. It shows 15 Cadette inspectors (including Betty Masket and Mary Sprow) standing in front of a Helldiver or lying flat on its wing. They are all wearing dark lipstick and are dressed to kill, in pumps and skirts rather than the slacks and coveralls they wore when crawling around doing inspections. Three Curtiss-Wright engineers in proper dark suits stand with or squat next to them. I first saw this photo when Betty brought it to our group rendezvous in Dallas. She had it on loan from Jackie Warren Davis, another Cadette inspector, who also lives in Chevy Chase. This picture, I found out later, had far more door-opening power than any crowbar or charming verbal pitch I could ever come up with.

The Gander on the Golden Egg

No matter how many closed doors I ran into while searching for an insider's perspective from within the company's management or its engineering departments, I couldn't stop hoping that something definitive would surface, like the notes of a plant manager or personnel director, something that would let us know what value Curtiss-Wright really placed on their acquisition of female engineers.

Promisingly, Nolan Leatherman gave me the name and phone number of an engineer he'd worked with at North American. He told me this man could be of real help to me as he was the grandson of a man I shall call "Guy I" (for reasons that will shortly become evident), the engineer who oversaw the amazingly fast construction of the Columbus plant. It sounded like my prayers were about to be answered. I couldn't wait to speak with Guy III.

The *Fly Leaf* issue Nolan had sent me about Curtiss-Wright's expansion in 1941 said the new Columbus plant was 1.2 million square feet and was built and ready for occupancy in approximately ten months. Ten months —the same amount of time my mother's Cadette group had been given to absorb all that engineering information. This company sure got things up and running in the wink of an eye.

In 1950, in a similar eye-winking manner, as the airplane division was closing because they "ran out" of government contracts, a huge pile of plane designs and photographs was spirited out of their offices and into the hands of Guy I's son. This cache included documents from the St. Louis and Buffalo plants, which had closed right after the war when the airplane division decided to consolidate in Columbus. In other words, this was the mother lode of all Curtiss-Wright airframe plant documents from WWII.

Guy II (whether with official consent or just a wink) took possession of thousands of photos, designs, and other corporate documents. When he died, Nolan explained, his son, Guy III, claimed possession of the collection. At retirement, he moved it all to his new home in another state.

I thought this could be a real bonanza. While interviewing the Cadettes in Texas, I had kept my fingers crossed: Guy the Third would be my Deep Throat, providing the kind of documents about the Cadette Program I needed most. Maybe he would even turn up pictures of my mother and her friends in the plant. Curtiss-Wright's airplane division could *never* have been so callous as to dump all evidence of the women engineers who stepped in to fill positions in testing, design, liaison work with the line, drafting, and final preflight inspection. Their service to the company was too important.

What I wasn't really registering yet was that at the height of the war, Curtiss-Wright Columbus employed over 24,000 people, working three shifts around the clock. Even though there were 365 Cadettes working in the plant, they had almost no consciousness of their own numbers. Over and over I heard surprise from Cadettes when I mentioned how many of them were in the plant. Most of them only knew and socialized with others from their own training group. For example, the 92 Cadettes from Minnesota never made contact with (or even knew about) those from Purdue (groups numbering 80, 98, and 77) or Iowa State (16) or the University of Texas (2). Even the different Purdue groups didn't really mingle.

Far stranger was the fact that Lester Hall, an assistant project engineer on the Helldiver through the end of 1944, said he never even knew there *were* women engineers in the plant.[19] I concluded from this that senior engineers like Les were working at a significant physical remove from the main engineering department, which functioned as a highly skilled draftswoman pool.

The women in that pool, after ten intensive months of training, could read engineering orders and quickly draw the changes with technical precision. Many of these women never even left their drafting tables. But others (liaison engineers in particular) regularly traveled between the engineering department and the production line. Some even made trips through the long, enclosed outdoor walkway to Building 3A, a large sub- and final-assembly building. Several Cadettes told me they worried about getting lost in their travels between the engineering department and the line, so they would create a mental diagram of their route and try to retrace it exactly.

When I look at the picture of the Cadettes on the Helldiver wing, I wonder how these beautiful women could ever have gotten lost, even in a huge plant. The men working on the line, no matter how busy, would surely have noticed them: the ones I've seen were drop-dead gorgeous, especially when wearing skirts and dark lipstick. And since they were doing technical rather than physical work, they didn't have to pull their hair back in nets. The men on the line would somehow have managed to stop and point any "lost Cadettes" in the right direction.

So where in that huge conglomeration was my mother? In a little cluster of desks designated "Service Engineering" somewhere in the middle of the vast open engineering room with its rows upon rows of drafting tables. She was just across an aisle from the big desks used by salesmen and lesser company managers, an area known as "mahogany row," according to the plant manager's secretary, Arlene Kelly. (Arlene told me she never got to leave the manager's office, so she didn't know about the Cadettes either.)

With only six Cadettes in the pilot's handbook section of Service Engineering, my mother and two of her best buddies, along with three other women I've never heard named, must have felt like they were huddled on an island in the middle of a huge storm of people and paper. Fifty years later, when my mother was asked by the reunion committee about her work in the plant, she wrote, "I have no idea what I was doing there." I think she meant the size of the operation overwhelmed her. Even though engineering was not her calling, I know she would never have been permitted to work on the pilot's handbook if she were not technically informed and a capable editor.

Shortly after my return from Dallas, I finally called Guy the Third. At first, I thought he really was "the man." He talked nonstop about his grandfather, the plant, the planes, the phenomenal success of Curtiss-Wright. Yes, he'd heard of the Cadette Program. He even recognized the name Warren Bruner and said Warren had been a good friend of his grandfather, though he didn't recall seeing any documents about the Cadettes. He promised to peruse the huge collection of boxes to see if there was anything in his grandfather's correspondence or in the extensive photo collection on the plant and the Helldiver.

Just to be certain I knew how substantial his holdings were, he told me that the Smithsonian's National Air and Space Museum had asked him to donate them for its Curtiss-Wright Collection. He bragged that he had told them no, he was saving them for his daughter, who is a pilot. Most of the call consisted of a recitation of technical details about various warbirds, followed by the academic achievements and engineering successes of both his parents and himself. Of my 45 minutes on the phone, the exchange about the Cadettes took maybe five.

I waited for Guy the Third to contact me but got no word. Three weeks later I decided to politely inquire by phone if he'd had a chance to look in the boxes yet. He became irritated.

"I don't like it when people start thinking they're my boss and can tell me when to get something done. Especially if they think they're going to make money from things that belong to me. But yes, actually I did find a few items. I'll scan them for you and send them on."

I received no scans, but he did add my name to his email list for patriotic and Christian fundamentalist postings.

After six weeks, I had received no scans. I finally sent an email to ask if he was still planning to help with my research. I got no reply, but shortly after that the unsolicited emails stopped.

I asked at various museums, including the Smithsonian's National Air and Space Museum (NASM), whether there was any legal recourse to recover documents from World War II that would be of historical interest to the American people, especially when many of them had been created and paid for as part of government contracts. Everyone I spoke to said no, there was nothing to be done except wait for him to die. Seeing as how he's two years younger than I am, it's likely to be a long wait.

One of the stories Guy III told me was that there is a complete Helldiver buried under the tarmac behind Building 3 (the primary plant building his grandfather helped construct). He said a Helldiver had come off the line and was sitting out back when a pusher vehicle ran into it, damaging it so badly it couldn't be repaired. They were in such a rush to meet production quotas, he said, that rather than let it take up precious space, they dug a hole and buried it.

I passed the story along to pilot Ed Vesely in Houston. If it was true, he'd have access to hard-to-find spare parts for the CAF's Helldiver. He inquired of Guy III directly whether it was true. Guy III said, "Oh yes, absolutely, but you'll never get near it because you have to have high security clearance due to all the EPA contamination issues you'd invoke by disturbing the soil." He claimed that he himself had that rating.

Ed quickly put the story out of his mind.

Seven months later, I talked to an engineer named Otto Acker who had worked in the Columbus plant all through the war. He assured me there was zero truth to the rumor.

"Stories of that magnitude get around," he said. "And I never heard it. Nope. There was never a Helldiver buried whole at Columbus."

Rosie the Irreverent

One of the mementos I had brought home from my New York theater trip in 2008 was a poster from a woman comedian's show that caught my eye one afternoon as I walked through Greenwich Village. The comedian was pictured in classic Rosie the Riveter pose: a bandana holding her hair back and one arm crooked at the elbow to show off her big bicep. The main distinguishing feature, however, was that the hand in the poster was clenched into a fist with the third finger in the air: "Rosie the Irreverent." Unfortunately, I was already booked for the night of the show, but I grabbed the poster for my wall because it was, well, riveting.

So in June 2009, when I finally got to the Rosie the Riveter Memorial in Richmond, California, I didn't think I was going to be particularly reverent. But was I in for a surprise. The memorial was built on the site of Kaiser Shipyard #2, one of five huge factories operating in World War II around San Francisco and San Pablo bays. Shipyard #2 had built a large number of Liberty Ships for transporting munitions and supplies during the war.

The memorial itself was 442 feet long, the standard length of a Liberty Ship, with planted flower beds to indicate where the hatches had been. A walkway extended down the middle from stern to bow, spaced with chronological plaques and photos. The stern was a standing metal abstract with windows for pictures and writing about women and minority workers who had struggled to get hired by factories dedicated to the war effort. According to one of the many plaques reciting events, changes in war-work legislation, and quotations from workers, up until the invasion of Normandy on D-Day (June 6, 1944), more people died in American factories making ships, planes, tanks, munitions, and other equipment for the war than in combat overseas.[20]

I was stunned! I had never heard my mother or anyone talk of so many disabling injuries and deaths in the factories. Other than Mary's big cut to her arm, none of the Columbus Cadettes had said a word about physical dangers in that plant. Of course they were in the engineering department most of the time and weren't witness to what happened on the production line on a daily basis, except for those first few months when they got to do inspections, so perhaps they just didn't see other work-related accidents.

As I walked the length of the ship to where its prow, in the form of a curved wooden observation deck a couple of feet above the sand, touched the water, I felt I had been unjust in my assumption that Rosie the Riveter and Wanda the Welder had been mere peons in the war machine. In fact, the challenging manual labor they did seemed more meritorious than some of the low-level tracing and drawing the Cadettes were assigned. (The biggest threat to Cadettes at their drafting tables was arm cramp and boredom.) After all, what was technical sophistication worth compared to the incredible courage it took to crawl deep into small spaces in dark ship hulls with only a lantern and your tools? Or to stand with your neck crooked back and weld iron plates while molten slag pours down. One woman worker stated: "It took many years for the small white scars to go away from the hot rolling slag."

But as I stood there reading the plaques, I saw again, with even greater clarity, that the reason to resurrect this story about women aeronautical engineers was not just because their work was more technical or sophisticated. What kept *me* crawling deeper into *my* dark little space was what "Ms. Think Purple!" had urged me to consider: How would the world look and feel if women contributed fully half of the creativity and production expertise for all of the world's designs? Would there even *be* Liberty Ships? More important — would there be world wars and killing in such great numbers if most women weren't relegated to subservient, less-than-full-partnership roles? My mythic image of the Cadettes as the Sisters of Icarus made me wonder again if, given the encouragement and the funds to imagine and explore and experiment, my mother, her friends, and the other Cadettes would have been able to use all that math and aero-engineering knowledge to some completely different end than producing the machinery of war.

The Flying Pancake came whizzing past the corner of my eye again. What a wonderful shape. No wonder the UFO enthusiasts often picture alien vehicles that way. What if all these Cadettes could have been employed after the war to make personal flying vehicles that were completely safe and very slow, not trying to rush over great distances and destroy a target, but simply help you run errands or go to the dentist? How could we get control of the skies out of the hands of war-makers and into the minds of home-makers who seek to preserve rather than destroy the human family?

Such a big question — and "Ms. Think Purple!" nowhere to be found. I had, however, made the virtual acquaintance of a young feminist professor of engineering education at Purdue named Alice Pawley who seemed like a potential ally in my quest to restore the Cadettes to aeronautical engineering history. I didn't have to be a scientist to see this through. I just had to have enough vision and like-minded teammates to stand strong in the face of the naysayers and are-you-out-of-your-mind-please-go-away-sayers who scoff at a wave of such magnitude before it even begins to roll ashore. I had sent a long, impassioned description of my vision of the "Cadette history recovery project" to Professor Pawley and was still waiting for a reply.

In the meantime I let the currents sweep me north toward Seattle. There was an assistant curator at Boeing Field's Museum of Flight I need-ed to talk to who would, I hoped, continue to fire me up. I was still looking for evidence that Curtiss-Wright hadn't just trained over 900 women in aeronautical engineering to maximize company profits and squeak by on the backs of their "junior engineering" efforts. If I could just find proof that at least one engineer or manager had given due credit to the Cadettes' accomplishments on the job, I'd be able to deliver up this chunk of hidden history with the glow of Kryptonite still on it rather than just dust and decay. These women had not served their country in vain. Nor had they been given access to the secrets of flight for just a day. They had actually been handed a key to early aviation design, and no one but no one, if I had anything to say about it, was going to hide or pocket that key again — without acknowledging the distinct smudges of the Cadettes' fingerprints all over it.

The Boeing Bounce

My plan in Seattle was to casually drop by the archives where the assistant cura-
tor I'd spoken to about Burdette Wright worked. I didn't know where he was
located, just somewhere at Boeing Field near the Museum of Flight. I didn't
even know if I'd be welcome, but it seemed unlikely I would be turned away.

Boeing Field, the original World War II heart of the now-sprawling
company, is south of Seattle's downtown and covers many thousands of
acres. Boeing's present-day production facilities are actually a distance
from this site in two separate Seattle suburbs. By happenstance, Barbara's
sister's house, where we were staying, was fairly close to the back side of
Boeing Field. So that's how I approached it — through an old, somewhat
derelict neighborhood. As soon as I drove onto the property I could see
the Museum of Flight's fancy multistory glass-and-steel complex, which is
about four times bigger than Dallas's Frontiers of Flight Museum. Once
inside, I asked the first person I saw wearing a museum uniform how to
reach the archives. He directed me through the museum and out the back
door to an old two-story brick building behind the museum.

The youngish man who opened the door back there was John Little,
the assistant curator I'd spoken to months earlier. I introduced myself and
he clearly remembered our conversation. I supposed he didn't often get
inquiries about Curtiss-Wright's Cadette Program. We sat down at one of
the research tables and talked about the old Curtiss-Wright plants and cor-
porate offices and where in the world they might have stashed the records
on the Cadette Program.

John clarified, however, that the facility we were in was not Boeing's
archives but the Museum of Flight's Research Center, which had no con-
nection to Boeing. They had an extensive archive and library on aviation
but none of the proprietary records Boeing inherited when it acquired
Curtiss-Wright's patents. Seeing my disappointment, he said he could give
me the name of one of the curators at the actual Boeing archives.

"Their archives are in a thermonuclear-bomb–proof shelter half an
hour east of Seattle's downtown," he said. "I've only been there once, but it
was very dark, certainly not a place I'd want to work."

"Hmm — they must have some really important material to be so worried about security," I ventured. But clearly, I would not be just dropping by.

I repeated the story I'd heard from Curtiss-Wright's corporate headquarters about a flood ruining their stored documents, and he said, yes, he'd heard that, too. I also told him that the Cadette Program had been coordinated from the airplane division's main offices in Buffalo, but that since they had closed the Buffalo and St. Louis plants right after the war, they must have moved all their corporate records from both those plants to Columbus, where the airplane division was being consolidated.

John said he might be able to locate some material of interest for me in the library, just beyond a set of double doors. I tagged along with him toward those doors, and as he was about to go through them, they opened from the other side and the main curator, a tall man in his 60s, walked through.

Dan Hagedorn said he was on his way to a late lunch. But after he found out what I was researching, he stayed to talk because he, too, is fascinated by Curtiss-Wright.

"I worked in Buffalo from 1970 to '77," Dan said. "During that time I checked out all the major libraries, newspapers, and university archives, looking for stuff on Curtiss-Wright. I even ran several ads in local newspapers, asking anyone with information about the Curtiss–Buffalo operations in World War II to contact me. I received maybe three responses, none of them terribly useful. It was almost as if Curtiss-Wright hadn't been a major element in the local landscape."

I was amazed to hear of this informational vacuum. Having Google-mapped my way down to close-up views of Curtiss-Wright's old Buffalo plants and the buildings that housed their research department and corporate offices, I knew how big their presence in Buffalo had been during the war. If the curator of a reputable aviation archive couldn't find evidence of Curtiss-Wright in Buffalo, how in the world was I going to locate material on the Cadette Program, which was even more marginal? Surely they would have packed it up and sent it along to Columbus with everything else. Or would they dump it because the program was done? Maybe though (and this thought carries me to this day), the Cadette Program coordinator, Warren Bruner, took home some (or all) of the records because nobody else wanted them.

Following the train of thought John and I had been riding, I shared with Dan my picture of how Curtiss-Wright's records converged on Columbus from Buffalo and St. Louis and then shifted east to the company's engine plant at Wood-Ridge, New Jersey, where the flood had supposedly consumed a great many of them.

"I'm pretty certain that flood is apocryphal," Dan said. "I don't believe they ever had one. They just don't want to deal with it."

The little gnome inside me who gets excited whenever my gut intuitions are validated jumped up and down so hard I thought its gyrations might be visible to Dan. Then the history fairy who flits through my posterior lobe started reminding me that I'd seen a blog called "Lost in Jersey," full of photographs and stories written by a guy who had gone hunting for dead and decrepit historical sites throughout the state. One section of the blog focused entirely on the Wood-Ridge facility. If anything from the Cadette Program *did* wind up in New Jersey, the prospect of looking for it at Wood-Ridge was dark and dangerous — if you put any stock in the posts on that blog.

The site's creator described World War II underground bunkers, interconnecting tunnels, and abandoned test cells that he had personally seen and explored. Blog entries by a series of young intruders about nocturnal escapades into the forbidden spaces of *other* New Jersey sites were frequently vague or contradictory. But when it came to Curtiss-Wright's engine plant at Wood-Ridge, their stories became truly disturbing.

As with all Curtiss-Wright facilities from World War II, Wood-Ridge was built with government funds and was therefore officially the property of the Defense Plant Corporation (later known as the War Assets Administration). It encompassed 140 acres and two dozen buildings. The engine manufacturing plant itself covered 30 acres. The night-raiders exploring Wood-Ridge described its decrepit infinitude as having large chambers with very weird acoustics, sealed-off doors, flooded tunnels with floating barrels of toxic waste, and rooms full of machine parts, entire engines, and boxes of papers. They claimed it was all pitch dark and went down two to three stories belowground.

The blog version of this plant was like a not-quite-sealed time capsule from World War II, full of gunpowder, grime, and groady goo, but promising room after room of underground possibility. All I could think was, "I'm going to need a hazmat suit, several assistants, lots of lights, and tools to break down those sealed doors and pry open boxes. Yes, I will find those Cadette records. And no, I will not turn back on account of toxic water. Somebody has to do it. Why not me?"

My real-world skeptic, the one who keeps the bouncing gnome and the history fairy in check, began to question my sanity: "This is going to take years and probably any number of legal assists just to gain access. You'll be broke and contaminated and what if you don't find anything?"

I woke up from this three-way internal conference call and found I was still talking to Dan Hagedorn at the Museum of Flight's Research Center. He was giving me a number of recommendations for continuing research in Buffalo, including State University of New York (SUNY) Buffalo and the former Cornell Research Facility (CALSPAN) that had once been part of Curtiss-Wright, which housed one of the first really big wind tunnels.

We walked halfway across the main room and were standing in front of the entry door when two new guys walked in, one of them the co-author of a book I'd heard about several times called *Curtiss-Wright: Greatness and Decline*. A review on Amazon had faulted it for whitewashing corporate management's irresponsible behavior, so I had avoided buying it. But after meeting Edward Young, I was ready to give it a second chance.

When Dan introduced us, he said, "Ed, here's someone I want you to meet. She speaks fluent Curtiss-Wright." I had to laugh: the history of the company often does feel like a lost or forgotten language — perhaps even a dead one.

When I told Ed about the Cadettes, he said he didn't know anything about them.

"You're not the first," I said lightly, but I was upset that someone so versed in the company history had never heard of the program. His book had been published 11 years earlier, and I wondered if maybe he or his co-author had actually included some teensy little reference to "women engineers" (without calling them Cadettes or even engineers) and Ed just didn't remember it. But when I later bought his book and scoured it for anything that might be corporate management's veiled reference to the Cadettes, there was indeed nothing.

The Boeing archives lead turned out to be a total dead end: the archivist claimed they had never had any Curtiss-Wright documents whatsoever. But I left Seattle feeling that I had been officially scanned and accepted for membership by a significant chapter of the aviation-history-buff clan. If I could pass muster on hallowed Boeing ground, I could pass anywhere that my investigative flat feet might take me, even though all the aviation-history-loving men, no matter how curious and cooperative, kept coming up empty-handed on the Cadettes.

Turning East: Augie the August

When I came back to Taos I set my sights on another, longer visit to the National Archives and Records Administration (in Washington, D.C., and College Park, Maryland), as well as the Smithsonian's National Air and Space Museum. But I needed an insider's help. I decided to call Curtiss-Wright again.

This time I spoke to company historian Paul Ferdenzi, who referred me to the communications director, Michael Stock. Both of them repeated the probable apocrypha about the "flood," although in this version it was the result of a broken water main. Finally I asked Mike if he could tell me how the donation of their historical records to the Smithsonian had been handled. He directed me to a curator at NASM named Phil Edwards.

Phil responded right away with a long description of what was in the Curtiss-Wright Collection at the National Air and Space Museum and how best to begin my probe of the National Archives. "College Park will be your best bet," he said. "But don't expect too much on your first visit and give it plenty of time."

He also advised me to make an appointment at NASM's Preservation, Restoration and Storage Facility in Suitland, Maryland, which is southeast of Washington, D.C.

"And do it soon because they're going to be moving to a new facility so they'll be shut down for several months. They have a large collection of Curtiss-Wright photos, because I saw them when they first arrived at NASM in 1969. In fact, I supervised the accession of all the Curtiss-Wright historical documents. Unfortunately, there are almost no corporate administrative records. They're not required by law to keep them."

I was thrilled to finally find somebody who had seen the stuff when it first came in 40 years ago. Phil invited me to NASM's main facility on the Capitol Mall so he could show me the collection of Curtiss-Wright's in-house newspaper for employees, the *Curtiss-Wright-er*.

Since I'd be in striking range, I thought about visiting the Wood-Ridge, New Jersey, engine plant. During the war, the engine division had retained its old name (Wright Aeronautical Corporation) among Curtiss-Wright engineers, a holdover from the old competition between companies formed by Curtiss and those formed by the Wright Brothers. Even so, over the main entry to the plant at 32 Passaic Street (thanks again to Google Maps), you can make out the remnants of the old Curtiss-Wright sign, missing the 'CUR' of Curtiss and the 'W' from Wright.

A large property-development company has acquired the site, so I called their corporate office; they told me to look at several online news pieces about plans for the site. One of them listed an engineer who had worked there for 30 years, including the WWII years. He had retired in 1969 when the plant closed. I checked phone listings for the area and found him.

August Zoll was just sitting at home as if waiting for my call, though actually he keeps busy, in his late 80s, volunteering at the local aviation-history museum. He had heard of the Cadettes, but only after the war, from another volunteer at the museum who was a Cadette. Before she died, she donated the same Curtiss-Wright recruitment brochures I had received from the Glenn H. Curtiss Museum.

I told Augie the engine division had opted out of the Cadette Program.

Curtiss-Wright Cadettes, entering class, Purdue University, 1943. Full Cadette Class of '43 roster available on the website: wildharepress.com/flyingintoyesterday.

Betty Lu (later Ricki) Cruse, age 14, October 1938, Daisetta, Texas.

Betty Lu (Ricki) Cruse, Stephens College, age 17, 1941.

Ricki Cruse, graduate, Curtiss-Wright Cadette Program, December 1943.

Ricki and Reuben Lenthe, with son, Roger Drew, September 1946.

Wild Bunch Reunion, Dallas, 1991. L to R: Peggy Upham, Beth Benson, Ruthe Mellott, Ricki Lenthe, Mary Sprow, Betty Masket.

Wild Bunch with author, same hotel, 2009.

"Flying Pancake" in flight, February 22, 1943 (prototype being refurbished at Triumph Aerostructures – Vought Aircraft Division, Grand Prairie, Texas, Dick Atkins, team leader). Photo credit: Vought Archives.

Wild Bunch Cadettes Peggy Adams (Upham), Beth Benson (Wehner), Betty Henson (Masket); and Jean-Vi Lenthe, model workshop, Frontiers of Flight Museum, Love Field, Dallas, Texas, March 2009. Photo credit: William McWhorter, Texas Historical Commission

Curtiss Wright Cadettes
Purdue-1943

JO JOHNSON

JAYNE ALLEN

ELOISE LAPP

Purdue 1943 Cadettes: Josephine Johnson (Jackson) and Jayne Allen (Abney) with slide rules in mechanical drawing class; Eloise Lapp (Ruby) in flight simulator training.

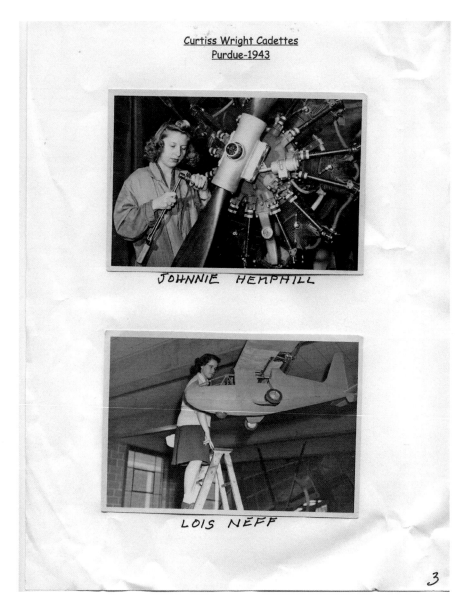

Curtiss Wright Cadettes
Purdue-1943

JOHNNIE HEMPHILL

LOIS NEFF

3

1943 Cadettes: Johnnie Hemphill (Coyner) practicing engine teardown and rebuilding on Curtiss Cyclone; Lois Neff (Haynes) inspecting airplane model in wind tunnel laboratory.

Warren Bruner, coordinator of Cadette Training Program, September 1943 to August 15, 1945.
Photo credit: Hobart and William Smith College

Ruth Cleverly Klick, Cadette Training Program supervisor and first hired interviewer, August 1942 to September 1943.

Curtiss-Wright-er *(employee newspaper), September 29, 1944. Class of '44 Purdue Cadettes ("slide-rule commandos"): Jane McWhite, Nancy Donovan, and Marian Smith in shop class; Sue Barber (Kilgo), Catherine McKnight (Muesenfechter), and Lavinia Wicker (Spilman) at drafting tables.*

George Palmer, senior aeronautical engineering student, with Cadettes (Class of '44), teaching aerodynamics class, Purdue University. Dorothy Wurster (Rout), keeper of Cadette history and 1994 50th reunion organizer, stands directly behind his left shoulder.

George Palmer with Cadette sweetheart Minna Burgess (Connor), Purdue Class of '44.

Jay Smith (Betty Masket's great-nephew), writer for Model Aviation Magazine, *after Jean-Vi's Purdue talk: "Slide-Rule Packin' Mamas," November 12, 2009.*

Purdue aeronautical engineering professors emeritus George Palmer and L.T. (Larry) Cargnino, November 9, 2009.

Author Jean-Vi Lenthe, after her talk at Purdue's Engineering Education Department, November 12, 2009.

Curtiss-Wright Columbus airframe plant, engineering department, June 1941.

Above: Les Hall, assistant project engineer, SB2C Helldiver, at his drafting table, Columbus, Ohio, 1943.

Above right: Standing in front of an SB2C. Les was sent aboard a carrier to watch Helldiver trials; he was issued a uniform and special documents granting him permission to board a U.S. Navy ship because government regulations forbade nonmilitary observers during the war.

In the "bone yard" behind Building 3, SB2C Helldiver final modifications and preflight inspections continue through the night, Columbus, Ohio.

Helldiver test pilots in front of four-blade propeller model SB2C-4, Columbus, Ohio.

Curtiss Fly Leaf *cover, July-August, 1944, featuring model of Helldiver SB2C-4 with three-blade propeller.*

Program cover for "Anchors Aweigh," a musical production by Curtiss-Wright employees in Columbus, May 10-11, 1943.

SB2C Helldivers lined up behind Columbus plant, 1944.

Last flying SB2C Helldiver, owned by Commemorative Air Force, Cactus Squadron, at CAF "Airsho" in Midland, Texas, November 2009. Photo credit: Linn McKeighan

Columbus Area Cadettes, 2009. Standing: Anne Rill Yates (Iowa State '43), Nova Anderson Weller and Kay Atkinson (Purdue '45). Seated: Mary Lou Stuber Wright and Dorothy Wurster Rout (Purdue '44).

Jean-Vi and Ricki, 1999, Moorhead, Minnesota.

Class of '45 Cadettes at Purdue, residents of Curtiss House (one of three fraternity houses used by the Cadette Program). Photo credit: Nova Weller

Columbus Area Cadettes receiving framed photos of their sister Cadettes (inspectors) while on tour of former Curtiss-Wright airframe plant, November 5, 2009.

Curtiss-Wright Cadettes 50th Reunion, Columbus, Ohio, October 17, 1994. Full reunion roster available online at the website: wildharepress.com/flyingintoyesterday.

"So that was why no one talked about them at the plant during the war," he said.

Later I found out that Curtiss-Wright did in fact allow women to work on engines at Wood-Ridge. When it became obvious how competent they were, the engine division created classes for them inside the plant, the reverse of how Cadette training was handled for the airplane and propeller divisions.

Augie described the Wood-Ridge engine-plant layout for me, which moved my image of it back above ground and made it sound manageable. This plant, with Augie's help, had produced many thousands of reciprocating engines. When they closed it down, he was there.

"So do you know where they kept their historical records from World War II?" I asked.

"Sure, I know exactly which room they were in. I was there the day the Smithsonian backed their trucks up to the loading ramp and took them away — photos, drawings, papers, everything. They completely emptied that room."

I breathed a sigh of relief. "So there's no other place in the building where there might be more records?"

"Oh, no," he said. "I don't think so. I went all through that building at the end."

He sounded so clear and reasonable that I decided to let the "Lost in Jersey" blog float away on its bloated miasma of invention. Especially now that I knew that a huge percentage of the main plant space was currently being rented by several large businesses. Most of the old relic was still commercially viable property, not the complete howling-dogs-in-the-moors swampland the blog had conjured up.

"Thank you so much, Augie. You've made my day."

He laughed. "You're welcome. Come by and see our museum if you're around."

"Oh, I will," I said. "Just promise you'll be there."

"I'll be here," he said. "I'm gonna be around for a long, long time."

Something about keeping WWII aviation history alive seems to invigorate these old engineers and should be bottled.

Boogeying with Betty

In mid-September of 2009 I went back to Washington. Betty picked me up at the Baltimore airport and drove me to her house in Chevy Chase. Barbara was always saying I should get Betty to let me drive, but after multiple visits to Betty's homes in Maryland, North Carolina, and Chincoteague Island, Virginia, I still haven't managed to wrest the wheel from her hands. Betty's determined little Smoky Mountains–bred butt is in the driver's seat, dagnabbit, and that's where she's gonna stay.

The night I arrived, Betty and I sat at the small island counter in her kitchen, and I sketched out for her what I had deduced about the movement of all the Curtiss-Wright records around the country, who the main players were, and what I hoped to find in the Suitland repository that Phil Edwards had told me to check out. I'd made an appointment to visit the next day.

Betty kept shaking her head in wonder. "It's only been, what, six months since Dallas? Sounds like you've been all over the country."

"Really," I said, "it's just the miracle of phones and the Internet, plus a few actual trips."

Betty could see that tracking down evanescent (and possibly nonexistent) documents had become my new mission in life. She didn't know about the abusive relationship in college that had sidetracked me from pursuing a career as a reporter all those years ago. But the flame under the truth-seeking young woman who had chosen to major in history and journalism in the first place had been reignited to blast-furnace temperature by this investigation into Curtiss-Wright and the search for my equally courageous young mother.

As I sat with Betty, I remembered how my mother and I huddled together over college catalogs in my junior year of high school, trying to determine which school was best for me. Mom leaned toward the University of Missouri, which had a decent journalism school and was in the same town as Stephens College, where she'd renamed herself Ricki. My preference was the University of Colorado in Boulder, which had a mediocre reputation for journalism but would enable me to ski my buns off in the Rockies. We compromised on Northwestern, a Big 10 school with an impressive academic reputation and the prestigious Medill School of Journalism.

What was going to transform me from a small-town, provincial girl into a big-city reporter was a question my mother and I never tackled at all. But here I was, 35 years later in Chevy Chase, taking on the most important story of my life. Betty found my efforts so impressive she glowed with second-mother pride.

Early the next morning, Betty and I drove the Beltway to Suitland, Maryland. We found the National Air and Space Museum's Preservation facility in a well-hidden series of aged Quonset huts behind a cyclone fence with a very relaxed (i.e., empty) guardhouse next to the driveway. Behind the fence were all the artifacts in need of repair, cataloging, or just plain storage, and none of them were considered worthy of tight security.

We followed a guard through the reception area into a warehouse, past a large number of dusty old decrepit planes, out the back door, and 50 feet up a paved road to one of the Quonsets. For the next two and a half hours, we sat in a small room with a wooden library table, eight chairs, and four bustling curators.

They offered us three-ring binders listing the contents of their repository. We picked some we thought might pertain to our research, and then a curator retrieved them for us. After several different requests, it became obvious that the documents and pictures in this Curtiss-Wright collection (which was not very extensive) were almost exclusively from the St. Louis and Buffalo plants; they contained nothing about the Cadettes. The biggest hole in the collection was the Columbus plant. Even though Phil Edwards had warned me not to get my hopes up, I expected to find at least a smattering of Curtiss-Wright administrative files relating to the Helldiver. I found nada. Zilch. The side-door leakage out of Curtiss-Wright Columbus into "private ownership" seemed to have been devastatingly complete.

As a last resort, one of the curators offered to pull up scans of photos from the Columbus plant for us. But after waiting patiently for his overloaded computer to sort through the thousands of photos, what he came up with were shots of the not-quite-finished plant before anybody actually occupied it or manufactured anything. All the photos were of huge empty buildings with piles and piles of construction materials.

Rather than come away empty-handed, I asked for a copy of a photo that Curtiss-Wright's public-relations bureau had retained since 1931. It was a gorgeous shot of a 19-year-old named Charlotte Hodgkinson, who wowed everybody by flying solo at the Curtiss Field in Valley Stream, New York, after just 76 minutes of instruction. Her jaunty, raised-arm salute and wide-open smile looked like the kind of confident gesture any of the Cadettes might have given if they had been allowed to "take off" in aero-engineering after all their training. Something about her reminded me of my own bravado in the previous 12 months. Thinking about it kept me aloft during my next round of research, which came close to grounding my entire flight into aviation history.

NARA and NASM: The Info Chasms

That weekend, Betty's younger daughter came to visit and they went off to Betty's beach house in Virginia — a double-wide trailer on Chincoteague Island. On Monday, I began another week of solo research, traveling by subway and bus between Chevy Chase and the two National Archives facilities.

The bottom line about doing research at the National Archives and Records Administration (NARA) is this: unless you are willing to go there every day for five years, you're not likely to understand its layout or its retrieval system. As far as I can tell, a good percentage of the staff have been there less than five years themselves.

A veteran researcher I met at NARA told me that only a few years ago, after you established that you were a reputable researcher, you could walk back into the storage areas and browse hands-on. Now you are at the mercy of the "pull" system, which is just slightly less torturous than medieval body-stretching machines. You look through guides for numbers in a filing system that has been altered several times over the years and quick-like fill out a slip before one of the cutoff times for requests. Then you sit and wait.

Eventually a rolling library cart loaded with up to 14 archival boxes is yours to paw through — carefully, of course.

I already knew that the World War II collection had been slashed in two, with a line drawn at the end of 1942. Supposedly, everything before that date was in Washington on the Capitol Mall; the rest was at College Park, a full hour away. But that's just a neat-sounding description for what is in fact a huge mess, especially since the Navy (my primary target because the Helldiver was a Navy plane) had changed its own contract numbering system in the beginning of 1942, with the change scheduled to take effect on July 1 of that year. Unfortunately, the two dates of most significance for me fell right in the twilight zone between July 1 and the end of 1942. In that six-month period, all hell broke loose in the Navy filing system, and curators at both College Park and the Mall were completely baffled by the difficulties I had locating documents with 1942 dates.

The two agreements that launched Curtiss-Wright's Cadette Program were both signed in late 1942 — by the Army on November 30 and by the Navy on December 7. Phil had instructed me to ask for the SB2C contract and any correspondence about it between the Navy and Curtiss-Wright. He thought that funding for the Cadette Program was probably a line item (or "add-on") on one of the many "supplements" to the original production contract, which was signed on November 19, 1940. The Helldiver, in other words, had been trying (and failing) to fly with the Navy's fleet for two years before C. Wilson Cole, the director of Curtiss-Wright's Engineering Personnel Board, decreed that women must be trained in aero-engineering.

I made wild guesses about which files to request from the last half of 1942. When a monstrously heavy rolling cart appeared, I would lean my full weight against it and push it over to an official researcher's desk, quickly scanning the many file folders in each of the boxes. By the time I'd been doing this for a few hours, I could rifle through 14 boxes in such short order that I'd be back at the "pull-delivery desk" to return the whole cart in about half an hour. Then I'd have to wait at least another hour for yet another cart to appear. This was all in College Park.

Downtown NARA on the Capitol Mall was more casual about retrieving, not so wedded to the time clock. But their pulls were delivered two floors up in a hushed research room where I made a huge boo-boo on my first day by letting the top-heavy cart get the better of me, sending all the boxes crashing to the floor. None of the boxes opened, but I got stern looks all around.

I shot daggers back at the researchers and archivists glowering at me and returned my cart to the desk, grabbed my shoulder bag, and headed huffily out the door for a much-needed cup of coffee. I can't tell you how many hours of pull-and-release fun I endured at the National Archives; but it was clear that if I continued, I would go insane in such a straitjacketed system, with two different orderlies tightening the straps, one downtown on the Mall and one at College Park.

My only relief was two visits to the National Air and Space Museum's main branch, also on the Mall, where Phil Edwards showed me the *Curtiss-Wright-ers*. They were so old, yellow, and dry that as I gingerly turned the pages they shed their edges like teensy bits of confetti all over the carpet under the table. You might think I'd be delighted that NASM was so much looser about protecting documents than NARA had been, but I was actually horrified. I did my conscientious best to leave these crumbly newspapers mostly in tact, marking pages for Phil to hand over to the professional photographer who comes in to scan fragile documents every few weeks.

In the public-access shelves of their library, I finally found an article I'd been looking for everywhere: "The Ohio — Curtiss Airplane Connection: Curtiss-Wright Airplane Division in Columbus, 1940-1950," by Richard A. Morley. I copied all 20 pages of it gratis on their ancient machine and called it a day.

Though I wasn't bringing home the kind of profound or illuminating pages I'd hoped for, it was better than the big zero I kept coming up with at NARA. Then again I had pretty much exhausted NASM's potential, whereas the National Archives had simply resisted my initial assault.

After four days of research I emerged with the ability to correctly pronounce BuAer (beuw-air), the abbreviation for the Bureau of Aeronautics, which controlled the Navy's aviation program in World War II. I could also throw around phrases like RG72 (Record Group 72), which was largely where you would find BuAer's records. But my biggest coup was that I now knew the correct contract number for the SB2C: NOa(s) 1609. This was after it was renumbered — not on July 1, 1942, but on May 31, 1943. Getting this correct number would later lead me to a copy of the Navy's summary of the entire life of the Helldiver contract, from exciting inception to hellish design problems to prolonged tardiness of delivery to alterations and improvements in later models.

I filed a Freedom of Information Act request with the Department of the Navy when I returned to Taos at the end of September. In exactly one month, I received a copy of the SB2C contract summary. With the trembling anticipation that I would finally see documentation that the Navy, at least, had played a real role in the Cadette Program, I read through every page. I found exactly three sentences about the Curtiss-Wright Cadettes and not a single mention of the final price paid to Curtiss-Wright to administer the program.

These were the lines: "To alleviate this problem [the shortage of engineering personnel], the Corporation instituted a program for training capable girls, known as 'Cadettes,' in the elements of aeronautical engineering. These expedited programs were set up in several universities known for their aeronautical schools. At the conclusion of the training these Cadettes were brought into the plant, where they absorbed a volume of the detail work."

Clearly, the Navy was not prepared to take any responsibility for approving or overseeing the Cadette Program. If Warren Bruner hadn't written that the Navy and the Army agreed to C. Wilson Cole's proposal (which opened the door for that initial $2 million in government funding), one would never know that the American people are legally entitled to a true accounting of the program's history. Its privacy is *not* protected by the proprietary interest of a private corporation.

With my copy of the summary, I found a cover letter suggesting that I speak to Daniel A. Jones at the Naval History Heritage Command (the Navy's archive and library at the Washington Naval Shipyard). He was relatively new at the Command and listened raptly to my detailed story about the Cadettes. I told him about my attempts to find the original agreement the Navy had signed. He was very sympathetic and said he would look further for records on the Cadettes.

"By the way," he said, near the end of the call, "that SB2C contract summary was only recovered and saved by accident. It was on a loading dock, destined for the dump."

All the pages and pages of numbers recording exactly how the government's money was spent were not found with it.

Wrangling for Warren

On my first day at College Park, an independent researcher overheard me talking about my Curtiss-Wright Cadettes search and how I hoped to find traces of the only person from the program who held out real promise: Warren Bruner. All I had was Warren's name and a Washington address typed on the back of two issues of the *Cadette Register and Digest* from 1950 and 1953 that Betty had sent me. They had both been mailed to Purdue's Cadette class of '43.

A name and a 56-year-old address. That's what I gave the researcher, John Arnold, PhD. I also told him that Warren had coordinated the Cadette Program out of the head offices of the airplane division in Buffalo, New York.

Dr. Arnold oversaw a small crew of researchers. They started pulling up a wide assortment of Washington, Maryland, and New York newspaper articles that talked about someone who might or might not be the Warren Bruner I needed. (I knew from an Internet search that, historically, there had been at least three men by that name on the East Coast.) The Warren Bruner who surfaced most often in Dr. Arnold's quest had been a very congenial, politically active consorter, a progressive and principled ideas man who circulated in some very significant government circles. But this Warren Bruner also had an ornery streak, having chosen to spend five days in jail rather than pay an $8 municipal fine because he had allowed his dog to run free during breeding season in the small Maryland community where his family (actually, his wife) raised chickens.

The same Warren Bruner had attended a reunion of former employees of President Roosevelt's Resettlement Administration, which helped Americans who were displaced by the Dust Bowl find jobs and housing in federally funded "Green" communities. He had been the procedural division director, a national position, even though the Resettlement Administration only lasted two years before it was absorbed (and quietly muzzled) by the Farm Security Administration.

In late 1945, Warren was sighted (by the author of a social column) moving his family to upstate New York from longtime digs in northern Maryland because he now worked at the Hobart and William Smith College near Geneva in the Finger Lakes area. This was substantiated by another article a few years later about a young Imogene Bruner (presumably his daughter) who had performed music in a radio broadcast while enrolled at that same school.

After hearing a few of these stories, I asked Dr. Arnold whether he'd located any actual descendants, which is what I was paying him for.

"Unfortunately, what I found is an obituary notice for an Imogene Bruner in the Bronx, age 79, dated April 2, 2009."

If this was in fact Warren's daughter, I had missed her by just six months.

"Out of curiosity, what was her birth date?" I asked.

"September 20, 1930," he replied.

"That's amazing: I was born on September 20th."

Since Dr. Arnold had exhausted the money I'd given him without finding me a walking-talking descendant, I decided I would try to continue the search on my own. And at this point I became very appreciative of College Park NARA's one saving grace: once you'd proved you were a citizen and worthy of their trust, you could actually sit down and use the public institution version of "Ancestry.com" on one of their computers for free and for as long as you liked. That's how I discovered some other weirdly coincidental information about the Bruner family.

Warren Bruner's Washington address from the early '50s, for instance, was actually the home of two sisters with the last name Peck. This was my maternal grandmother's family name in St. Louis. The Warren Bruner family had lived in the late '20s (according to the census report for 1930) in a small town in Illinois just over the hill from the hippie farm where I lived after dropping out of journalism school in 1972. The town was called Libertyville and was so tiny that only people who lived within a few miles of it even knew it was there.

Then an even stranger coincidence came to light: one of the building materials used by the Resettlement Administration in its "green communities" was something bravely experimental that would last forever and always look good. Lustron, as it was known, was made of a porcelain-enameled synthetic material. It sold in prefab walls that provided great insulation and came in a variety of floor plans, with built-in wiring, plumbing, and major utilities. Lustron houses were considered an affordable answer to the returning vets' needs.

These "everlasting" homes, however, threatened to drive the building trades out of business. So the trades made an effort to undermine the company, and their efforts apparently worked. The Lustron Company went bankrupt only two years after it had moved its manufacturing operations into two large buildings that had been vacated at the end of the war. And who leased these buildings to them? The War Assets Administration. And where was this space? In Buildings 3A and 3B of the Curtiss-Wright Airplane Company in Columbus, Ohio.

How in the world could all of this information-seeking about Warren Bruner have led in such a tight circle right back to my mother's factory?

When Betty returned from the beach after my week of zigzagging between College Park and the Capitol Mall, I was waiting.

"Hey, Betty," I said. "We've got another mission."

"We do?"

"Yes, we need to visit a small town named Greenbelt just east of College Park. The Resettlement Administration under Roosevelt constructed it in the '40s."

"Actually, I've heard of it," she said, "but I've never been there. Let's go."

So we drove to Greenbelt on my last full day in Maryland and got a good taste of the innovative, community-minded spirit of the three Green communities that the Resettlement Administration had completed before the project (way too socialistic) was aborted.

Now that Betty was available to drive me around again, we went to see Jackie Warren Davis, the Cadette who had provided the fabulous photo of the Cadette inspectors on the Helldiver. She lived half an hour away and was happy to have us stop by. She made scans for me of close-ups of Cadettes at Purdue in the machine shop, at drafting tables, and with a flight-simulator training panel. Then she let me interview her.

At the Columbus plant, Jackie had worked as an inspector with three men. She said that when they found problems, they'd have somebody come fix them. Then the inspectors (including Jackie) would stamp them "fixed." (Clearly, this stamp was what Betty never got to see — if it was there — on the plane where she found the faulty clearance around the hydraulic line.)

Jackie was on the 4–11 p.m. shift in final inspection, right at the end of the line, just before the Inspector of Naval Aircraft (INA). She said her job was not to inspect engines, except for oil leaks and loose bolts, but she did inspect bomb bay doors, control panels, and the wing-fold.

Her most interesting story was about how she overcame her father's resistance to the idea of her studying aeronautical engineering. He had been quite dubious when he first heard about her application to the program.

"But then I went with him to a dance in Washington, and a man came up to us and told my dad he'd heard that I was going to be in the Cadette Program. He shook my hand and congratulated me, and he was just beaming. Dad was so impressed, he let go of his doubts about my participation."

I later wondered if the man at the dance was Warren Bruner. He seemed to show up in such diverse and leading-edge places during the 1940s. At Hobart College in upstate New York shortly after the Cadette Program closed, Warren served as director of admissions *and* head of the "Career Determination Program," a service that didn't exist on college campuses yet. He espoused the idea that college-bound students should consider working for a year or two before embarking on their studies to gain a better idea of what they really wanted to do with their education. This was a novel concept for the late '40s and early '50s.

Warren Bruner was an outspoken and unusual man. I could see why he'd been chosen to coordinate the Cadette Program once the first round of training was up and running. I felt in my gut that he would not have let those Cadette files get away from him. He cared too much about the women engineers, as was obvious in his remarks to them in the Cadette *Registers* I'd seen. And the fact that he was dedicated to keeping my mother's class in contact with each other 10 years after they'd been at Purdue told me this was a man with real heart.

Several months later, I found further evidence that this impression was correct. In yet another Cadette *Register* mailed to another Purdue group, Warren said:

"They need engineers as badly now as when you were doing your stuff. Here's your chance if you want to get back in the game. Or maybe you can steer someone else into it. While engineering is still not primarily a woman's field, it is not so tough for a girl since *you* broke the ice. And *you* know it is plenty challenging."[21]

I also found several mentions in the Cadette *Registers* from other participating schools that Warren was working on a book about the program. He had a publisher lined up and was collecting names of Cadettes who wanted to buy the book when it came out.

"So!" I thought. "He *must* have had the ancillary files on the Cadettes!"

The key to my project was finding a living Bruner who had seen Warren's personal effects at the end of his life. Even if his youngest child — whose name was uncannily similar to my original name (Gene) and who shared my birthday — had expired, surely some other Bruner was out there to find.

Before leaving Washington, I sent an email to one of Hobart's vice presidents asking if they could please look in old personnel files for living descendants of Warren Bruner. I had a feeling I was not going to get a response, but I had to start somewhere.

One piece of indubitably synchronistic luck fell into my lap in Washington. The official NARA website features a list of independent researchers. On it, I found an old friend I hadn't seen in 25 years. The last I knew,

Jeremy Bigwood was in El Salvador working for the international press, taking the most damning photos of government-sponsored violence imaginable. Now he was in Washington specializing in Freedom of Information Act (FOIA) research, the toughest kind. I called him to arrange a meeting. Over dinner at a restaurant near Dupont Circle, he gave me a great pep talk with insider pointers about dealing with archival mysteries. He also persuaded me that I shouldn't hesitate to use FOIA whenever I met resistance from the keepers of government (especially military) documents — which is how I got up the courage to solicit that copy of the SB2C contract summary when I got home to Taos.

After dinner we walked to Warren's last known address because it was just a few blocks away. We thought maybe we'd get a sensory hit about what he'd been doing there as a guest of the Peck sisters, even though they were long gone. As we stood in front of the three-story house, which I'd only seen through the slanty-eyed camera vision available with Google Maps' pedestrian-view function, I felt a tad foolish. The place had obviously been divided up and reconfigured in the intervening years. It was squeezed between two other ordinary row houses with equally inscrutable exteriors. Dr. Arnold's leads about Warren were far better than anything I could deduce from looking at a house full of strangers who'd never even heard of Warren Bruner or the Pecks.

Jeremy and I took a quick peek, and afterward he escorted me back to the subway. As I descended the super-long escalator into the bowels of subterranean Washington, I waved back up until he disappeared, happy that there were charming scofflaws like him in the history-dredging game with me, willing to commiserate, conspire, and collude in the grand project of opening unjustly locked doors. I had accepted a challenging mission, and it was no longer just: "Find my mother among the Cadette ghosts of Curtiss-Wright." It was now subtitled: "Everyone in Washington's hiding something — especially from themselves. Let's find out why." And I'd be back again.

But for now I needed to turn tail on this "warbird" saga and wing my way home to northern New Mexico's mountains, where the most important things flying, now and always, are ravens and crows.

The Real Imogene

When I got home from Washington, I decided to try again to find Warren Bruner's kin. Since I'd never received a response from Hobart College's personnel office about their former director of admissions and Career Determination Program, I thought I'd see what came up if I looked up history of flight or theory of flight in the Hobart class listings.

Almost immediately, I found a professor who was teaching a class in the basics of flight and encouraging his students to think imaginatively about constructing unusual aviation designs. He sounded like my kind of guy. When I called, he listened to my story and then referred me on to the alumni office. I thanked him and hung up: another likely dead end. I knew Warren's daughter had gone to school there, but from the obituary Dr. Arnold had given me, I also knew that Imogene Bruner was dead. There couldn't be more than one person with such a distinctive name.

I called anyway. The woman who answered was the alumni fundraising coordinator. I told her about my book and that I was looking for relatives of an alumna who was apparently deceased. She said she'd be glad to look into it for me. But when I gave her Imogene's name, she became so quiet I thought the phone had gone dead. After a long pause she spoke again.

"Everyone in this office knows Imogene. She's a very enthusiastic alum. In fact she was just at a reunion here back in May. I'll ask around. Hold the line."

While I was on hold, I looked up the date of death for the "Imogene Bruner" in the obituary and it was four months *before* Hobart's May reunion.

"I think you are mistaken," said the woman when she picked up again. "No one in this office has heard of her death."

I got a sudden sparkle of hope that maybe there were actually two Imogene Bruners in the world, and the one I sought was still alive!

The alumni office agreed to forward an email to her. I composed a few paragraphs for them explaining who I was, what I was doing, and why I hoped to speak with her, and ending by saying: "I hope you are the correct Imogene." Then I waited for a week with no reply. I finally lost patience and decided to just look for her phone number on the Internet and give her a call.

She answered on the second ring.

When she heard who I was, she said, "Yes, I'm the Imogene you're looking for. When I got your email, I just cried and cried. I was so moved by your attempt to publicize the important role my father played in the Cadette Program."[22]

She told me she'd always felt close to him but it had been difficult to see him, partly because he was on the road so much for his work, but also because her mother, who had the upper hand in their family, ridiculed him relentlessly for not doing "anything real" in life, like farming, which was her mother's background. (So the farm just down the road from my Northwestern dropouts' farm near Libertyville, Illinois, belonged to his wife's family; it had been a haven for Warren and his young brood during the '30s.)

We had a long, emotional talk about how sad she was that her brothers had sided with their mom in denigrating their dad.

"I was young, maybe 13, when he ran the Cadette Program, so I was kind of vague about what he was doing at Curtiss-Wright," Imogene told me.

Though she studied at Hobart after he got hired there (tuition was free for children of faculty and staff), she'd been so absorbed in her studies that she hadn't really paid much attention to what her dad was doing at Hobart either. After college, she married and moved to Tucson, so Warren became an even more distant figure.

"Mom ragged on him to the bitter end, but he never left her," said Imogene. Mrs. Bruner, however, only outlived her "reprobate" husband by a few short months.

Imogene also became the target of her mother's ire, especially toward the end of her life, when she disinherited her only daughter. With such a painful family background, Imogene had determined that one of the most important things in her life was to make peace with each of her three brothers before they died.

"I finally earned their respect," she said. And now she is the only one left.

As Imogene talked, I became aware of a close parallel between the stories of her father and my mother. After she quit teaching, my mother was the one with no power or status in our family. She was constantly razzed by my father for her lack of practical knowledge, stuff he had learned as a boy on a farm. And one time when I called him many years after she retired, he even referred to teaching (which I was trying to break into) as "not real work." The irony was that in the act of reinstating my mother as a valuable player in her younger life, starting with the Curtiss-Wright Cadette Program, I was in fact helping "rehabilitate" Imogene's dad's reputation as well.

Imogene had no idea what finally happened to her father's personal effects and professional papers after he died. When her mother passed away and the house was being cleared out, Imogene had no legal access and she hadn't yet reestablished her relationships with her brothers. This mirrored my situation in the estate battles with my siblings after my parents became incompetent, which resulted in my being barred from the house in Moorhead. Terrible as it was for both of us to lose connection with our families and no longer be welcome in our childhood homes, even more terrible for me as I spoke with Imogene was the premonition that, more than likely, somebody in Warren's own family had dumped his — and the Cadette Program's — history as I had unwittingly helped dump my mother's.

Imogene halfheartedly agreed to call the widow of one of her brothers, who still lives back East, on the slim chance that she might know whether any of Warren's papers had been kept. Then I heard nothing. For weeks. After appealing to her by phone and by email three times each, I finally got an email from her apologizing for not being in touch. She'd just come from the funeral of her youngest son, who had died tragically in his late 40s.

I gasped in sympathy and took a giant step backward. It was time to let the dead Warren Bruner and his secrets rest. If he (or his effects) ever chose to surface again, it would be on his timetable, not mine.[23]

Don't send my girl to Lockheed
The dying mother said
Don't send her to Consolidated
I'd rather see her dead.
But send my girl to Douglas
Or better still to Bell
But as for dear old Curtiss-Wright
I'd see her first in hell.

Cadette Song 1[24]

Chapter Five
Going Back to Bexley

The Columbus Aviation History Clan

Even though I wasn't getting anywhere with finding Curtiss-Wright's corporate records, I did have a promising date at Purdue. Just before my trip to Washington, I had emailed Professor Alice Pawley again. I was hoping to find out where she might be heading with her feminist-oriented take on engineering education and whether we might form an alliance. I told her I was farther along in my research and would love to tell her about it.

She emailed back that she was definitely interested in hearing more about it and had an additional idea: "Would you be interested in speaking at our weekly seminar? We have folks (both faculty and grad students) interested in engineering education history, and it could be a friendly and helpful audience. People from aero/astro would be welcome to attend also."[25]

My heart leaped. I couldn't believe I might actually have an invitation to speak at my mother's alma mater. I wrote back to accept for November 12th. During my research quagmire in Washington, however, I started worrying: How was I going to present the Cadette story to her seminar when I kept coming up empty-handed at the National Archives? I decided to focus on the drama and excitement this story evokes whenever women in particular hear about the unusual opportunity in aviation the Cadettes had been given—even though it didn't continue, for most of them, past the war.

Since I would be in Indiana, I decided to swing through Columbus, Ohio, first. I needed to see the plant where my mother had worked and get a feel for her other stamping grounds in Columbus. In order to gain access to the old Curtiss-Wright plant, I decided to arrive in the company of Cadettes, who'd more than earned their right of return. I asked various members of the Wild Bunch to meet me, but they were either too busy or too recently reunited to want to do it again so soon.

So I called Dorothy Wurster Rout, coordinator of the 50th Cadette reunion, to schedule a videotaping rendezvous with her and other local Cadettes. I told her that afterward we would tour the old Curtiss-Wright plant, if I could arrange it. Dorothy had sent me a two-page letter earlier in the summer encouraging me in my pursuit, twice-repeating the line "More power to you," — so I knew she'd be on board. She was clearly aware of her memory lapses, and her nervous laughter about it peppered our phone conversations. So just to be on the safe side, after I told her the date for the videotaping, I got her husband Chuck on the phone to confirm the information. I told him I'd be interviewing as many Cadettes as I could round up in that area on Thursday, November 5th, at my hotel suite in downtown Columbus.

He said, "Great. I'll get Dorothy there."

I took my list of addresses from the 50th reunion and started calling. First was Mary Lou Stuber Wright, Dorothy's friend from the Purdue class of '44. They'd been best buddies during the training, and after the war both went back to Ohio State to finish their degrees. When I called Mary Lou, she said, "Yes, I'll definitely come."

Next I found Anne Rill Yates, who had gone to the 10-month training at Iowa State. She didn't hesitate three seconds before she committed.

I knew I couldn't do everything myself in a town I'd never even been to and getting the spacious hotel suite at Hilton's Doubletree seemed like enough of a commitment, so I asked everyone I talked to for help. No one balked. They just jumped right in, even though they were from three different Cadette training groups and didn't really know each other, unless they had worked with Dorothy on the committee for the 50th reunion.

That's why a Purdue class of '45 graduate named Nova Anderson Weller was so quick to join in. It seemed that she had become the official keeper of Dorothy's Cadette memory, because Dorothy had given Nova custody of the thick files Dorothy had once accumulated as they planned the reunion. During the gathering, I noticed that Nova was just quietly and attentively present, patiently holding the space, while Dorothy giggled musically whenever she couldn't remember a date or name. All the other Cadettes knew how much work Dorothy had done to keep records on the program's history and update biographical information on the Cadettes, not to mention coordinating the 50th reunion. They all appreciated her devotion.

In the notes she sent out after the reunion, Dorothy, in a lively state of mind, quoted some gems she'd brought to the gathering but hadn't included in her speech because she'd accidentally turned two pages at once.

"If you remember, I tooted a horn and waved an American flag to say that after years of the depressing WWII, the Curtiss-Wright Cadettes appeared on the scene. Maybe, just maybe, WE saved the USA and the world. I started at the Columbus plant in January 1945 and the war ended seven and a half months later. We Cadettes must have done something right! Discounting the atomic bomb, it had to have been the Curtiss-Wright Cadettes who made such an impact! If we were employed now as young women, we would be in NASA working on a Hellspace project."[26]

I found one more Purdue class of '45 graduate named Kathryn (or Kay) Atkinson, who had portrayed herself as "not particularly worthy of interviewing." But at an important moment on the big day, she wound up center stage and wasn't the teensiest bit shy about telling her story.

At this point, while making dozens of phone calls to strangers, I had no idea what a fabulous conglomerate of talkative, funny, amazingly sharp women I was assembling. A few of them were still in their early 80s because the age minimum had been lowered for the second and third rounds of Cadette training. Some, I was to discover in the interviews, had never even graduated from high school when they started the training at Purdue.

Because none of the Cadettes from different groups comingled on the job, none of them knew my mother. But all of their paths and work assignments had intersected within the holy walls of Curtiss-Wright Columbus. Ricki's feet had trod the same steps and walkways theirs had, and that made them wartime kin.

I moved on to arrange meetings with a wide assortment of men who cared about Columbus, the Port of Columbus airport, and World War II aviation history. This included my great phone friend Nolan Leatherman; a retired TWA pilot named Don Peters; a ramp agent for US Airways, Jim Thompson; Bill Tylka, the manager of Odyssey Aviation, a local fixed-base operation (FBO) that repairs corporate jets (located in Building 3B, the old Curtiss-Wright modification facility); and a dedicated local historian named Richard Barrett.

In the process of locating all these people, who often knew each other because of their shared interest in aviation, I contacted the Ohio Historical Society, the Columbus Historical Society, the custodian of a collection from a private aviation museum that had once been located at Port of Columbus, the metropolitan library's downtown branch, and Joe Blundo, the local paper's outspoken columnist, hoping he'd write us up.

When I'd first imagined visiting Columbus, I'd pictured a small town along a river with charming neighborhoods and a modest airport just outside the city limits, alongside which Curtiss-Wright had built its humongous plant. I knew Columbus had probably grown since the 1940s, that it would be slightly more bustling, but I thought it would still be rather provincial. Ohio State University (OSU), which I knew to be big and home to a team named the Buckeyes, was in my mind just one of the settings for a movie I had seen in my teens — *Goodbye, Columbus*. Never was anyone more quickly disabused of preconceptions than was I upon flying into Port of Columbus Airport on a sunny Tuesday afternoon with a perfect vista of the never-ending suburban developments stretching in all directions from an original small-town hub.

I'd been warned by a local Taos gallery owner who also runs a gallery in Columbus that it would not be 1) safe to walk around downtown near my hotel at night or 2) easy to go anywhere without a car. I didn't walk around alone at night, mainly because I was too busy in my suite preparing for meetings. But I ignored her advice about the car and found that everyone I met was more than willing to chauffeur me around and show me the sights — if I asked for a ride at all. Their warmth and good-natured tour-guiding made the whole transportation thing a non-issue.

The hotel I had picked offered a lovely view of the river and the old Romanesque Supreme Court building across the street. It was also centrally located and big enough to accommodate the ever-growing numbers who would shortly materialize in my suite. All I had to do was order up a coffee service from the hotel kitchen, and the Cadettes and history buffs would provide the rest.

Columbus, one might think, has five unemployed students and one aviation history buff per square yard. However, there is substantial economic activity in the town. Besides being home to OSU (the biggest state university in America) and the Ohio State Capitol (with its plethora of government offices), it's also host to the Battelle Corporation, one of the largest scientific research and development companies in the country. Battelle, in fact, provided employment to several of the Cadettes after the war.

And then, there's Schottenstein Property Group, which just so happens to own my mother's old plant.

I'd never heard the name Schottenstein, though if you're looking for college sports and other entertainment at OSU, you'll be walking into the Schottenstein Arena. Or if you own a small commuter-jet company, like Republic or American Eagle, you'll be renting space from Schottenstein in what's left of the original high-bay hangar Curtiss-Wright built in 1941, a breathtakingly spacious area that's just one small end of the original 1.2-million-square-foot plant known as Building 3.

I'd seen a picture of the original entry to Curtiss-Wright's Columbus plant at 4300 East Fifth Avenue, and it was very elegant, with the company name in clean, tall, sans-serif letters above the doors. This entry was etched in my mind for life, even though someone had removed those letters many years before. So I knew what the steps looked like where my mother and her friends had entered the building, five days a week (and sometimes six), from January 1944 through August 15, 1945. I longed to walk unimpeded up those steps right through the doors into my mother's history. It was just a matter of getting Schottenstein Property Group, the monster mega-company, to say "yes."

I consulted a friend about this dilemma.

"Just start at the top," she said. "That's what I always do."

I called the company and asked to speak to someone in the president's office. I was put through to the voice mail of two different female executive assistants, and neither of them called back. After a day or two of this, I once again got the main switchboard operator, a polite young man with a very sweet voice. I decided to reverse direction and work from the bottom up.

"Listen," I said, "You were so kind and helpful the last time I called, but I'm just not getting any return calls from the president's assistants. Is there anyone else you think might be able to help me? I know you must talk with everyone there. What do you recommend?"

He hesitated for just a moment and then said, "Well, I'd call Michael Broidy, the vice president of corporate affairs."

"And what does he do?"

"He handles all kinds of visits made by people doing business with the corporation."

"But this isn't exactly business."

"No, but he's a nice guy. Let me give you his extension."

Not being fluent in corporatese, I had no idea what the job title "VP of corporate affairs" really covered, but I was game.

I called Michael and told him I was working on a project, trying to resurrect the history of the women Curtiss-Wright had trained in aero-engineering.

"I was wondering if you'd mind if a small group of these women, who are now all in their 80s, take a brief tour of the plant."

"Possibly," he said. "Why don't you write it up and tell us how many people will be on the tour and what you want to see, and I'll look into it."

"Sure, no problem," I said. "I'll send it to you this afternoon."

I wrote up a customized version of my usual impassioned pitch that this had been a great and unusual program. I even requested that he imagine what an amazingly different world we'd be living in if fully half of the engineers were women. I was worried he might think that part was overkill, but what the hell—I badly wanted to get inside those doors, and I had no reason to think he was a stuffed corporate shirt. He certainly hadn't talked like one.

I attached a copy of the fabulous photo of the Cadette inspectors on the wing of the Helldiver and sent the email. When I followed up with another email a couple days later, Michael replied that it looked like a go, but he was still waiting for final clearance from security. I tried not to worry that defensive corporate machinery was going to come down and crush his cooperative intentions.

Two days later, with still no word from him, I called to politely inquire whether our "little visit" had passed under the behemoth's radar (i.e., security). And sure enough it had.

"Do you want me to contact the local TV stations?" he asked.

"Sure," I said, "why not?" I'm not a big media fan and mostly don't expect them to get things right, but if he wanted to invite them, he could be my guest. I didn't really expect them to show up.

In the meantime, I made plans for a preliminary view of the Curtiss-Wright acreage, asking whether Bill Tylka, the Odyssey Aviation manager, would mind if I stopped by to see his premises and take a look at the other plant buildings nearby. He said he'd be glad to have me come by after I landed and would show me around personally. It was amazing how quickly the mention of anything to do with World War II aviation opened doors in Columbus. Jim Thompson, the ramp agent at US Airways (and aviation history buff), also wanted to do (it seemed) anything I asked. I didn't know how to assess all this over-the-top enthusiasm I kept encountering. But I decided to take one step after the next and trust it would turn out right.

Jim had said he wanted to greet me when I landed and would take off from work to do so if he could. However, we never crossed paths that afternoon, even though we both earnestly looked for each other, because my plane was quite early. But no worry, I called Bill and asked for a ride.

"Sure," he said, "I'll pick you up at the Southwest arrival door in ten minutes," which belied how completely busy he really was. "How will I recognize you?"

"I'm five foot two, on the thin side, with two-tone hair. I'll be wearing a three-quarter-length black-leather jacket and a burnt-sienna paisley scarf. I'll also have a stack of luggage and briefcases that no one my size should be pushing around."

"Perfect," he said. "I'll find you."

Bill drove up in his large, black, leather-seated SUV in 12 minutes exactly, and we drove the few miles of frontage road between Port of Columbus Airport and Curtiss-Wright's old plant. Finally, those famous front steps of Curtiss-Wright I'd studied so assiduously loomed into view a stone's throw from my passenger seat. I nearly swooned with satisfaction, having logged so many Google Maps hours on the Internet trying to establish an intimate acquaintance with this old, but still rather sprightly, relic.

Bill casually cruised the length of the never-ending Building 3. Then he drove in circles around the old power plant, the transportation building, and the remnants of a shed formerly used for painting the planes. After I was thoroughly overwhelmed by the giant scale of everything, he parked in front of the Odyssey Aviation building, which had been the site of Helldiver modifications. He told me he'd been in town about eight years and was slowly renovating and upgrading the entire building. He was clearly as enamored of Curtiss-Wright's aviation history as I was.

After a brief tour of his company's offices, we started a walking tour of the remodeled, repainted hangar in the next space, where expensive corporate jets were being serviced. When we got to the far end of that hangar, we went through a door into an equally big unoccupied space. At the other end of it, Bill became about as excited as any boy who's just received his first model airplane. Without warning he suddenly scrambled up some stairs in total darkness.

"I'm going to try to turn on a light so we can go through this door up here," he said. "Wait till I get the light on. I want you to see this landing over the old hangar floor, the one part of the old Curtiss-Wright and North American days that's never been retouched."

I waited at the bottom as long as I could while Bill groped in the dark trying to locate the switch. Then I just started up the stairs, fingering the peeling walls of the stairwell, stepping carefully up the concrete steps as it got darker and darker. I was certain I would emerge in the light if he at least got the door open — and he finally did, just moments before I reached the top. There, opening wide before us, was that ancient preserved room with its wide hangar doors and high ceilings. The dusty walls were still full of gobs of alligator-skin paint, and there were rails in the floor for moving the planes. The two of us hung over it all on a catwalk platform, like a shop foreman and his assistant checking on the movement of the production line.

Except of course for one big difference: there was nothing but empty space below and not a single solitary sound. None of that clanging and banging and shouting over the noise of electrical tools as the airplanes inched down the line. No smell of metal and dust. No roar of fans and belts and a million other buzzing, battering sounds that would deafen you if you weren't crazy careful about wearing earplugs. Up here, it was deathly still.

After a few minutes of reverence, we turned and walked back down the stairs, making our way in silence to his pilots' lounge with its cushy leather couches. After I reviewed the small pile of Helldiver production-line photos he handed me to look through, Bill offered to drive me to a print shop so I could scan them.

On the way downtown, he did a leisurely loop through old Columbus neighborhoods and, without even having to ask for it, I got to see the old governor's mansion. I'd heard about this place. My mother and Betty and several other Cadettes had been temporarily quartered there when they first arrived in Columbus. It was an impressive two-story mansion on a beautiful tree-lined street. The setup sounds like a sweet deal, but Betty had told me that the old man who managed the place at the time and was supposed to watch *over* them instead tried to watch *under* them. They couldn't wait to move on.

"It's unfortunate," Bill said near the end of the tour, "that I'm going to have to miss the plant tour. I have to go to Chicago on Thursday for business. But you folks should feel free to use the Odyssey lounge after the tour."

I thanked him for his generous donation of time and space, and of course for the fabulous tour of the modification building.

"You're more than welcome," he said. "I wish I could do more."

He drove away and left me standing in front of the hotel. I took a deep breath and inhaled my good fortune at having found such congenial company right out of the gate.

I settled into my suite and made a few phone calls to confirm my arrival. Yes, Dorothy Wurster Rout and her husband Chuck were all set for our meeting on Thursday. Richard Barrett, historian and former North American engineer, agreed to meet me in the morning at the Metropolitan branch of the Columbus library, an eight-block walk from my hotel.

Columbus was rolling out the red carpet for a visiting unknown, apparently because I'd learned the town's aviation password: Curtiss-Wright.

Is Curtiss-Wright-er?

The November weather held out, and the next morning was beautiful. I started up the street toward the library and discovered a print shop halfway there, where I arranged for an inexpensive banner to use as a backdrop behind the Cadettes during interviews. The owner located a copy of the Curtiss-Wright logo on the Internet and added "Engineering Cadettes" beneath it on a bright-red background with white lettering. He said it would be ready at the end of the day.

The downtown branch of the Columbus library was old, with an imposing façade; but it had been greatly expanded a few years earlier. The interior atrium of the new section was open and airy, unlike the dark drear of so many old municipal libraries. In the elevator to the third-floor periodical section, I saw a man with square black glasses and an absolutely nononsense face. He was unmistakably my local historian. He saw me looking at him and immediately introduced himself.

Richard Barrett was in his late 70s. He had worked in engineering (at first North American, then Battelle) and was all business. When we got off the elevator, he made no attempt at small talk and led us straight to a research table to unload our briefcases. He then walked to a closed door, knocked, and an invisible reference librarian's hands delivered the *Curtiss-Wright-er* collection into his safekeeping.

There were two volumes, and all the pages were in primo condition because they had been carefully bound and were non-circulating. This collection contained the entire year and a half's worth of issues that had been missing from the National Air and Space Museum. I was finally seeing the full coverage, thin as it was, of the Cadettes generated by the one and only employee-oriented newspaper at the Columbus plant.

We spent the next hour and a half carefully thumbing through issues, recording dates and page numbers where Cadettes were referenced, and both taking photos of each relevant page. Now that I had access to both volumes, I could no longer doubt my first impression of Curtiss-Wright's limited coverage of the Cadettes. As before, the new articles were exclusively trumpeting: "The Cadettes are Coming! The Cadettes are Coming!"

I wanted to scream: "They're not the cavalry, for god's sake! So they arrived already. *Then* what did they do?" Apparently that question never occurred to the PR department's scribblers. Warren Bruner, however, provided an in-house view of what happened to some of the Cadettes after they started working in the plant. He pointed out that a large portion of management and supervision knew very little about the capacities of the women and that their morale as Cadettes had been excellent, their record as a whole outstanding: "Consequently, the girls were placed under line supervisors, some of whom were not aware of the schooling the girls received, and few of whom appreciated the need for some finesse in handling the high quality assistance they were being given."[27]

After we finished at the public library, Richard drove me to the State Library of Ohio, a big, characterless, metal-frame building with a high ceiling and rows upon rows of efficiently arranged metal shelves. I went right up to an idle librarian.

"I'm looking for information on a Curtiss-Wright program from WWII that trained women as aeronautical engineers. I'm sure you know how big Curtiss-Wright was in Columbus. There should be some pretty good materials here. Can you help me?"

The librarian got a strange gleam in her eye and barely said anything, just started typing madly on her keyboard. I wasn't sure if she was thrown by the topic or just relieved to have a challenging research assignment. After 15 minutes, she had pulled up an extensive computer list with a number of items I'd never seen before. They weren't, alas, located in this particular library. Still, I was impressed with her research skills.

"Wow. Fast work!" I said. Even when I thanked her, the Sphinxlike gleam didn't go away.

Richard swung by a grocery store on the way to the hotel so I could pick up some items for the next day's Cadette reunion and taping. He even waited outside the print shop while I collected the banner. Then he deposited me at the hotel's front door, saying he could not come to the hotel gathering, but he and his wife would try to come on the afternoon plant tour.

I never saw him again.

When I got home to Taos, I found copies of the photos he'd taken of the *Curtiss-Wright-er* in my email. His pictures were infinitely sharper and steadier than the pictures I had taken. Writing and publishing four volumes of local Columbus history with mountains of photographs had given him a steady hand.

At Battelle, Richard had known a few of the Cadettes personally, including Nova Anderson Weller, who did classified work as a mechanical engineer. But overall he knew almost nothing about the Cadette Program. So he didn't say much while we were photographing those newspapers, except for one statement, delivered very quietly, almost without inflection, while looking down at one of the articles he was photographing.

"You know, you really shouldn't refer to them as engineers."

I looked away and said nothing; but at that moment, I made a silent vow to prove him wrong.

Otto the Octogenarian Dancer

One important informant I spoke with in Columbus was 88-year-old Otto Acker, the engineer who had put to rest the story that an SB2C had been buried out back of Building 3. Otto worked at Curtiss-Wright all through the war and had been recommended to me, by at least three different aviation buffs, as a man who'd been in the thick of it and was still quite sharp.

I called Otto twice and asked him to come to our Cadette party. When he finally returned my call, it was 11 o'clock on the night before the big to-do. He told me he had just come in from dancing at Schmitt's, a famous sausage house and microbrewery in German Village.

During our late-night interview, he told me he had worked closely with one Cadette in the wing and fuselage section and knew two or three others, one of whom he was sure had stayed on after the war. He couldn't remember her name, but she had continued working there even after North American assumed control in 1951.

Then he told me a story that made it hard for me to sleep that night.

In 1945, while the Curtiss-Wright airplane division was regrouping and consolidating its manufacturing and engineering at the Columbus plant, Otto left the company to work for Goodyear. In late 1950, as the airplane division was closing down, he stopped by the plant to say goodbye to his old coworkers.

"I found them shoveling boxes and boxes of stuff out the back door of the plant into a big dump truck. They were all real happy to see me and told me to just climb up and take my pick. Said I could have whatever I wanted — photos, drawings, company reports. But it was just too big a pile. I felt sick seeing how much good stuff they were throwing away. Years later, I could've kicked myself for not jumping in and trying to salvage some of it."

What Otto saw in that truck was a big percentage of the combined corporate records from the four Curtiss-Wright airframe plants, all red-tagged for oblivion. I had to wonder whether the person(s?) who gave the order to dispose of all those documents wasn't trying to keep one step ahead of the hounds of hell — a.k.a. the ghosts of the Truman Committee. My hopes of ever finding Curtiss-Wright's records about the Cadettes grew very dim. I now knew for certain that the master bombardiers at Curtiss-Wright had dropped everything they had on whatever airplane division records remained after Guy II spirited away the precious designs and photos he wanted. The fact that the Helldiver's story eventually resurfaced with such resplendent detail (in that remarkable book Betty had shown me, first published in 1998) was nothing short of a miracle. To me, the

SB2C now seems more like a graceful phoenix rising from the ash than a Big-Tailed Beast.

Otto never showed up at our party. I heard he'd caught a cold.

Hell-Jivers

The next morning, I prepared to greet the Cadettes. Having never laid eyes on any of my guests, and nervous about hosting so many at once, I was relieved that the first to arrive were Dorothy Wurster Rout and her husband, Chuck.

"Jean-Vi!" Dorothy said as she greeted me. "You look just like I pictured you!"

My image of Dorothy hadn't really gelled over the phone. But she was big and jolly-faced and immediately assumed Queen Central status in her flowing purple dress. (I had to wonder: was she *thinking* purple as well as wearing it?) Her husband took up a remote position on the couch in front of the window while she hunkered down near the food table.

Dorothy had no sooner settled into her chair than I heard knocking on the door. "Just help yourself to coffee or tea," I told her as I moved toward the door. These 80-plus types were awfully punctual.

All the rest of the arrivals came very fast: first another Cadette, followed by an engineer, a history buff, the cameraman, Nolan, two more Cadettes, a retired pilot, the US Airways ramp agent (with three dozen of the thickest bagels I've ever seen), and finally, the last Cadette.

I quickly lost track of which names went with which faces — except for the Cadettes, because I stayed near them and kept at it until the names stuck. Imagine my extreme embarrassment when I had to go up to a robust, balding, flush-faced but very serious gentleman who was talking to Chuck and ask his name again. It was Nolan. He had introduced himself when he came in, but seeing his face a second time had not triggered name recall because he in no way resembled the image I had conjured during our many phone calls.

I was mortified. Nolan had been nothing but kind and helpful during my initial unstable steps. It's entirely possible, however, that Nolan had the same reaction to me. He'd asked me my age some months back and I was pretty sure my bounding-rabbit energy didn't match his image of a 58-year-old.

I slunk back to the food table, which the Cadettes were hovering over, and admired the pile for its quantity, if not its nutritional value. This was white flour and sugar heaven, interrupted only by some fresh fruit Nova had brought. Everyone was chattering and chewing a mile a minute. I walked from room to room, grinning and listening in here and there, staying on the move to be sure everyone felt welcome.

The vibe in the room was so bright and energetic, I was reminded of a photo I'd seen in the *Curtiss-Wright-er* of an in-house band that played at the plant's social events in 1944 and '45. They called themselves the Hell-Jivers, an apt description of how this happy bunch of Curtiss-Wright aficionados was carrying on in my hotel suite.

I was glad I'd turned over the camera work to Arnett Howard, the volunteer shooter who'd been recommended by at least two of the aviation-history guys. He was a local black R&B bandleader of considerable renown who also happened to be a member of the Columbus Historical Society, making him one more of the legion of aviation history buffs overrunning this town. At least four other invitees were unable to attend, and a good thing, too, because with all the people, food, and film equipment (three cameras with tripods), as well as historical photos and documents spread through both rooms, there wasn't an extra foot of space.

We had agreed that, by 11 a.m., the gentleman history buffs, husbands, and retired engineers would remove themselves so we could film the Cadette interviews in peace. After we got them out the door, we started filming immediately. I'd created an abbreviated version of the questions I'd used in Dallas. The 15 minutes allotted to each of them was far from sufficient, but it was the best I could manage under the circumstances and would at least give a flavor of what these five graduates from other Cadette classes had experienced working for Curtiss-Wright.

I asked Anne Rill Yates, a 1943 Iowa State Cadette who was 22 when she entered the program, how the men at Curtiss-Wright treated her.

"I have only good things to say about Curtiss-Wright. I started in drafting but was transferred to production design. I think women in drafting probably contributed more than I did. I was always a little concerned about being able to do the job right because it was a magnificent place. And the airplanes were so much bigger than I had anticipated."

After the war, Anne moved away with her husband (an armaments project engineer on the SB2C). He lost his job and they moved back to Columbus so she could work at Curtiss-Wright on the Intercontinental Ballistic Missile (ICBM) computer program.

"I was a human computer," she said, "calculating trajectories."

"How would you say working at Curtiss-Wright impacted you?"

"In every possible way. As the child of immigrants from Yugoslavia who didn't speak English and arrived just after the stock-market crash, it was a difficult time. When I got to college and then had this opportunity, it changed my whole life. Truly."

Dorothy Wurster Rout (Purdue class of '44) told us she'd always been "an airplane nut" and had joined the Civilian Air Patrol (CAP) at the start of the war. Someone turned her name in to the Cadette recruiting office, and she was accepted. At the plant, she worked in the drafting department the whole time, working on the tail section.

When I asked about how it had been to work with male engineers, she said, "I really think they didn't object to women. I think they objected to my age, which was like 17. But I enjoyed it. I wanted to be there. I was very much geared to helping for the war. I felt I fit in. I was sorry Curtiss-Wright ended the program so abruptly."

After the war, Dorothy went back to selling jewelry in a department store, but also became the single most devoted keeper of the Cadette flame.

"I have pretty much been a women's liberator — or whatever you call them," added Dorothy. "Women have a place in almost any industry. I think we were a breaking point in the aviation industry."

Mary Lou Stuber Wright (Purdue class of '44) was the daughter of a Curtiss-Wright engineer who had worked on ejection seats.

"My dad would have loved for me to be an engineer. I didn't come through. But he did get me in the program. I was still in high school. I hadn't even graduated."

"What was the hardest subject for you at Purdue?" I queried.

"Analytical geometry. You had to figure curves on a graph. You had to turn something around and see what it looked like in the back."

At the Columbus plant, Mary Lou started as a tracer in the drafting department.

"It was in ink and I'm left-handed, so it was very difficult for me because my hand would go over the ink sometimes. They got me out of there. The rest of the time I was a checker. I just went over the drawings the girls had done to see if they'd missed a line. Of course for these small drawings it was easy to miss something. So you'd just send it back and show them what they'd missed.

"At that time," she continued, "they were tracing every drawing on linen, which seemed superfluous. Really. They had the drawings and then they kept changing them anyway, planes kept changing. Yet they had to do it permanently in ink on linen."

"What do you think about women in aero-engineering today, Mary Lou?" I asked.

"We started a trend," she said. "I just think it's wonderful that women can be in the space program. The world has opened up for women who have the ambition and the brains and the education. They can do anything that a man can do — almost."

"Amen, sister," cheered Dorothy from the other side of the table. Everybody laughed.

Kay Atkinson (Purdue class of '45) had leaped at the opportunity to join the program when she saw an announcement in the paper of her small town. She knew it was the only opportunity she would have to get a college education, because her parents couldn't afford it. She'd already graduated from high school and was working in the engineering department at a power-shovel company.

"What did you like best at Purdue?" I asked.

"I liked the machine shop. I loved working on the lathes. But when I first got to the Columbus plant, I was scared. The drafting department was such a big room. Once I sat down at a drafting table, however, I felt right at home."

Kay showed us the letter she received from Curtiss-Wright, dated August 18, 1945, three days after V-J day. She read us its pithy message: "Due to lack of work, your services are no longer needed."

"I got two other letters after that," she said, "special delivery, saying they were opening the factory back up and asking me to come back. But I never did."

Eventually she got work at Battelle in the engineering department.

"They couldn't call us 'draftsmen.' And 'draftswomen' didn't work. So they started calling us 'technical illustrators.' That's what I did until I retired."

In July 1944, Nova Anderson Weller (Purdue class of '45) was taking a summer class in physics right across the road from Curtiss-Wright Columbus when the teacher said, "There is an article on the bulletin board you might like to read."

"It was about a scholarship in aeronautical engineering at Purdue," said Nova. "It was exciting. I had taken flying lessons when I was younger. So I wrote it down and I wrote them and they accepted me. Just like that. I hadn't even graduated from high school. During the war, girls had to take nutrition. That sounded very boring to me. So I took what the boys had to take: war math. I wasn't sure the high school would accept that. But when I came home from Purdue at Christmas, I found out they'd given me a diploma."

When she started at the Columbus plant, Nova remembers, she and another girl sat for a long while in a hallway waiting to be fingerprinted.

"They had to drive us downtown to get special work permits because we were too young to work." She, too, was only 17.

Nova's assignment was to help redesign the Helldiver's instrument panel. She also did endless calculations for a book being written by one of the plant's top engineers, Frank Mallett, whose name appears in several Curtiss-Wright publications from that time.[28] After the war, Nova worked on numerical calculations for the flight-path pattern of the V2, the advanced rocket the Allies had found in Germany at the end of the war and brought back to the United States to analyze. Later, she went to Battelle and did classified work as a mechanical engineer until she retired.

My final question to Nova was, "What kind of impact do you think your work at Curtiss-Wright had?"

"We won the war," she said, with her no-nonsense, dead-on smile.

On the tour of Schottenstein's that afternoon, during a long interview with Nova, one of the reporters baited her.

"Wasn't it hard working around all the men?"

I could tell he expected her to get all worked up over gender politics. He wasn't interested in her tremendously disciplined engineer's mind.

She fired back: "I've never had any trouble with that. I respected them. They respected me."

The picture of her at Purdue in front of the frat house where they boarded her is so absolutely self-assured it always makes me grin.

Touring the Curtiss-Wright Plant

We were due at Schottenstein's front door at one o'clock. When I'd called to confirm the number of people we were bringing (about 12), Michael Broidy told me, to my amazement, that two TV stations were sending cameramen. He had also taken the photo I'd sent him of the Cadette inspectors on the Helldiver wing and made large framed copies for each of the Cadettes on the tour. He, of course, didn't know that none of these Cadettes had been inspectors or were even in the picture. But it was a grand gesture and I thanked him profusely.

Three of the history buffs at the party informed me that when they had heard I wanted to take a tour of the plant, they were sure I'd be turned down. In the decade since Schottenstein Property Group had purchased the building, there had been any number of attempts to have the company acknowledge the Curtiss-Wright (and North American Aviation) history of the plant. Someone even asked whether they would donate a tiny portion to create a Curtiss-Wright/North American museum. Every request had been denied, with the explanation: "We're looking towards the future, not the past."

So many people in Columbus had worked at that plant under Curtiss-Wright or North American that the cloud of resentment over Schottenstein's refusal was pretty dense. But I had heard absolutely nothing about this failed campaign. So when I went straight for the heart of it, via that sweet-voiced switchboard operator, I apparently hit the target dead on. Not only did Michael Broidy arrange for the TV stations to film it, he also enlisted all the employees in their corporate offices (about 90) to come down to the main lobby and welcome home the Cadettes.

When Dorothy, Mary Lou, Kay, Nova, and Anne walked through those doors, a huge round of applause went up, and it was all the theatrical recognition of the Cadettes and their World War II contributions that my mother and her buddies could have ever hoped for.

Unfortunately, I wasn't there.

Or maybe fortunately, because it makes me teary even now to describe the justice that was finally being done within those history-laden halls. I was seven minutes late and it had already happened by the time I arrived. But I could see the glow on the Cadettes' faces when I joined them in the lobby. Luckily, I had sent ahead my private cameraman, an Ohio State student volunteer, to film the tour, so I later got to watch most of what I'd missed.

My apparently foreordained tardiness to that tumultuous reception was the result of having ridden with Don Peters, a retired TWA pilot. Little did I know when I accepted his offer of a lift that his car was parked two blocks away from the hotel on the fifth floor of a curvaceous parking garage that would have challenged any driver trying to maneuver out of it, not just a man in his mid-80s in a long barge of a car.

When I got there, three-quarters of the corporate-employee welcoming committee had evaporated back to their offices, and a happily smiling Michael Broidy had already delivered the framed pictures to the Cadettes. All five women were lined up holding the pictures at one side of the lobby as the TV cameras rolled. And the Columbus *Dispatch*'s columnist Joe

Blundo had joined the crowd, though I was careful not to introduce him to Michael just in case Joe wanted to preserve his reportorial anonymity.

Three men who managed the facilities were poised to take us on a tour, so we didn't dally. We followed them across the large two-story lobby and down some stairs to the basement, which had high ceilings and large windows that started at shoulder level. It was the brightest subterranean space I'd ever been in.

I knew that the basement had been built to withstand bombing so they could continue at nearly full production down there, which of course had never been necessary. But the storage potential was mind-boggling, and one guy I spoke with who used to be the facilities manager in the '80s told me that he'd seen ramps going down into the basement from all directions to enable transportation of parts and subassemblies. The way that Schottenstein's had broken it up still didn't diminish the feeling of cavernous infinity.

"I have no idea where we are," said Mary Lou, as we all gazed at the enormous Schottenstein furniture showroom we were standing in. "I don't recognize any of this, do you, Dorothy?"

"No," said Dorothy, twirling around in wonderment and then following the group, while the leader pointed off into the far distance, announcing that the cafeteria was in that direction. I guessed it was probably in the same location as the original cafeteria, because it would be too expensive to move cooking facilities that had served some 24,000 people a day.

Our guide led us back to the elevator via a circuitous route that further disoriented us. But the TV cameramen kept right up with us, brightening the route with their camera lights. Amazingly, our entire party fit into the elevator, which lifted us to a landing between the first and second stories.

When we got off, our guide gestured toward a hallway that he said led back to an overlook above the original Helldiver production line. He assumed this largish troop of mostly elderly men and women wouldn't want to trek down a long, shabby, dimly lit hallway. But when I heard what was at the other end, I said, "Oh yes, let's go!" and started down the hall, leading the pack.

The cameras kept rolling, trying to interview Cadettes as they passed or paused. Both cameramen took turns saying they needed to interview me, but I was on the move, trying to make sure we saw as much as we possibly could on this magical journey into the past.

The hallway emerged as promised onto another catwalk platform like the one I'd been on two days earlier at Odyssey Aviation. You had to walk down about ten metal grid steps to get to a landing and I wondered if the Cadettes would follow, but every last one of them did. As we looked down into production-line central, knowing my mother's friends doing liaison engineering had come back here to check their drawings against the planes, I sensed that I had passed through a morphogenetic space that still held the impression of their young, agile, alert bodies walking briskly toward their goal.

"My mother must have stood here at least once," I told myself.

All the Cadettes were looking down the unending production line space, trying to remember what it had looked like with Helldivers moving down the rails. On the far side were endless double tiers of open metal shelving with enough schoolbooks and materials to supply the entire Northeast. None of the Cadettes were in a hurry to leave. Like me, they were still trying to take in the sheer size of the enterprise they had participated in. These spaces could never be subdivided enough to make them measurable on a human scale. In this building, a Herculean task for the enormously greedy and unquenchable gods of war had been undertaken and completed. How could any of these Cadettes not feel pride in their work here, even if just as "engineering assistants"?

When we returned to the other end of that long hallway, we followed the guide up a short set of stairs to the second floor and down a hallway with corporate offices on either side, where most of the cheerleaders in the lobby had come from. But as we walked down the middle of what had previously been an enormous open room occupied by Curtiss-Wright's engineering department, all the tight little cubicle walls fell away. And right about mid-center I paused to feel the vibe of the little pilot's handbook–editing group, with Betty and Beth leaning in over my mother as they looked over the pages together.

And that is where the cameras finally caught up with me for the interview they wanted. I decided to let 'er rip.

"Training 900 women in aeronautical engineering was a revolutionary idea. These women were all very bright, quick studies. That's why they were able to absorb two and a half years of standard aero-engineering curriculum in just ten months."

"What are you going to name your book?" asked one of the cameramen.

"Probably 'The Sisters of Icarus,'" I answered.

"Why?" he pursued.

"Because they're the ones that stayed on the ground in World War II, while the men went up and burned their wings."

I heard the Cadettes guffawing behind me when they heard that. I was amazed they found it so funny. To me it was a simple statement of fact.

I could have talked all day about this program, but I was saving the details of how their phenomenal absorption of "male subjects" had impressed faculty at all seven universities for my talk at Purdue.

Our last stop on the tour was the high-bay hangar at the far eastern end of the plant, which was still in use by three different commuter-jet companies for repairs and maintenance. Their airplanes looked like toys in the enormous echoing emptiness.

One of the tour guides we'd been assigned told us that when Schottenstein's contractors decided to shore up a weak seam in the floor between the end of the production line and the high-bay hangar, they uncovered 100 toilets side by side in a row under the cement. They'd all clearly been designed for men only because they had no walls. It was a vivid reminder of what an enormous population of workers it took to produce these planes.

Finally, we'd seen enough. We took all the bagels and cream cheese Jim had brought and regrouped in the Odyssey's Internet lounge, enjoying the afterglow of a day well spent. Then we went our own ways, Nova, Jim, and I driving back to my hotel suite to watch the five o'clock news just in case our tour made it onto the screen. And sure enough, there we were — in living color on one of the local NBC affiliates for a generous two minutes.[29]

Four weeks later, Joe Blundo, the Columbus *Dispatch* reporter who'd gone on the tour with us, finally published his story about the Cadettes: "'Girls' Once Had Designs on Aviation Careers."[30] I received copies of it from five of my new Ohio friends. Everyone in Columbus knew that the Cadettes had been historically reconstituted. Now—to make sure the rest of the country got the news as well.

Goodbye, Columbus

I spent two more days exploring Columbus in hopes of catching a closer glimpse of my mother's personal tracks. The morning after the plant tour, I watched the longest Veterans Day parade I'd ever seen, right below my hotel window. Then Nova Weller took me to the Franklin Park Conservatory, a large airy space with a fabulous plant collection and colorful blown-glass creations in the ceilings and in almost every room.

Nova had recently retired as one of their volunteer photographers. To the conservatory staff who greeted her warmly, I reintroduced her as a TV star, telling them how to find the clip of her and the other Cadettes on the Internet. The staff hadn't even known about Nova's brief but glorious career as a Cadette. They mainly recognized her as someone with a buoyant spirit and a fine eye for color and composition.

Nova drove me to the approximate location where I thought Casa Dingy had been. According to Betty, it was at the end of the streetcar line on Main Street in Bexley. Peggy had always inadvertently added "Heights" to Bexley. A local Columbus resident chuckled when I used the same combination. "I'm sorry, darlin', but we don't have any hills in old Columbus. There couldn't have been a Bexley Heights." Peggy had unconsciously elevated the status of their shabby old house to match its more elegant neighbors—and her high, happy memories.

In the '40s, Bexley had been right on the edge of town. My Mom's friends all said that Ricki had found the house for them and that she was very good at "that kind of thing." The fact that they hung the name "Casa Dingy" on it indicates it might not have been such a great find, though it was clearly homey enough to help them feel like lifelong family. There was also, Beth told me, so much gritty soot in the Columbus air back then, from all the coal the city depended on for heat, that it was a struggle to keep the clothes on your back — or on your clothesline — from turning black. Being in upscale Bexley didn't protect them from it.

Most of the neighborhood where Casa Dingy might have been has been torn down and "upgraded" into four- and five-story apartment buildings with street-level stores. The only business still there that I know my mother frequented is the Drexel Movie House, where I'll wager she took in at least two films a week on her days off.

Saturday, November 7th, I found myself alone in German Village in a big park, standing before a statue of the German poet Schiller. It would have been my father's 90th birthday. Even though this trip was not about him, I knew that after their first few meetings at Purdue, he had courted Ricki in Columbus while on leave from the Navy. I also knew that as soon as he got back to the Naval base in Jacksonville, Florida, he called her to propose marriage over the phone.

"Your mother," said Beth, "was apparently feeling some doubt. She talked to Rube for a long time and then asked him to wait a moment. She put down the phone, went over to the sink, and threw up, making him wait in extreme suspense. Then she came back, picked up the phone, and said 'yes.'"

Betty said she, too, had witnessed this.

I found this funny — and pretty sad. I might have wished for a more romantic story of how my mother's 57-year union with my father was launched. But since this trip was about revisiting and honoring my mother's adventurous pre-marriage life, I have to stick to what really happened — at least according to the Wild Bunch.

Mary Sprow, in her heyday one of the most outspoken of the Dingies, claims my mother was at one time engaged to three different guys.

"She would call them each collect," Mary claimed, on a tape her daughter Cindy made for me after she got home from Harlingen. "And they never refused the charges."

"I always admired what a fantastic dancer your mother was," Betty told me. "She knew this one sailor named Dude who used to swing her high up in the air. He'd swing her this way and swing her that way and swing her right over his head. Later she was going out with a guy named Rich and got engaged to him. But none of us liked him. We thought he was a phony — and shallow."

"So how did she remove herself from Mr. Rich — and the two other fiancés — so she could marry my Dad?"

"I don't remember exactly," said Betty. "But when it was time, she just did it."

After twelve months of Service Engineering at Curtiss-Wright, in late December of 1944, Ricki left Columbus and never came back.

As I stood in front of the Schiller statue in German Village, I remembered what Beth had told me when I first called to make arrangements for the Dallas reunion.

"It's too bad your mother and I both married squareheads."

"What do you mean — 'squarehead'?" I queried.

"Oh, you know — German men. They're so stubborn and controlling."

Beth had learned how to deal with hers, apparently (she divorced him after 30-plus years). But my mother never did. She began talking about leaving my father soon after she and I returned from Hawaii. On various occasions throughout the second half of their marriage, she asked my older brother and I to help her do it. She'd lost whatever had allowed her to take flight in the arms of those young dancing men in Columbus so many years before.

Thanks for the memory
Of moment, lift, and drag
Along with coke and fag
Of lab reports and drafting sports
And metatarsal sag
Oh thank you so much

Cadette Song 2 (excerpt)[31]

Chapter Six
Perdu at Purdue

Alma Mater (Nourishing Mother)

*I*t was time to go on to Purdue. The story I heard as a child was that Purdue is where Mom and Dad met. She was training to be a Cadette (whatever that was), and he was working as an airplane mechanic. And this was where? West Lafayette, some backwater town in Indiana dissected by a muddy brown river named Wabash, like the famous Cannonball that brought some of the Cadettes to town.

On that blizzardy day in February when she arrived from Texas, Ricki probably wanted to just get back on that train and return south. But she had just turned 19 and had already attended three other colleges, so she was not about to admit feeling *perdu* at Purdue.

On an icy morning soon after her arrival, all of the Cadettes gathered on risers in front of one of the engineering buildings for a company-arranged photo shoot. Mom stood on the right-hand side at the end of row two, wearing a full-length fur coat, one of only two Cadettes so enrobed. Her family's fortunes tended to fluctuate from high bottom to occasional middle and they could never have afforded this luxury. But she wore it in this picture. By the time she posed for the graduating picture ten months later, you couldn't tell if she still had it because she was tucked so completely behind another Cadette in the fifth row. My guess is she would have positioned herself at the end of a row again if she still had that coat.

I had never seen pictures of Mom's class before I received, in late fall of 2008, a small package from Purdue Aeronautics and Aerospace Professor Alten (Skip) Grandt. In this entering class picture, her lips are pressed firmly together as always, and she's smiling in a composed and quietly serene way—the smile I've seen in almost every picture taken in her adult married life—refusing to laugh or bare her teeth. It was the self-possessed, ladylike expression she had perfected and always put forward when she knew the camera was aimed her way. Only at the very end of her life did she open those lips to smile right at the camera, but by then she didn't know the date or where she lived.

I couldn't help but marvel at this young East Texas woman standing there without knowing a single one of the other 97 Cadettes, ready to make the most of whatever happened in the next ten months. I knew that when she changed her name from Betty Lu to Ricki it was because she'd made up her mind that she was never going to be mistaken for "just another Southern belle." Her own mother, Genevieve Peck, was also raised in a financially precarious situation by the descendant of a very prosperous St. Louis patriarch. Genevieve had developed a passion for the dance hall and wanted to be a paid singer; but her strict, proper parents said absolutely not.

Genevieve's love of music and dance had instead infected her three children: my mother, her sister, and her brother. This dance hall passion, combined with a wild, you-can-do-anything-you-damn-well-please streak from grandfather Buck's East Texas ranchers side of the family, drove the three Cruse children toward creative careers that each flamed out when they were still relatively young, though they all carried the torch for high-spirited, high-kicking dance the rest of their lives.

My Aunt Gene taught choreography in Jacksonville, Texas, until her mid-40s when her doctor husband betrayed her and she tried to overdose on insulin. Uncle Bud danced on Broadway after leaving the Navy and then decided that even though by nature he was "a little light in the loafers," he couldn't sustain a career on "the boards." And Ricki captured the limelight with her high-school theatricals for eight short years.

All three of them felt deep disappointment about not being more successful in the arts. They each gave different reasons for retreating, but it seemed that something in the Peck-Cruse genes decreed, "You must eventually withdraw so you don't outshine everyone else in the family."

The Ricki I knew was the bright star outshining all my own achievements. I knew that I was not ever to outperform her. And I got that message not just in so many words. She actually challenged me one time when I bemoaned the difficulty of the artist's path by saying, "What makes you think *you* can succeed in the arts? No one in this family ever has." I was stunned and wounded by this out-loud statement of the Cruse family's defeatism.

So as I rode a Greyhound bus from Columbus toward the Purdue campus in the fall of 2009, nearly 66 years after my mother graduated from the Cadette Program, I decided to keep my eyes on engineering and not even look at liberal arts. All the time I'd spent capturing the stories of Cadettes — looking at airplanes and factories and production lines, talking to engineers and historians and museum curators and university librarians — was going to culminate here in the engineering-education department. I might not get another chance to bring the story of the Cadette Program home to one of its main points of departure with the wisdom and cherishing I needed it to carry.

Regardless of what I might find out about by my own mother's aptitude for engineering, I still needed to keep in mind that unlimited possibilities in science and technology for all young women with creative minds and caring hearts had stood in the doorways of these engineering classrooms in the person of Curtiss-Wright's Cadettes.

In the background, they had all been listening to President Roosevelt's urgings to build an "arsenal of democracy." Industrial America was being completely retooled for war production. The Cadettes, the faculty, and the male engineering students were all united in purpose and a belief in the future of a free world. No one was worrying that America's frantic preparations might create an indestructible, mega-profitable war machine, whose power and reach even General (and then President) Dwight Eisenhower would find alarming after the war.

I got off the overlong bus ride Sunday evening and looked wearily around as soon as we few passengers had been disgorged. Professor Alice Pawley had promised to meet me but was nowhere in sight. I called her cell phone and she said she was minutes away. So I just looked up at the starry night sky and piled my luggage higher. Suddenly, there was Alice, medium height, ash blond, with a warm smile and a whole lot of spring in her step, greeting me and taking my huge roll-on bag, which had expanded beyond the Greyhound weight limit from all the mementoes and Cadette documents (plus banner) I'd acquired in Columbus. I had barely managed to cram it all in, and Alice was kind enough to hoist it into the back of her car.

We went off to a local hangout that served pizza with surprisingly interesting toppings (ours was vegetarian Thai) and sat down to talk. I tried to fill her in on my overall research as quickly as I could because I knew she was leaving for an out-of-state conference in a few days and wouldn't be at my talk. So I gave her a condensed version of my Washington investigations and the plant tour in Columbus, plus some anecdotes about my mother's time at Purdue. The session was so short I didn't get to hear much about her teaching experience at Purdue, or any of her long-term dreams for women in engineering. I hoped, however, to see her again on campus before she left. Even with her large load of graduate students to oversee and engineering-education classes to teach, I thought there'd be time for at least one more focused chat.

Instead, I got a call from Alice the next morning that she'd been up all night with food poisoning. She wanted to know if I had it, too. Fortunately, I did not. In any event, it had thrown off her timing severely and she was racing to finish some charts she was taking to the conference. She gave me the name of the engineering-education professor (Matt Ohland) who would be hosting my talk and said she hoped it went well; maybe she could see the film of it afterward. It was obvious we were not going to sit down and talk again.

It took me a moment to adjust to the vanishing of someone who had seemed a star player in this academic universe, someone to introduce me to a few other faculty and students and generally smooth the path through these bookish thickets. But in this year of exploration I had grown accustomed to sudden changes of course.

I took a deep breath and tried to relax in my room at Purdue's Union Club Hotel (part of their extensive Memorial Union complex), looking through my notes for the names of other people on campus I was planning to talk to and studying the campus map so I could find them *and* the multiple libraries and collections I needed to search.

My hotel was conveniently located right on the edge of campus, within an easy walk of the engineering buildings. I figured out that once you stepped through the back door of the hotel, you practically fell into one of the most important parts of their library system (as long as you didn't mind falling up three stories) — the new and very commodious Archives and Special Collections Research Center. I planned to make tracks over there the next day.

One of their many collections is the George Palmer Putnam Collection of papers on Amelia Earhart, whose airplane for her 1937 round-the-world flight, a Lockheed Electra, was financed by the Purdue Research Foundation. She called it her "Flying Laboratory."

As part of the bargain, Earhart became a counselor in the study of careers for women and an advisor in aeronautics for Purdue. Had she succeeded in her mission, she might well have opened the door for women in aviation at Purdue much earlier than the Cadette Program did — and *kept* it open, unlike Curtiss-Wright. Ironically, Amelia was flying her plane east over the International Dateline, just like the Japanese did toward Pearl Harbor, when she disappeared, permanently, into yesterday. Unproven rumors that Amelia was actually spying on the Japanese — and went down near the Dateline — resonated eerily with my search for evidence of the Cadettes' role in engineering the Helldiver.

As I realized how closely linked Purdue was with Amelia's final, fatal mission, it occurred to me that somebody needs to pilot the spirit of women aviators — and aero-engineers — back over that strange line of temporal demarcation in the opposite direction, i.e., toward tomorrow. It would be a bit like relocating aviatrix Beryl Markham's *West with the Night* bravado from Africa to the Pacific. I wasn't sure whether I would find the kind of support for such wild and woolly projects at the current aero-engineering department, but it couldn't hurt to look.

Would You *Please* Put Down Those Damned Needles!

I had a date scheduled after lunch with a professor emeritus from Purdue's engineering department who shared the first two names of Amelia's husband. George Palmer is an almost-90-year-old spitfire who actually taught aerodynamics to the second class of Cadettes. He would be picking me up in front of the hotel to drive me to the home of another professor emeritus from that department, a spry six-foot-tall gentleman in his mid-90s named Larry Cargnino. I planned to film the two of them discussing what they knew about the Cadette Program. Though Larry arrived at Purdue in 1945, shortly after the last Cadettes graduated, he had shared an office with E.F. Bruhn, the professor who directed the second and third rounds of Cadette training at Purdue after Professor K.D. Wood, who supervised my mother's class, had departed. Both Bruhn and Wood were known to have loved the Cadettes, but only K.D. Wood had written a charming, funny poem about them ("Henson, Benson, and Bond," page 190).

On a warm November day in West Lafayette, George pulled up in his pickup under the canopy in front of the Union Club and tossed me a copy of his impressive "short resume" to peruse as he drove, very rapidly, to the retirement neighborhood where Larry and his wife lived. When we got there, I quickly set up my tripod and camera, positioning George and Larry in two cushy chairs, determined not to miss a word from these two living legends with direct (or almost direct) connections to the Curtiss-Wright Cadettes.

It turned out, however, that though they were very willing to probe their memories, other than one or two anecdotes about the Cadettes, they were both a little short on detail. George only really knew Cadettes from the Purdue class of '44, the July through December group that also went to Columbus when they were done. He was a senior engineering student at the time and taught Cadettes how to use the wind tunnel in one of the two sections offered on aerodynamics.[32]

George showed me an absolutely charming picture of himself with several Cadettes, including Dorothy Wurster Rout from Columbus. They were grouped around him at a classroom table where he demonstrated, with his glowingly handsome young face lit up in a broad smile, a controllable-pitch propeller. He clarified that they never worked at tables like this or on machines in his class. It was just a promo shot.

The other section of aerodynamics was taught by Paul Homsher, another senior engineering student, who was also George's best friend. Paul, George said, worked for Curtiss-Wright in St. Louis and still lives there. This was good news because I hoped to visit that plant, which is still making airplanes, though it's now operated by Boeing.

Both George and Paul fell for a Cadette in the other's section and both got pinned to their dream girl. Unfortunately, their pin-mates later dumped them. Each of the men eventually found suitable wives, so they had no hard feelings about their "runaway Cadettes."

Neither George nor Larry had firsthand experience with my mother's class of '43, whose Cadettes endured the intensely concentrated ten-month curriculum. All Larry really knows (and he freely acknowledges this) is received legend or anecdotal material from E.F. Bruhn, who loved to tell stories about the women and some of the funnier antics he observed. Bruhn, Larry claims, thought the women were pretty good students, but in Bruhn's official end-of-program summary is an unflattering story about the Cadettes at Purdue, which calls their scholarly propensities into question: Bruhn said several faculty had complained that over fifty percent of the women "knitted in class."

I first read this story a year earlier in the material about Purdue's Cadette Program I had received from Professor Grandt. It had been included, pretty much as originally written by E.F. Bruhn, in a book that professors Cargnino and Grandt (and one other aero professor) had compiled on the history of aviation at Purdue, which was poised to be reprinted in the coming year.

I had checked this rumor out with every Cadette I met from all three classes at Purdue. Not one of them remembered seeing anybody knit in class. They undoubtedly did knit at other times because there was a big campaign in America to get women to make scarves and sweaters for the troops. A class of '43 Purdue Cadette named Edna Wigley Short added a different slant to this story when she submitted her bio for a 1995 update of the '43 class: among her many happy memories was a math professor (J.N. Arnold) who learned how to knit so he could be "one of us."

The ongoing portrayal of women sitting in engineering classes with long sharp needles clicking away under their desks instead of pencils scribbling numbers and formulas on notepads depreciates the seriousness of the Cadettes at Purdue. I have seen equally chiding initial reports from several participating universities about the Cadettes' fragile physiques or girly squeamishness in shop classes when first confronted with heavy metal lathes and woodworking machinery. But these reports disappear in later commentary, which compliments them on how well they adapted to a world of boy's tools and toys — *and* aeronautical ideas — that had never welcomed them before.

In our first phone conversation, George had confided that he thought the department back then had a lot of machismo, and there was even one professor (a German man, whom George declined to identify) who flat-out refused to teach "girls." So I knew George was sympathetic to the Cadettes and disliked the disparagement. But I was distressed that Purdue's official book on their engineering history was going to perpetuate this unsubstantiated story of less-than-scholarly behavior (knitting) by Cadettes on their campus.

When I finally gave my talk at the engineering-education seminar, I presented, as evidence that Purdue's first-round Cadettes had been anything but ditzy, the impressive results of the testing done at the end of their 10-month training (described above in "Hatching the Cadette Egg").

During a meeting with Professor Grandt, who had gone out of his way to provide me copies of the few photos and documents on the Cadette Program that had been retained by E.F. Bruhn, I asked whether he would consider, in the second edition, substituting the information about the Cadettes' test scores for the apocryphal anecdote about knitting. He replied that the updated version would only add new material and new achievements; it would not attempt to alter old entries.

Even though Professor Cargnino may not be in a position to make significant changes to the section on the Cadettes, we had a wonderful exchange just before I left his house. He had mentioned early in our taping session that "today's girls are more oriented toward math and science, earlier in their education."

So I asked him the million-dollar question: "What if women aeronautical engineering students were given an opportunity to create something completely different that was *not* for war use?"

Without missing a beat, the professor responded: "They would handle it beautifully."

Purdue University Airport

George and I had agreed to tour the Purdue Airport right after the taping session with Larry. I had no idea what a treat I was in for.

He drove up the long, tree-lined road toward the main gate and let me out to walk through it alone. He was going to park close to the building that housed the aerospace science laboratory and the machine shop. He told me to come find him there after I finished exploring the two original airport buildings from World War II.

I knew my father had worked for the Purdue Aeronautical Corporation for almost a year and a half, starting in March 1943, until he was drafted into the Navy on July 24, 1944. By the time he left the Navy, he had earned the rank of aviation machinist's mate, first class.

It wasn't quite like *Casablanca* crossing the tarmac toward the big hangar on the right, with its administrative wings on either side, but I did feel some deep excitement about walking into a place where my dad had worked. I heard from one of the '43 Cadettes that their class had gone out there one day to watch an engine being taken apart, and the light finally clicked on that this was where my parents first laid eyes on each other.

The details of who set up their first date, however, are fuzzy. Betty claims she and Mom doubled with my dad and another guy. The fun begins with the fact that Betty was my dad's date for that evening and Mom didn't care for hers. So at the end of the evening, Mom leaned far forward from the back seat to give a good-night kiss on the cheek to my dad, ignoring her date. Betty, showing early signs of being the reliable friend she was for the rest of Mom's life, just moved back and let it happen.

"Really," she told me later with a grin, "Your father was not my type."

I looked through the glass panels in a door on one side of the hangar and saw a small class grouped in the far back left corner, so I stepped quietly through the door into the hangar. The place was chock-full of large machines and stacks upon stacks of aircraft and engine parts, with only just enough room in the aisles to slip through diagonally to the corner, where a professor and his young male students were gathered. I slowly made my way there; it was clear they were just finishing an engine-maintenance class. I told the instructor (Professor Mike Davis) why I was there, and he welcomed me to look around, saying he'd be pleased to give me a short tour through this and the other original building as soon as he finished.

While I waited, I wandered back up toward the front through the equipment, thinking there must have been a lot more open space in this hangar when my father worked here, with room for half a dozen small planes to be serviced at once. The light wasn't that strong, but through the windows in the hangar door I could see across the tarmac to the other WWII-era building, made of old red brick with a tower on top. Next to it were parked two medium-sized commercial planes (including one FedEx jet), which I was told were for instruction only. There is no commercial service at Purdue Airport anymore.

I ventured back outside through the small side door, and a student who was emerging said they were going to be opening the hangar door in a second if I cared to see the whole space at once in full daylight. I said, "Yeah, great, I'd love to." So I backed up from it until I could get the whole thing in the frame of my video camera, and I filmed as the massive glass and wood door swung slowly up, thinking that my dad must have watched that door in action a couple thousand times in his 17 months on this job. The door, which is amazingly wide, still functioned smoothly, if a little creakily, after all these years.

Professor Davis, a former USAF pilot, joined me and led me across to the other building. He steered me into a hallway that had a row of engine test cells on the right side. These rooms were basically unaltered from the '40s, except for more modern testing equipment and control panels. After I followed him into the first cell, he pointed through the glass to an enormous jet engine bolted to a torque stand.

"We're about to test that," he said.

I stepped back a few feet in consternation.

"Later," he laughed. "You can relax."

The original cement-block walls and cooling-system pipes lent everything an authentic feel. No one had bothered to spiff it up with paint in all these years, but I guessed that with the rough usage these cells were getting, there would be little purpose to that.

The instructor then showed me the stairs leading up to second-floor classrooms and a few administrative offices. This was the Aviation Technology School and was far more hands-on instructional and trade-school-like than the purer aeronautical research labs on campus.

I walked outside and down a narrow space between the buildings, slipping into the door George had indicated. I found myself in a large, machine-filled shop with heavy old drills, lathes, presses, and worktables that had been salvaged from World War II Navy ships. They'd been installed here because they still functioned quite efficiently in this instructional setting. This wasn't the high-tech end of the building, but it was certainly impressive to someone who'd never spent much time around heavy machinery. I could imagine my mother's intimidation at first encountering even half of an array like this.

Next stop was a massive wind tunnel just on the other side of chainlink fencing that separated all that precious equipment from the rest of the space.

Having never seen a wind tunnel up close, I had no idea that it would look so much like a combination of an enormous camera bellows, factory venting duct, and super-sized vacuum-cleaner hose. It was made mostly of wood and glass and ran almost the full interior length of the building, with room at one end to duck under and get to the back side. A painted sign read "Boeing Wind Tunnel, 1950, built by George Palmer and his students."

George told me that the smaller wind tunnel, used to demonstrate principles of aerodynamics to the Cadettes in 1944, had been transferred to another college. He designed and built the current one to replace it. He also directed the entire Aerodynamics Testing Laboratory. We started up a flight of open wooden stairs to a long balcony overlooking the wind tunnel so he could show me all the model planes hanging from the ceiling. They had all been tested there.

One of the models was a passenger jet with the name Serendipity painted on its fuselage. I couldn't resist telling George the mythic background of serendipity, how the island of Ceylon (now Sri Lanka) had originally been known as Serendib, and that early sailors passing by each sketched something entirely different, so its true shape (as well as its exact position off the tip of India) was unknown. Therefore, there were many ways you might wind up at Serendib, but almost never by deliberate charted course. If you did find it, or at least one side of it, and deduced that you were on the same island everyone was talking about, your incredible luck would be regarded as "serendibitous" — and probably not repeatable.

George seemed to find this interesting and told me that at one time in the '70s, just about every aviation company used the word serendipity in advertising their products.

"It was just a fad," he said.

I was delighted the topic had come up, because I intended to feature serendipity in my talk at Purdue to explain how I had fallen back on "intuitive science" during my research whenever hard digging hadn't turned up enough reliable evidence.

Looking down on the wind tunnel, I was still having difficulty apprehending its true dimensions and shape. It seemed too amorphously overextended and puffed out to be useful in testing airplane models, especially with all that artificially generated wind. But glancing up at the hanging models above us on the balcony, I realized that some of them were quite large and would need such a big wind chamber to simulate high velocity, strong wind, and crosscurrents. In any event, when we left that room and went into the much newer supersonic testing chamber across the hall, I realized that the old tunnel was positively quaint by comparison.

George was gleeful in both rooms, clambering around nimbly and showing me everything, though he did have some slowness in his knees on stairs. He showed me, however, how his mother, who had lived to 106, dealt with this in her last decade: walk backwards down stairs. It's slow, but it saves on impact. So we practiced until I got the knack, knowing how grateful I would one day be that I had toured the Aerospace Science Laboratory with George.

When we'd seen almost everything, George dropped me on campus at the front door of the Potter Engineering Library, with instructions to look up Charlotte Erdmann, the collections coordinator. He drove off as fast as he had gotten me there. I felt certain we were destined to be friends.

Charlotte's Engineering Web

I found Charlotte Erdmann rather quickly back in the stacks after someone at the front desk pointed me in her direction. She had a quietly disarming smile and the roving focus of someone who spends a lot of time scanning everything around her while fielding nonstop questions and requests. George had told me she was the best, partly because no one else had been around as long. She listened to my spiel for a moment or two and then quickly took me in hand, leading me through a maze of bookshelves, up and down stairs, in and out of underground-but-windowed study rooms, and finally into the online fishponds, where she handed me a really good pole.

Under her expert guidance, as I typed in the right variables, we hooked descriptions and locations for a variety of periodicals and engineering journals and other abstruse titles I'd been looking for, even a few from the list I'd been given by the librarian at the State Library of Ohio who'd had that Sphinxlike gleam in her eye. Most of what we found on the shelves, however, was not terribly meaty. Back in the main research room near the entry, Charlotte directed me on an advanced computer search of archived administration records that one can only access while on campus and that only she knew how to find.

Thus, triumphantly, we reeled in some board of trustees meetings notes from October 1942 that showed their initial approval of the Cadette Training Program. Then we got evidence that in October 1943, as the first round of training (i.e., my mother's group) was winding down, the trustees felt that the Cadette Program had been highly successful. They gave most of the credit to Curtiss-Wright and their "good job of selection," plus the fact that they maintained close contact with the teaching program. There was no general commendation of the women enrolled in the program because of course they hadn't yet graduated.

But it seemed like a good strong beginning, and if I'd had half a brain, I would have called in some pizza (not Thai, just in case) and kept this research party going into the following day, feeding Charlotte whatever she asked for to keep her engaged. But I'd already seen and heard so much that day—between George, Larry, the airport, and the ghosts of both my progenitors—that I didn't understand how badly I needed to stay put. I was giddy with the kind of "finding success" I had never experienced at NARA, our local municipal library, or the library at the University of New Mexico's Taos campus. With Charlotte's help, all filing systems began to seem reasonable and fairly accessible.

Charlotte was the best "archival finding aid" I'd encountered on this entire journey—and I was too tired to stay. She did say one thing as I was leaving that was almost as valuable as having had her eyes beamed into the dark of my subject for two whole hours: contact Sharon Whitlock in the engineering dean's office. As she glided back toward her dusty web I called out my sincere thanks, but she had already slipped into shadow.

Very Special Collections

The next morning (and once a day thereafter during my stay in West Lafayette), I visited the Archives and Special Collections in its fancy new quarters, making the acquaintance of five different archivists.

I spent quite a bit of time looking through the Lillian Gilbreth papers for notes on a very important speech she had given. This mother of twelve, whose brood was the subject of *Cheaper by the Dozen,* had been (along with her equally famous husband) a pioneering industrial engineer. After her husband's premature death, Lillian led the way in experiments with efficiency methods for household work in order to free women for other activities.

She had also been on the engineering faculty at Purdue for a number of years, including during the Cadette era. Lois Neff Haynes, the Waco Cadette, told me that for the class of '43, Dr. Gilbreth had hovered like a mother hen, encouraging them to finish the training and take advantage of this unusual opening for women in aeronautical engineering.

"If not for yourself, then do it for your daughters," Lois remembers her saying.

What I wanted was the notes for the "remarks" Dr. Gilbreth had delivered at the class of '43's commencement ceremony. From conversations with Wild Bunch Cadettes, I knew that not everyone in that group knew just how important Lillian and her work in home efficiency (and as an advocate for women in engineering) had been. They were focused, after all, on making things fly, not capturing them in a Hoover.

As I put in my requests, the librarians, who were mercifully not swamped by other researchers, fetched them for me in near-record time, at least compared to the response speed of other libraries I'd been in. In this manner, I found a great variety of Cadette photos, catching them in classrooms, labs, dorm lounges, dorm rooms, at drafting tables, in the shop, looking at models being tested in the wind tunnels, sitting at large instrument-simulation panels, and of course standing in rows upon rows in front of dorms and fraternity houses where they stayed, or on risers as in my mother's entering and exiting group shots. They were talking in front of Heavilon Hall, strolling through the wide-open grassy spaces between buildings near John Purdue's grave, listening to lectures with pencils (not knitting needles) in hand, scrambling up on top of each other to get to the higher mailboxes in Wood Hall's lobby, playing bridge, singing at the piano, entertaining young Navy men, helping each other solve mathematical problems, working with triangles and slide rules (always slide rules), and just overall dominating the campus.

At least that's the impression the pictures give. In reality, they were only there in groups of just over or under 100, at three different times. There was one exception: for three months in the fall of 1944, two of these groups overlapped and close to 200 Cadettes were on campus at the same time.

The Bruner Report states that the faculty realized they needed to emphasize visual aids and hands-on shop experience to help the women get comfortable with the mechanics and materials of airplane manufacturing. At each of the universities, the Cadettes gamely took on the shop machines and made small ball-peen hammers. Also, everybody made a model airplane, assembling it in front of class, the same exact model, until there was a table covered in them.

In *The Cadetter,* a compilation of writings and drawings by Cadettes at all seven schools published periodically during their training in 1943, Jeanne Moorhead of Purdue summarized their model-making experience:

Did you ever see an airplane with a negative dihedral? With landing gear lacquered with nail polish? With a "man in the moon" face on its nose? No? Well neither had Professor Wood until his job terminology classes turned in their model airplanes. We built and built and built for four weeks these monuments to the wonders of aeronautics. Spars, longerons, struts, formers, and glue were the common subjects of conversation at dinner, at breakfast, and on the way to classes.

Before long we knew why Curtiss-Wright had asked us to turn our inventions over to them. Lucy Hanse's collapsible landing gear that withdrew into the plane when it landed is sure to be the thing of the future, as is Betty Ahl and Johnny Hemphill's invisible plane covering that simply isn't there at all; so think of the weight saved. Other equally ingenious but less conspicuous innovations were made until poor K.D.'s head was spinning. But they were planes, they passed inspection, and who is to say that from them may not evolve the wonder plane of the future. Yes, the Purdue Cadettes are real aero engineers now.

This of course reminded me of how Richard Barrett, my *Curtiss-Wright-er* researching companion at the Columbus library, challenged the Cadettes' "engineer" status. I knew there had been some initial concern after the program was launched about whether the Cadettes appreciated the serious commitment they were being asked to make in exchange for all this free training. One Cadette from the University of Texas, Fairy Jane Frazier, spoke very clearly about their ready responsiveness to the opportunity, when she said, "We'll be able to express our gratitude in a very concrete and aero-'nautical but nice' manner that will be written in planes and signed with long hours of hard work."

Things were moving so fast in the 1943 training that one Cadette who was later interviewed for a master's thesis said: "The big joke was, you dropped a pencil, bent over to pick it up, and missed a whole course in algebra."[33] It bears repeating: they covered two and a half years of upper-division engineering curriculum in 10 months. This was mainly possible because they took no courses other than engineering.

Somehow my mother managed to keep up. She'd always seemed to be a good student, graduating as valedictorian from high school and then going for a year to a private girls' school. And, as I already knew, she had to have placed in the top third in math at the University of Texas, where Curtiss-Wright recruited her, to be accepted into the program.

A few weeks after I returned from Purdue, I finally managed to get a copy of my mother's grades from the great dark vaults below Hovde Hall, where Purdue stores its business records and student transcripts. Though I did not know it while I was walking around that campus, the transcripts made it clear as day that my lively, dance-loving mother did not have *her* nose to the grindstone as much as my father did out there at the airport.

Although grades were given in numbers, not letters, her overall average was about a C+. She wasn't hustling very hard, at least not in terms of her studies. From what her Cadette buddies told me, Mom would not have survived engineering mathematics without Betty's help. When it came to shop, she was also foundering, and once again Betty came to the rescue, making her ball-peen hammer for her. I picture my mother in the machine shop in slacks with her hands on her hips, elbows out, looking drop-dead gorgeous among the heavy shop machines, but trying not to touch them — ever.

Since she wasn't working at getting good grades, what *did* she do with her head?

In Purdue's 1944 *Debris* yearbook, I found a picture of my mom that may answer this question. It was taken in front of Wood Hall and was the third group shot I found her in. This photo only includes the Cadettes who lived on her floor. Ricki's in the front row, in a heavy plaid wool (not fur) coat, facing directly forward, eyes securely shut, hands folded. Everyone around her is smiling sweetly for the camera. She alone has pulled back inside, her posture perfectly upright, as if she wants to open her eyes and look around but isn't sure she can bear to see more of this campus or deal with these demanding engineering classes. Those sassy, pursed-but-not-quite-pouting lips are holding everything together, and it would take more than bricks to get those shoulders to relax.

It's hard to say what kind of weather they were having. The women in the second row are wearing open-collared cotton shirts, but the two on either side of her are enveloped, like her, in large wool coats. Hers, however, is the only one buttoned tight straight up the neck, helping to hold her ramrod straight.

If it's possible for a child to inherit a combo of revulsion for large-scale academia and miserable, stiff-spined forbearance just by having her mother pose publicly for one picture like that, it completely explains the love-hate, edge-lurking ambivalence I have felt about big university environments since my J-School days.

This is why I'm so enjoying all my dodging and darting through light and shadow on the campus of Purdue University, where, praises be, I am not going to receive a grade. I just want to fill my bucket with dirt and build that Cadette Mudwoman higher and higher into the sky, until her authority can open any door I knock on.

Beni and the Boys

I could have remained sequestered in special collections, resisting the youthful and invigorating energy racing back and forth across the Purdue campus, but I decided to venture out and hear a lecture Alice Pawley had told me about by a Stanford professor who wanted to ask, "Has Feminism Changed Science?" in front of a large noontime audience.

I walked into the building and remembered I had not given my cell phone number to Ross, Beth Wehner's grandson, whom I was meeting for lunch. I frantically scouted the lobby for a student with a laptop who could email him and wound up meeting one of Alice's PhD students. She sent off an email on my behalf and recognized my name because she'd been looking forward to my talk.

She, too, was waiting to hear Stanford Professor Londa Schiebinger, so we walked together into the lecture hall. Though the typical bulleted Power Point presentation usually leaves me numb, her lecture did provide some new tools of persuasion about the importance of including women in the discovery phase of science and engineering, rather than in the "make-us-something-to-eat, won't-you, we've-got-to-watch-these-beakers-and-vials" middle or the "clean-up-that-broken-glass, dearie, the-experiment-is-complete" tail end of the creative/inventive process.

Yes, the discovery phase. That's where we women belong, right alongside the men. But if it's so obvious, why are there only 15 men in this room of 100?

But I can't wait around to ask the question. I'm off to lunch with Beth Wehner's grandson Ross, who called back while I was in the lecture. Over a watered-down bowl of vegetables and noodles, I chatted with the sweet young grandson of this "Slide-Rule Packin' Mama" I would soon be describing, in some detail, in the talk Alice had invited me to give. First off I told him how Beth had used her slide rule, holding it out in feigned ignorance of its workings, to seduce young male engineering students in the hallways after class when all the other Cadettes had gone.

"Could one of you boys tell me how this thing works?" she would ask, looking as clueless as any slide-rule-ignorant, eyelash-batting blonde could manage.

It always got results. She was unapologetic about its effectiveness, laughing because her father, a mechanical engineering professor at the University of Texas (who actually taught machine-shop class to that school's Cadettes), had shown her how to use a slide rule when she was quite young. Not only that, she was an ace in mathematics and had noted very early that the male-to-female ratio at Purdue was excellent for her half of the gender divide, compared to UT, where she'd been studying before Purdue.

"Texas was just dismal," she said, "All the men had gone off."

A campus still teeming with male students, even short-term, was fine by Beth.

In tandem with my brunette mother, they were a one-two punch walking down any street. According to Beth, my mother used to arrange double dates for them as often as possible, making sure their outfits were coordinated to show off their light and dark features. Which sounds conniving, but something must have worked out right because here I was sitting in a booth facing Ross, the tow-headed descendant of the blonde half of that equation, while I represented (at least partly, through the aid of a bottle) the brunette.

I wondered later if he'd thought I was glancing crazy for having barreled through my recitation of the Cadette story in such a short time over lunch. But he sent me an email that put my anxiety to rest: "You know so much about my grandmother's history, most of which was new to me today. It was cool for me to imagine what life was like for her so long ago, yet in the same place where I am now. I need to have her share more stories about her life with me."

I sighed in relief. If you have a rapt, quick-feedback audience, getting so carried away is not nearly as deflating afterward as it is when you've been transported completely out of reach while everyone was looking away. I viewed it as a successful trial run for the material I would be delivering the next afternoon.

The Golden Beacon

When Professor Pawley invited me to speak to her seminar, she asked me the title of my talk and how I wanted to be introduced. I had a title ready for her ("Slide-Rule Packin' Mamas"), but it took me several days to decide who or what I was in this show. I finally settled on poet/activist and independent scholar. She seemed to accept this label without qualm. I had figured her to be open-minded, but just to test the limits of "the new academia" (in this case, feminist engineering education), I wrote her an email explaining that my true work is mythopoesis, the moment of creation, because the roots of mythic stories and scientific discoveries are deeply intertwined under the ground.

She never responded to that directly, but she also didn't tell me to please stay home. I decided to structure my talk so it would satisfy both liberal-arts- and engineering-based attendees: a little to the left and a little to the right of midpoint on the rational/imaginal line. I would start with a full mythic wallop to introduce the talk, followed by a spoofing apologia for not being a hard scientist.

So I delivered a two-page introduction about Daedalus the inventor, his son's crash into the sea, and the "Sisters of Icarus," who are never quite mentioned by the Greeks. I cross-referenced with the myth about how King Agamemnon sacrificed his daughter Iphigenia for a wind, so his ships could sail off to the Trojan War, a conflict almost as famous as World War II. Then I suggested that perhaps the Curtiss-Wright Aeronautical Engineering Cadettes had actually been the Sisters of Icarus in disguise. I gave them to understand that alternate myths say Iphigenia wasn't really sacrificed because Artemis, the goddess of the hunt, swooped down at the last minute and substituted a deer. My message was that the shining light of brave young women can never be sacrificed to the gods of war. I didn't know how many of them would care about this. But for my own peace of mind, I had to start there.

"I am not an engineer," I continued. "If I am an independent scholar, then you might say my chosen field has been the Science of Imagination. At one time I even referred to myself as a 'Scientist of Caprice' and 'Chief Explorer of Possibilities,' which gave me permission to make things up as I go, though it did make finding professional employment a little dicey. Having attained a master's degree in poetics on the basis of my thesis on 'Voudoun and the Oral Tradition' made my resume an even stranger stew."

Then I told the students, faculty, and staff in the seminar, that I was only standing in front of them because I had followed the guiding principles of serendipity and synchronicity.

"One helps you recognize that you're always in the right place; the other, that you're always right on time." I looked around the darkened room, hoping George was out there somewhere so we could exchange a grin, but I couldn't spot him.

With my mytho-professional status firmly established, I launched into a mélange of investigative journalism and history, topped off with an irregular sprinkling of personal memoir.

For visuals, I had plenty of shots of Cadettes on all seven campuses, though not in the plants because, other than the one inspectors-on-the-wing shot, those are so scarce. I also showed pictures of the Helldiver, its production line, its pilots, and Building 3, including the gigantic engineering room at Columbus as it looked before the Cadettes turned up.

On the grease board behind me, I had hung my banner from Columbus and drawn a map to show where this research had taken me within the continental United States. (Matt Ohland had advised me that the people attending this seminar would be especially interested in my discovery process. "Ah," I thought, "the discovery phase — I'm all for that.")

I brought ten copies of the Cadette curriculum from Iowa State to give away and a set of drawings for a model of the Helldiver to display, courtesy of Jay Smith, Betty's great-nephew, the one who had sent the book that opened my eyes a year earlier to the seriousness of the Cadette Program. Jay had graciously volunteered to drive two hours to bring those drawings, have lunch, and hear my talk. His stepson Joey, a 17-year-old electrical-engineering student in his *junior* year at Purdue (no small feat), also joined us.

Now that I was deeper into my talk, I could look around and see who else was in the audience in this tiered seminar room. I was cheered to see the PhD student who'd helped me contact Beth's grandson, the aero-engineering professor who had sent me the first batch of Purdue documents (Alten Grandt), and two of the librarians from special collections who'd been most enthusiastic in their assistance (Sammie Morris and Stephanie Schmitz).

I could have been nervous, but I wasn't. From the enthusiastic response I had received in my many tellings of this story, I knew there was something of intrinsic value about the Cadette history, whose surface has barely to be scratched to bring new life up from below.

Besides, I loved wearing my blue Western flap-pocket shirt with two official badges from the Commemorative Air Force, one telling my name and the other calling me a colonel. Tacked above the CAF title was my turquoise and cobalt-blue Helldiver pin from Peggy. And as I stood in front of the seminar, I could feel all six of the Wild Bunch Cadettes standing right beside me. I was only holding up the golden beacon three of them had entrusted to me at our Dallas reunion. My job was to switch it on and let it shine.

After an hour's talk, I hadn't quite finished, but I knew I'd said enough, running over the published statistics on the program and then moving through my outline. Over half of the group stayed for questions and answers. At the end, all ten copies of the 1943 Cadette curriculum flew away. I felt like I'd delivered "the goods" — or at least all the goods I'd been able to gather.

I wrapped up by offering my vision of the future.

"My hope is that women studying aeronautics, wherever they may be on earth, will finally bust loose and create a personal flying vehicle. I predict that the PFV will be round (maybe pancake-shaped) and made of a soft material that renders collisions harmless. As a poet, I'd like to suggest a name for this vehicle: *The Flutterby*. *The Flutterby* will only rise far enough off the ground to get to the dentist or the store. And it will be powered by something other than fossil fuel. It won't fly faster faster, farther farther, and it won't try to reach the moon. In fact, it won't be designed to fly free of earth's gravitational field at all because its designers like it just fine down here."

"When that happens, women aero-engineers will no longer be known as the Sisters of Icarus, staying on the ground, wishing they could fly, and sadly shaking their heads as another brother falls into the sea. They will take their place as designing equals with the man who first invented those wings of feathers and wax. And all the newspaper headlines will trumpet: 'The Daughters Are Coming! The Daughters Are Coming!'

"Yes," I confided, "the Daughters of Daedalus will soon be graduating from an engineering school near you. In fact, don't look now, but I think they're already here."

Chapter Seven
Ricki's Goodbye

Get What You Want

*B*ack in Taos in time for the holiday season, I was gratified by the results of my trip north: I'd found tracks of the young Ricki and reported my investigative findings on the Cadettes at Purdue. I was almost ready to write the book "Ms. Think Purple!" had politely pressured me into writing. Only one thing held me up: I was still waiting for my mother's final goodbye.

Expecting Ricki's spirit to show up in New Mexico in the dead of icy cold winter, the thing she'd hated most about life in the North after her hot Texas childhood, was highly unlikely. Not that amazing things didn't sometimes happen in those long, frozen Minnesota nights. In fact, on one of them, I'd received something akin to a blessing from her when I least expected it.

In the late 1990s, not long after a neuropsychologist in Fargo diagnosed my mother with "diabetic dementia," she had been removed from our family home to the "memory wing" of a nursing facility in Moorhead. Less than a month later, my father also became functionally debilitated after a blood clot worked its way up to his heart and blocked his blood flow, cutting off oxygen to his brain. He wound up living upstairs from Mom on a floor for patients who needed even more medical supervision.

As soon as my father joined her, my siblings and I began a legal contest over our parents and their estates. For almost three years we allowed lawyers to play tennis with our fate. Midway through the third year I wrote an *ex parte* letter to the judge, begging him to please mandate *family* mediation. He wrote back that Minnesota state law didn't permit him to do this in an estate case. He waited a suitable length of time and then quietly suggested to his court-appointed referee that we might try eight hours of *legal* mediation — a whole different ball game.

Whenever I visited my mother in the nursing home during this time, I could tell, by her few but anxious observations, that other siblings had filled her mind with fresh stories of chicanery and vengeance. To counter this, when I left I always gave her a big hug and said, "Take care, Mom. And don't worry — we really are going to work this all out." Usually, she'd nod dubiously and wish me good night. But one frosty winter evening when we children were in the thick of our legal mediation, she took me totally by surprise. Right after I repeated my goodwill departure speech, she sat up on the edge of her bed, took hold of both my shoulders, and looked me straight in the eye.

"No, *you* take care. Get what you *want*."

I almost melted through the floor. I couldn't remember the last time she'd spoken so encouragingly to me. After she turned 60, she became progressively more passive and worried nonstop about when my grand bohemian adventure would be over and why I still persisted in writing and performance when I clearly wasn't going to make a living at it. But here she was, speaking from the deepest part of her heart, telling me to satisfy myself and not let this estate battle or my siblings run all over me.

Tears gushed into my eyes and my heart twisted in my chest. Mom had clearly been watching our legal drama with far more moxie than anyone thought she had left. No matter how dim her lights might be about time and place and who was president, her heart still beat with fervent hope that the warring factions in her family would finally make peace.

Crawfish and Crab

In February 2010, three months after my return from Purdue, I finally figured out how I might persuade my mother to make one last appearance, though I knew I had to act quickly. People from "the Greatest Genera-tion" were expiring rapidly: my mother and the sixth Wild Bunch member, Ruthe Mellott, had already stepped over the line of mortality drawn in the sand. I decided to visit the only surviving member of the Wild Bunch I had never met: Mary Sprow in New Orleans. I figured that putting together all four of the remaining "Casa Dingies" at once just might spur the spirit of Ricki Cruse to rejoin the living one more time. With generous help from Mary's daughter Cindy, I began to organize another reunion.

I wasn't particularly happy about going to New Orleans, and not just because the wrecked neighborhoods were still unrestored four years after Hurricane Katrina. My main hesitation was being near the Mississippi Riv-er in such a showy town with its disparate strata of wealth. It brought back a heavy cluster of family memories.

Upriver in St. Louis, Charles H. Peck, my mother's great-great grand-father, had left behind a large fortune tied up in a tangled legal web that fed only a few of his descendants and a whole lot of local lawyers for over 105 years. Some of his money finally trickled down in equal distribution to the remainder of his living descendants. But my mother died eleven months too soon to be one of them. The fumes of that fortune — taunting and unavailable — had hovered over Grandmother Genevieve's side of the family and gave my grandmother, my mother, and her siblings the indel-ible impression that they came from money. Therefore, they had only one real responsibility in life: to keep up appearances until their ship came in. I blamed Charles H. Peck for my mother's inability to grasp that certain opportunities in her life would guarantee her economic independence — like aeronautical engineering.

Even so, I needed to brave the mighty Mississippi's broad sweep and meet the last of her close Cadette friends. On a Thursday night, exactly one year after the interviews in Dallas, I walked off a plane at New Orleans' Louis Armstrong International Airport back into the illustrious company of Cindy and the three other Cadettes, who had all flown in separately.

We were lucky: we arrived in time for the first sunny weather New Orleans had seen in months. Plus, the Saints had just won the Super Bowl, so the whole city was in a good mood. Early the next morning we showed up at the National World War II/D-Day Museum so their on-site historian could interview each of the Cadettes in a padded, topnotch video studio. The next day, we did the French Quarter, starting with beignets piled half an inch high with powdered sugar, followed by a tour in an open horse-drawn carriage, narrated by a spunky woman who was a long-term French Quarter resident. At our urging, she gave us the unexpurgated version of New Orleans' seedy history and made us all very merry. Then it was time to get serious and drop in for our first short visit with Mary.

We all knew this weekend might be the last time we'd see Mary alive. She'd begun to have seizures and was taking medications that sedated her into periods of extreme vagueness. But when she saw the other Cadettes, she spoke their names without hesitation, her eagle-sharp eye tracking them, even though her head stayed still. I was fascinated by the strong and beautiful line of her profile sweeping broadly back, her lank gray hair hanging down in straight lines behind her, the smooth fair skin of her cheeks as she followed our conversation and questions, responding unexpectedly with sudden statements of historical fact and halting but lucid questions of her own.

Mary was the Cadette who'd nearly had her arm sliced off by the dive brake, the scar of which I finally got to see. It was a dark red arc about three inches long just below the elbow on her very thin right arm. Strikingly tall Mary, who'd loved to wear high heels that made her even taller and more regal, whose hair was piled high and luxurious in every picture I saw of her, was now paralyzed on her left side from the stroke. This tragic turn of events had happened only a few weeks before I began this quest for "All My Daughters," my personal title for the companion play about World War II women that Arthur Miller never wrote.

I would never see Mary at full tilt, but it was easy to imagine her infectious laugh and magnetic energy. Even after being with her for just an hour, it became abundantly clear that she had been the social hub and warm heart of the Wild Bunch. It also emerged that her warm, playful (though now senile) husband Don had given them the name.

Ricki's Goodbye

Before she moved to New Orleans, Mary had lived in Houston for many years and often did favors for my mother, who now lived in the Far North with my father. Being such a good friend to Ricki, Mary would often go shopping with my Grandma Genevieve and look out for Grandpa Buck. During those years, she was far more involved in my grandparents' daily lives in Houston than my mother was. Even Cindy, who'd tagged along as a kid, knew my grandparents better than I did. Genevieve and Buck rarely braved the Minnesota cold.

One of the more mysterious moments was when I asked Mary, in front of the other Cadettes, what she had done after the injury. She couldn't answer, which we all wrote off to the stroke making certain things impossible to articulate. But none of the Cadettes could remember either. Mary had not worked with my mother on the pilot's handbooks, they were sure of that. And she had not been in drafting. So where was Mary and why couldn't anyone in the room, including her daughter, who had listened to her tell vivid stories about the Curtiss-Wright episode for many years, remember what her next assignment had been, especially since it was for the duration of the war? This was exceedingly strange, because she had been such a lively presence in their lives for so long that they had never considered that they might not be able to account for where she was in the plant after that select group of Cadettes were taken off inspections.

We called on her at home three separate times, only once being at mealtime, and it was a repast I will never forget. Ten of us — including all four Cadettes, Cindy, her partner Lisa, their daughter Sophie, Cindy's sister Connie, and their dad Don — had a prolonged feeding frenzy on boiled crawfish and crab piled half a foot high on newspaper the length of a dining table. It was so New Orleans spicy it made my cuticles burn trying to liberate the edible insides from the shells. Mary watched, assisted by a nurse's aide who helped the fork reach Mary's mouth. Mary still has a good appetite, which makes everyone hopeful she'll stick around a good while yet.

At one point, Mary amazed everyone by asking Cindy, "Who's that one in the middle?" while gesturing in my direction.

"That's Ricki's daughter," Cindy replied. "You remember Ricki, the good-looking brunette from Houston? This is her daughter Jean-Vi."

"Yes, but this one's prettier."

That took my breath completely away. My mother — beauty queen, valedictorian, "Southern Belle" in her college yearbook, fabulous dancer, male magnet — was *not* the fairest of them all? I had always felt my appearance ranked a poor third (after my mother and my sister) on the distaff side of our family. And here I was being yanked to the top. From out of the distant reaches of Mary's stroke damage came this lovely compliment.

My lips smarted from the hot pepper on the crab, my eyes burned with tears. The spirit of my mother, whose glittering vapor trail I'd been following since I could remember and who'd brought me to this room by her strong friendship with these other Cadettes, was no longer requiring me to stay just slightly behind her polished lead.

Even when she had faded back into the shadows behind my father after leaving her teaching job, the loss of her theatrical luster hadn't dimmed my memory of the sparkle and challenge in those warm hazel eyes. She'd been so admired for her charm, beauty, fashion sense, and teaching/directing talents that she couldn't ever turn and really see me. I was just her phantom companion, the adolescent daughter who sat beside her in the dark of the high-school auditorium, night after night, watching her create small miracles of music, dance, and drama on a small-town high school stage. Through it all, as I waited anxiously to be old enough to take her classes and join the action onstage, it never dawned on me that she might retire on the eve of my eligibility, leaving me with no theatrical guidance and permanent stage-fright, as well as an unquenchable passion for dramatic intensity.

What my mother could have done for me if she'd stayed on the job another couple of years was of absolutely no consequence on this boiled crawfish night. I had been fully welcomed into her life pre-theater, pre-marriage. I felt in some ways as if in fact I *was* her that night, with an opportunity to make it up all new to suit myself, never leaving the Helldiver factory to get married. And certainly not walking away from these dear, dear friends. When I really thought about it, I could see that my actual life choices — liv-

ing with women, remaining childless, working to promote women's rights
—had allowed me to be true to the vision of female bonding represented in
this room.

When I looked at the women around this table, I felt my heart vibrating
with hope that all women will eventually come down from the up-in-the-air
teeter-totter position we were shifted back to after the brief leveling provided
by war production in World War II. How could I not revel in the sisterly tide
flowing through that room and all around that seafood? I nodded gratefully
to Mary for having drawn us together because I could see that even though
her physical being may be slowly sinking, her smile and spirit will never
drown, even in this city so recently and tragically inundated.

After parting company with the Cadettes in New Orleans, I finally
understood that I alone could initiate the goodbyes that my mother had
failed to speak. So as the plane lifted skyward above Louis Armstrong Air-
port, I bid a silent farewell to the mother who had left me so dramatically,
both when she dropped her teaching and directing career *and* when she
died in a matter of hours. I waved goodbye to that Ricki and to the dutiful
young daughter still waiting for her chance to shine on the musical stage.

Then I turned to embrace the younger Ricki I'd found in the company
of Mary, Betty, Beth, and Peggy—the Ricki who'd busted out of macho East
Texas and traveled north to Purdue to take the bull of aeronautical engi-
neering by the horns, even though that bull spoke a language she couldn't
relate to and eventually bucked her off. I marveled at the fact that even as
she was being thrown up into the air, she was brave enough to befriend
five other women and affirm those bonds for life. *That* Ricki would be alive
forever, dancing up the length of Mary's crawfish-and-crab-covered table,
kicking her legs toward the ceiling, telling us to "Go ahead, girls, get what
you want. Just fly, fly, fly."

Epilogue

On the way back to Taos from New Orleans, I got off in Dallas with Peggy because we had a date with an old warbird — one that had only briefly left its nest. She drove us to a large aviation facility just west of Dallas where Vought Industries is housed. One of the old metal buildings in the far back corner currently contains the original prototype of the famous Flying Pancake, officially known as the V-173. The V is for Vought, Chance Vought, the inventive engineer whose company manufactured my favorite alternative WWII plane.

A gentleman at the National Air and Space Museum had told me the Pancake was being refurbished and would be on static display at Frontiers of Flight at Love Field. So I contacted the Vought Retirees Association that was working on it and got approval for a visit. Peggy and I both had to have security clearance, which surprised me because no other plane or museum I'd visited had required it. But this plane belongs to the Smithsonian, and they are very protective of it. Frontiers of Flight will have it for ten years and then it may have to be returned to the Smithsonian.

This presents some very vexing problems because the process of transporting the Pancake to Texas from Virginia, where it had been stored in a half-wrecked state, was so daunting it took a year to figure out how to do it. They had to get permission from every state it traveled through and then build a box tailored to its unusual round shape (diameter 23.2 feet) and tilt it at enough of an angle to get it under overpasses, but not so horizontal it would lift off.

They succeeded, and for many months a small team had been rebuilding the Pancake in a large hangar where several other Vought-designed planes had also been restored. I was trembling with delight as we entered the premises and could hardly sit still in the office of the project leader, Dick Atkins, a retired Air Force pilot who loves this plane passionately and is co-authoring a definitive historical book on it.

Epilogue

He was very interested to hear about the Cadettes and meet Peggy, so we spent a half hour talking and then cruised the Pancake in the hangar, where it is flipped onto its side. It was completely in tact but sported two shades of paint: half cobalt blue, the other half primer white. The final color, a bright yellow as in all the models, was soon to be applied, though Dick told us they'd temporarily suspended work due to technical difficulties that he did not specify.

This was the version of the Pancake designed in the '30s, tested in the early '40s, then redesigned. The sleeker, more efficient model was built but never tested because of the ascendancy of jet engines. After it was targeted for the scrap pile by the government, they dropped wrecking balls on it and nothing happened because the design was so strong. So they went at it with blowtorches to weaken it and then delivered the coup de grâce, leaving no trace of the beautiful sleek Pancake that succeeded the clunkier apparition flying sideways in its cradle at this hangar.

One drawback is that the pilot has to climb in through the underside of the cockpit, which is a glass-paned cone through which he also has to look down at a 45-degree angle as he takes off. In the videos I've seen of the Pancake's flight tests, it looks like a strangely tilted bird running up the tarmac on two extended legs and one tiny tail wheel. The outer sides of the round body each sprout tiny upright flippers like a sea otter whose fins never quite finished growing. In one of its more amusing early designs, which you can see in a video of the first radio-controlled flights of the model, it has a hinged and floppy tail that looks like it could use some Viagra. But overall, according to several different reports, the Pancake was one of the most stable airplanes ever built.

Even though the man at NASM said the plane would only be on static display at Frontiers of Flight, Dick assured me that the Pancake will be completely flyable when they're done. But even if I learn to fly, I'm going to pass: as flat and charming as she is, she's still a warbird. I'll wait for *The Flutterby* instead.

Henson, Benson, and Bond
by Professor K.D. Wood, Director,
Purdue Cadette Class of 1943

Henson, Benson, and Bond one night
Sailed off with an old slide rule
Sailed with a crowd down Second Street
To Purdue's Engineering School
"Where are you going, and what do you wish?"
Miss Morrison asked of the three
"We have come to fish for the engineers
of this great University
Networks of charts and graphs have we"
Said Henson
Benson
and Bond.

Miss Morrison laughed and wrote a report
For the files of Curtiss-Wright
"We make them work eight hours a day
But we don't control the night"
All night long their charts they drew
Never afraid were they
They worked and plotted the whole night thru
So they could sleep the next day
I shall name you the three Cadettes
Henson
Benson
and Bond.

Now Benson and Bond are two little blondes
and Henson's a little brunette
And the old slide rule that carried them thru
is a thing to worry your head
So shut your eyes and draw the lines
and wonderful things you'll see
The Columbus boys will be surprised
but the old slide rule won't be
These are the girls that will carry them on
Henson
Benson
and Bond.

Author's Note

$\mathcal{M}$y initial curiosity about whether my mother could have par-
layed her Cadette experience into a career in aeronautical engi-
neering is still largely unsatisfied. But I did discover that, of the
many women who completed Cadette training and worked in the plants,
a substantial number went on to careers in drafting, teaching (math and
science), and other engineering and technology–related fields. They were
unable to complete aero-engineering degrees because universities again
closed that door to women, even though brilliantly promising light had
shone through it during the war. The women who saw and even basked
in that light at Curtiss-Wright developed a gleam in their eyes that would
not go away. All of the Cadettes I spoke with agree that they had an unfor-
gettable experience and that it gave them greater self-confidence and self-
esteem for the rest of their lives. Even in their mid to late 80s, they are full of
vim and vigor, especially when asked about their employment as Curtiss-
Wright Cadettes.

This story about my mother and her Wild Bunch friends, along with
the description of the planning and execution of the Cadette Program, is
necessarily limited in scope, as is my focus on Purdue as the main cam-
pus, which hosted the training of three separate Cadette groups, and the
Columbus plant, where so many of them worked. There are many other
daughters, granddaughters, and nieces of Cadettes out there who know bits
and pieces of the story as it relates to the other universities in the program
and the other plants of Curtiss-Wright. I welcome them to add to the mix
by visiting the website (www.WildHarePress.com/FlyingIntoYesterday).

I would also like to see a video made about the Cadette Program, freely
partaking of the material I have gathered as a foundation, including the
nine Cadette video interviews (and pictures of other Cadettes), photo-
graphs from the schools and plants, and documentation of the program
from professors, museum archivists and curators, and aviation historians.

There are also videotaped oral histories of other Cadettes in the archives at Iowa State University. I welcome creative co-participants in the project.

To research this story, I had to travel full circle back to my early ambitions and training in history and investigative journalism, both of which I abandoned when I realized how rigged they were toward reporting mainly on the activities and ideas of men. For over 30 years, I took refuge in poetics, mythology, dreamwork, and theater, trying to envision an alternate universe where the lives and experiences of women were fully valued. But now, well into the 21st century, it has become obvious that the campaign by male-dominated institutions to undervalue the female gender's vitality, ingenuity, and potential to contribute in every field of human endeavor continues unabated. In my opinion, every well-meaning, noble effort to restore the earth and its biosphere will fail until women are no longer prevented from demonstrating their power as movers and shakers, thinkers and creators — especially in ways that heal the planet and promote peace.

Bruner's summarizing comment about the Cadettes, that "a few of the girls in this program could, if further trained, compete with the best men in the business if prejudices were barred," says it all. In my estimation, *more* than a few women have always been ready. It's time to lift the prejudices and make space for women engineers to design a new aeronautical future — *and* a gentler, safer, healthier world. I'm betting that if younger women learn about the rapid comprehension and aptitude demonstrated by their Cadette sisters in World War II, they'll be more than ready to get down to the task at hand.

Author Mollie Gregory (whose new book on Hollywood stuntwomen is due out soon from the University of California Press) read an earlier draft of this manuscript and posed one of the most provocative questions I've heard so far: "Do you suppose there are women sitting in their kitchens today who are drinking because they can't be engineers?" She didn't need to specify aeronautical engineers. Clearly the question applies to women poised on the threshold of *any* field of engineering who still perceive that they are not welcome to offer suggestions about how the things in this world should be designed.

Author's Note

In parting, how can I ever express enough gratitude to the anonymous "Ms. Think Purple!" for guiding me onto this path? I hope she finds a copy of this book, which she urged me to write, and passes it along to another woman still waiting, as I was, for inspiration — and direction — from that regal light.

And just to set matters straight: I still haven't been to Japan, though I've been back to bathe in that "maternal current" off Hawaiian shores half a dozen times. On my last visit, which began on March 13, 2011, the Japanese "mother wave" had just come ashore — with *very* devastating results — on the Kona Coast. Whether we're all about to be swept into yesterday is anybody's guess. But if we are, I'm going to be carrying the bright and loving memory of my four Wild Bunch sister-friends — as well as Ruthe and Ricki — along for the ride.

Bibliography

Bix, Amy Sue. "From 'Engineeresses' to 'Girl Engineers' to 'Good Engineers': A History of U.S. Women's Engineering Education." *National Women's Studies Association Journal*, Vol. 16, No. 1, Spring 2004.

Bruner, Warren. "A Report on The Engineering Cadette Training Program of the Curtiss-Wright Corporation." December 30, 1944. Approved by Chief Engineer George A. Page on January 24, 1945.

Cole, C. Wilson. "Training of Women in Engineering." *Journal of Engineering Education*, October 1943, Vol. 34, No. 2. Paper originally presented at the 51st Annual Meeting, SPEE, Chicago, Illinois, June 18–20, 1943.

Corn, Joseph J. *The Winged Gospel: America's Romance with Aviation, 1900–1950.* New York: Oxford University Press, 1983.

Douglas, Deborah G. *American Women and Flight Since 1940.* Washington, D.C.: Smithsonian Institute Press, Smithsonian Studies in Air and Space, No. 7, 1990.

Eltscher, Louis R. and Young, Edward M. *Curtiss-Wright: Greatness and Decline.* New York: Twayne Publishers, 1998.

Grandt, Alten F., Gustafson, W.A., and Cargnino, L.T. *One Small Step: the History of Aerospace Engineering at Purdue University.* West Lafayette, IN: School of Aeronautics and Astronautics, Purdue University Press, 1995; second edition, 2010.

Hogan, Robert. Untitled master's thesis. Cleveland State University, 1997.

McIntyre, Natalie. "Curtiss-Wright Cadettes: A Case Study of the Effect of the WWII Labor Shortage on Women in Engineering." Master's thesis, University of Minnesota, 1993.

Morley, Richard A. "The Ohio-Curtiss Airplane Connection: Curtiss-Wright Airplane Division in Columbus, 1940–1950." *American Aviation Historical Society Journal,* Fall 1991, Vol. 36, No. 3.

Olds, Robert. *Helldiver Squadron: The Story of Carrier Bombing Squadron 17 with Task Force 58.* New York: Dodd, Mead & Company, 1944.

Perusek, Anne M. and Baldwin, Kenneth. "The Curtiss-Wright Engineering Cadettes." New York: *SWE (Magazine of the Society of Women Engineers),* March/April 1995.

Schiebinger, Londa, ed. *Gendered Innovations in Science and Engineering.* Palo Alto, CA: Stanford University Press, 2008.

Smith, Peter C. *Curtiss SB2C Helldiver.* Wiltshire, England: The Crowood Press, 1998.

Stoff, Joshua. *Picture History of World War II American Aircraft Production.* New York: Dover Publications, Inc., 1993.

Personal Acknowledgments

I am particularly thankful to "Ms. Think Purple!" for launching me on this trajectory. Though I have been unable to locate her or even find out where the conference she told me about took place, she crossed my path at a critical moment when it was still possible to locate Cadettes who were ready and able to tell it like it was.

For their honest and enthusiastic reporting of memories and facts about their participation in the Curtiss-Wright program, I am grateful to these Cadettes:

Class of 1943 — 1st Round: February 12 to December 14, 1943
(university attended during Cadette Program, in italics, followed by most recent city and state of residence) (using a code I found in several *Cadette Gazettes*, RC means respiration ceased):
Betty Henson Masket *(Purdue)*, Chevy Chase, MD
Beth (Beni) Benson Wehner *(Purdue)*, Austin, TX
Margaret Adams Upham *(Purdue)*, Richardson, TX
Mary Ullrich Sprow *(Purdue)*, Metairie, LA
Jackie Warren Davis *(Purdue)*, Chevy Chase, MD
Lois Neff Haynes *(Purdue)*, Waco, TX
Totsye Harper Winslow *(Purdue)*, Houston, TX
Nevaire Gambrell Richardson *(Texas)*, Magnolia, TX
Shirley Chase *(Texas)*, Webster Groves, MO
Juanita Cathey Sinclair *(Texas)*, Raleigh, NC
Ellen Sauer Thurber *(Cornell)*, Rochester, NY
Nina Stone Newton Kilgore *(Cornell)*, Avon, CT
Mary Hood Baltus *(Cornell)*, Tonawanda, NY
Nancie Baltus (Sr Mary Matthew) *(Cornell)*, Erie, PA
Mary Alice Stever Simes *(Penn State)*, Durham, NC
Dorothy Orndorff *(Penn State)*, Delta, OH

Ellen Holborn Post *(RPI)*, Springfield, MA
Harriet Talmage *(Minnesota)*, Willowbrook, IL
Barbara Wolf Bowers *(Minnesota)*, Dublin, OH
Mary Lou Teufel *(Minnesota)*, Maryknoll, NY
Lois Stender Rolke, via husband Bill *(Minnesota)*, Merrimack, NH
Mary Louise Converse Stamm *(Iowa State)*, Mantua, OH
Anne Rill Yates *(Iowa State)*, Gurley, AL (RC 2010)
Ethelyne Hendrickson Vea *(Iowa State)*, Richland, WA (RC 2010)

Class of 1944 – Purdue 2nd Round: July through December, 1944
Ann Meuser Books, Bartow, FL
Dorothy Wurster Rout, Columbus, OH
Mary Lou Stuber Wright, Columbus, OH

Class of 1945 – Purdue 3rd Round: October 1944 to March 1945
Kathryn (Kay) Atkinson, Columbus, OH
Nova Anderson Weller, Columbus, OH
Anne Callis Davis, Flint, MI

Descendants of Cadettes Who Assisted
Cindy Sprow, daughter of Mary Ullrich Sprow *(Purdue, 1943)*
Christelle Ellis, daughter of Ethelyne Vea *(Iowa State, 1943)*
Denise Luck, daughter of Mona Shuttleworth Mattingly *(Texas, 1943)*
Marian Jackson Smith, daughter of Josephine Johnson Jackson
    (Purdue, 1943)
Teresa Tanny, granddaughter of Juanita Lewis Gais *(Texas, 1943)*
Kathy Post, daughter of Ellen Holborn Post *(RPI, 1943)*
Jill Durkin, niece of Ruthe Mellott *(Purdue, 1943)*

Acknowledgments

For their assistance in tracking down this story, I want to thank these librarians, archivists, curators, and professors:

California
Elizabeth Tucker, ranger, Rosie the Riveter/WWII Home Front National Historic Park, Richmond, CA

Veronica Rodriguez, museum curator, Rosie the Riveter/WWII Home Front National Historic Park, Richmond, CA

Lester Hall, assistant project engineer, SB2C, Curtiss-Wright Columbus, Encino, CA

Indiana
George Palmer, professor emeritus, Aeronautical Engineering, Purdue

Larry Cargnino, professor emeritus, Aeronautical Engineering, Purdue

Alice Pawley, assistant professor, Engineering Education, Purdue

Matt Ohland, associate professor, Engineering Education, Purdue

Alten F. Grandt, professor, Aeronautical Engineering, Purdue

Charlotte A. Erdmann, collections coordinator, Potter Engineering Library, Purdue

Amy S. Van Epps, librarian, Potter Engineering Library, Purdue

Sharon K. Whitlock, administrative director, Engineering Department, Purdue

Sammie L. Morris, head and university archivist, Archives and Special Collections Research Center, Purdue

Stephanie Schmitz, special projects archivist, Archives and Special Collections Research Center, Purdue

Wanda A. Dutton, team leader, Academic Records, Purdue

Iowa
Tanya Zanish-Belcher, archivist/librarian, Iowa State University

New Jersey

August Zoll, retired aeronautical engineer, Wright Aeronautical
Corporation, Wood-Ridge

Mike Stock, corporate communications, Curtiss-Wright Corporation,
Parsipanny

Paul Ferdenzi, historian, Curtiss-Wright Corporation, Parsipanny

New York

Rick Leisenring, assistant curator, Glenn Curtiss Museum,
Hammondsport

Amy Rupert, archivist, Folsom Library, Rensselaer Polytechnic Institute,
Troy

Nancy Ward, archivist, CALSPAN, Buffalo

John Edens, chief librarian, University at Buffalo Libraries, SUNY, Buffalo

Ohio

Nolan Leatherman, retired engineer, North American Aviation,
Columbus

Richard Barrett, historian, retired engineer, Battelle, Columbus

John Scott, retired facilities manager, North American/Curtiss-Wright
plant, Columbus

Otto Acker, retired engineer, Curtiss-Wright, Columbus

Arlene Kelley, retired secretary to plant manager Jack Davey,
Curtiss-Wright, Columbus

Bill Tylka, manager, Odyssey Aviation, Columbus

Jim Peterson, ramp agent, US Airways, Port of Columbus Airport,
Columbus

Don Peters, retired pilot, TWA, Westerville

Arnett Howard, musician/bandleader, aviation historian, cameraman,
Columbus

Curtis Trueb, student and cameraman, Ohio State University, Columbus

Joel Greggs, commander, Helldiver Squadron, Association of Naval
Aviation, Columbus

Acknowledgments

Harold Baker, WWII gunner/radioman, SB2C Helldiver, Columbus

Michael Broidy, vice president corporate affairs, Schottenstein Property
Group, Columbus

Joe Blundo, columnist, Columbus *Dispatch*, Columbus

Cheryl Lubow, librarian, research services, State Library of Ohio,
Columbus

John Armstrong, special collections archivist, Wright State University,
Dayton

Texas

Maury Ford, exhibits manager, The Women's Museum, Dallas

Sharon Spalding, director of education, Frontiers of Flight Museum, Love
Field, Dallas

Dawn Letson, women's collection coordinator, Texas Women's University,
Denton

Dick Atkins, retired USAF pilot, project leader, Flying Pancake
restoration, Vought Retirees Association, Dallas

Patrizia Nava, special collections curator, McDermott Library, University
of Texas, Dallas

Ed Vesely, pilot, William P. Hobby Airport, Houston

Martha Dillard, colonel, Cactus Squadron, Commemorative Air Force,
Graham

Ted and Sharon Short, colonels, Commemorative Air Force, Midland

William McWhorter, WWII historian and cameraman, Texas Historical
Commission, Austin

Washington, D.C.

Mark Mollan, archivist, Navy/Maritime Reference, National Archives and
Records Administration, Capitol Mall

Carolyn Gilliam, reference librarian, Archives Library Information
Center, National Archives and Records Administration

Phil Edwards, technical information specialist, National Air and Space
Museum, Capitol Mall

Daniel A. Jones, librarian, Naval History Heritage Command, Naval Shipyard

Jeremy Bigwood, researcher, specializing in Freedom of Information Act searches

Washington

Dan Hagedorn, senior curator, Aviation Research Center, Museum of Flight, Boeing Field, Seattle

John Little, assistant curator, Aviation Research Center, Museum of Flight, Boeing Field, Seattle

For special favors and/or moral support, my personal thanks go to:

Rebecca Kroening, University of Minnesota archives retrieval, Minneapolis, MN

Imogene Bruner Helm, teacher and musician, Tucson, AZ

Susan M. Klick and Karen Frye, daughters of Ruth Cleverly Klick, Mechanicsburg, PA, and Leesburg, VA

Jay Smith, writer, *Model Aviation Magazine,* Betty Masket's great nephew, Muncie, IN

Gwyneth Ragosine, reference librarian, retired, Ashland, OR

Cherie Burns, journalist/author, Taos, NM, and Nantucket, MA

Rane Richardson and Carse McDaniel, my personal cheering squad, Albuquerque, NM

Jo Face, Ali Righter, Chris Wells, and Susan Ressler, my hiking buddies, Taos, NM

Chris Fairchild, who dared to "fly" with me via motor scooter, Taos, NM

Linley Solari, soul guide extraordinaire, who helped fluff out my wings, Taos, NM

Mary Simonini, bioenergetics/grief counselor and shaman, Taos, NM

Jacqueline Rickard, writer/artist/friend, who teared up when she first heard about this project and has fiercely kept me on track toward full disclosure ever since, Taos, NM

Acknowledgments

David Pérez, my content editor, who helped streamline the fuselage of my
   investigation, lighten its tail/tale, and drop excess family baggage until
   the story could (as he constantly reminded me) really soar, Taos, NM
Barbara Sheppard, love of my life, who soothes my war-weary soul and keeps
   my spirits up whenever my truth-hunting energy flags, Taos, NM

Endnotes

[1]"The Sisters of Icarus" was the name of a 2004 exhibition on women in aviation at the Zepplin Museum, in Zepplinheim, Friedrichshafen am Bodensee, Germany.

[2]"Engineering Cadettes of the Curtiss-Wright Corp.," Cadette Training Department, Curtiss-Wright Corporation Airplane Division. Recruiting pamphlet, January 1943, p. 11.

[3]Interview with Lois Neff Haynes, Waco, Texas, June 6, 2009.

[4]Smith, Zadie. *Autograph Man.* New York: Random House, 2002, p. 262.

[5]*Purdue Engineer,* March 1943. Every article initially published by the engineering departments at the participating universities called it an "invasion."

[6]Bix, Amy Sue. "From 'Engineeresses' to 'Girl Engineers' to 'Good Engineers': A History of Women's U.S. Engineering Education." *NWSA Journal,* Vol. 16, No. 1, Spring 2004, p. 12.

[7]Germany officially decried the use of German (non-Jewish) women for work in the war industries; they considered America barbaric for allowing its women to perform such "manly" tasks.

[8]Smith, Peter C. "Curtiss SB2C Helldiver." Wiltshire, England: Crowood Press, 1998, inside cover.

[9]Official Navy Summary of the SB2C Contract, issued in 1947. The summary states that there were 96,675 engineering orders related to the SB2C. As SB2C's assistant project engineer, Les Hall, informed me, "An EO is not necessarily a design deficiency; it could be a flaw on the manufacturing level, like a row of rivets out of alignment, which would take an EO to make the change."

[10]Ruthe Mellott was born and raised in the small mountain town of Woodsfield, Ohio, 100 miles south of Columbus. She lived most of her life after the war in Texas, settling in Conroe, just outside Houston, and served as assistant to the registrar at the University of Houston for many years. In her late 50s she finally married William H. Willson, who died 22 months later. One of her nieces describes Ruthe as "a perfect lady, just absolutely lovely." Ruthe never told her niece about her participation in the Cadette Program, although she went to every reunion (Jill Durkin, phone call, May 17, 2011).

[11]Curtiss-Wright Engineering Cadette recruiting pamphlet, ibid, p. 11.

Endnotes

[12]"Plane Defects Laid to a Wright Plant; Government Sues. Report of Truman Committee Accuses Factory in Ohio of Making Defective Engines." *The New York Times,* July 11, 1943.

[13]Natalie Marie McIntire, "A Case Study of the Effect of the World War II Labor Shortage on Women in Engineering." Master's thesis, University of Minnesota, September 1993, p. 29.

[14]Bruner claimed in his report (p. 54) that the actual cost per Cadette trained was closer to $2,000, but I have never seen proof of that.

[15]C. Wilson Cole, "Training of Women in Engineering," Journal of Engineering Education, October 1943, Vol. 34, No. 2. This paper was originally presented at the 51st Annual Meeting, SPEE, Chicago, Illinois, June 18–20, 1943. Cole was head of the Training Division, Wright Aeronautical Corporation; later he was supervisor of Curtiss-Wright's Engineering Personnel Bureau (EPB), whose offices were in Buffalo, New York.

In Cole's report, delivered halfway through the 1943 Cadette training, he said: "It is a foregone conclusion that 'on the job' training will be given to the Cadettes to supplement the preliminary material covered at the universities. Opportunity will therefore be open to each and every Cadette to be upgraded within the organization. This will be dependent solely on individual initiative and inherent ability."

But Les Hall, assistant project engineer on the Helldiver, who'd left the company in 1944 after six years because, he said, he did not approve of the company's manufacturing methods and management style, described the situation at the Columbus plant after Curtiss-Wright closed down its airplane division: "In 1951, when North American bought the plant — lock, stock, and barrel, I was sent back on assignment to indoctrinate the engineers in North American's methods. It was like walking back into my old house. They had rehired all the old engineers. It was a happy homecoming, and I worked there for six months."

Yes, North American had rehired all the old engineers from Curtiss-Wright — if you don't count the Cadettes. Possibly because they were nowhere to be found: During its last five years of airframe production, Curtiss-Wright had carefully used and discarded the few Cadette engineers they had retained or rehired after the war. Les never heard anyone mention the Cadettes — or their vital work — at the Columbus plant.

[16]Bruner Report, p. 48.

[17]A golem is an Eastern European, super-sized male figure made of clay, which could be summoned into action in defense of the Jews by rabbinical incantations.

[18]Other Cadettes I spoke to were asked to continue their work at the Research Department in Buffalo or stay on in Columbus to do computations for the engineers who were still refining the Helldiver or working on experimental aircraft.

One of them, Mary Lou Teufel (University of Minnesota), told me about working in the flight test section on data reduction from test flights for the SB2C dive bombers. "In 1944, there were no computers to manage this job. Our offices were right by the runway in Columbus. We were half deaf from noise of the SB2C engines running all the time. There was a camera in the cockpit facing the dashboard. It was 15-inch film, with the camera clicking every few seconds. Depending on weather, the pilot went up early in the morning and finished his tests about 10 a.m. Data on films and the Brown Recorder were ready for us in the afternoon.

"One of the other Cadettes suggested that if we worked the four-to-midnight shift, we could have data ready for the test pilot to see before he took off on his next flight. So we got moved to that shift. Early in June, the flight-test section crew moved to Buffalo to take advantage of the better weather there. On August 15th, we were at work when the announcement came that the Japanese had surrendered. We immediately stopped our work and joined the crowds walking along Delaware Avenue, celebrating. When we returned to Columbus, most of the Cadettes were terminated; but I was told that since I was in 'research,' I was not terminated. I stayed on until the following June (1946) and continued on the same shift" (email and phone calls, June 2010).

[19]Les Hall, phone calls, April 2009 and July 2010.

[20]*The New York Times*, Jan. 21, 1944. The article's title states: "Industry Deaths Since Pearl Harbor 37,600, Exceeding by 7,500 Number Killed in War." (These were the figures through January 1, 1944.) Also, a report from the Office of War Information (OWI) reported that 210,000 workers were permanently disabled and 4.5 million temporarily disabled. This was 60 times the number of military wounded and missing. By the end of the war, of course, the numbers were extreme in the other direction, with a total of 295,000 U.S. service personnel killed and an unknown number of wounded or missing.

[21]*Cadette Register and Gazette*, Purdue class of 1944.

[22]Imogene Bruner, phone call, November 2009.

[23]What surfaced instead of more information on Warren Bruner was a completely different picture of how the Cadette Program was launched — especially the

recruiting and oversight of the Cadettes themselves. I found out in December of 2010 that a woman named Ruth G. Cleverly had actually done a great deal of the initial recruitment and footwork. Ruth was a public-school teacher who, in 1942, signed up for a summer course in aeronautical engineering at MIT. When she completed it with the highest scores, Curtiss-Wright hired her to oversee the Cadette project. Beginning in September 1943, she worked closely with C. Wilson Cole, managing the recruitment process from the Curtiss-Wright corporate offices in Passaic, New Jersey. As the first hired recruiter, she hired the other recruiters. She then took trains all over the country to interview candidates on college campuses or at other centralized locations.

After the training began in mid-February of 1943, Ruth functioned as the program's coordinator, reading monthly reports that came in from all seven participating colleges, communicating with on-campus supervisors, cataloging progress reports on the Cadettes, and publishing a newsletter for the Cadettes (*The Cadetter*). In September 1943, when the first batch of Cadettes were in the second half of their training, she was informed that Curtiss-Wright was establishing an official Cadette Training Program coordinator position and moving the program's offices to the airframe division headquarters in Buffalo. The job, however, was not offered to her. From Ruth's personal memoir, provided by her daughters Karen M. Frye and Susan Klick: "I was told quite flatly that had I been a man, I'd have been made the new director, but there was *no way* the company would give that position to a woman! So I went as assistant director."

Curtiss-Wright hired Warren Bruner, who began his job on September 24, 1943. By mid-January of 1944, according to the memoir, Ruth "had had it." She got herself transferred to Curtiss-Wright's Research Laboratory, where she worked as assistant to the assistant director of research for the rest of 1944, doing public-relations work. She was making $4,000 a year, more than twice the salary of a teacher. She was also the only female executive at Curtiss-Wright, with a paid apartment, an expense account, and a car. But in January of 1945 she decided to exit the company and move to Boston to be closer to her ailing mother.

Bruner's December 1944 report mentions "the young lady who had done recruiting for the first program and then worked as assistant to Mr. Cole." He also notes that when they were trying to find recruiters for another round of training to begin in January 1944 (which didn't materialize), "after a month, there had been secured only one recruiter, in addition to *the one brought from Passaic, New Jersey ...*" His third mention of Ruth is in his description of how the Cadette training department was almost dissolved: "... permanent staff of the department ... had at that time shrunk to the head of the department [Bruner], *the interviewer obtained ini-*

tially from Passaic, the ex-Cadette, one typist…" In his final reference to her, he states: "During or shortly after this investigation [into whether the Cadette training department should refocus on company-related publications since the next round of training had been cancelled], *the recruiter and general clerk* left the department." This hardly gives due credit to Ruth's real work in the Cadette Program.

For whatever reason, Bruner could not bring himself to call Ruth by name, although he easily spelled out the name of every man who had any involvement with the Cadette Program. The idea that Curtiss-Wright refused to hire as program coordinator a woman who was smart enough to pass an aeronautical engineering course at the top of her class, had intimate knowledge of the Cadette Program from its inception, and helped recruit and then supervise the Cadettes during the first round of training, paints a portrait of a very conflicted management at airplane division headquarters.

[24]Grandt, A.F., et al. *One Small Step: the History of Aerospace Engineering at Purdue University.* West Lafayette: Purdue University Press, 2005; second edition 2010, p. 39.

[25]Alice Pawley, email, October 2009.

[26]Dorothy Wurster Rout, "Notes from the 50th Reunion of the Cadettes," December 1944.

[27]Bruner Report, p. 55.

[28]Examples of more sophisticated work by Cadettes are given in a master's thesis on the Cadette Program by Robert Hogan. One of the Cadettes he interviewed told him she had worked on a project to measure the airflow around the engine cells of a B36. She had also worked with an engineer to help design a thrust meter. Another (anonymous) Cadette stated that she worked in the electrical design group, "where I did harnesses, control panels, nothing really too inventive, but more advanced than doing prints…" Untitled master's thesis, Cleveland State University, 1997, pp. 19–20.

[29]http://www.youtube.com/watch?v=WevMPamNzN0

[30]http://www.dispatch.com/live/content/life/stories/2009/12/01/1A_BLUN01_--_for_dec._1.ART_ART_12-01-09_D1_H8FQ8A3.html?sid=101

[31]Grandt et al., ibid., p. 39.

[32]Hogan's thesis states that the Cadettes loved working with wind tunnels. "They tested airfoils, changed the angle of attack, the velocity of the airflow and numerous other variables in order to calculate and compare the efficiency of different wing sections." Hogan, ibid., p. 17.

[33]Hogan, ibid., p. 16.